C. DAVID MEAD
Professor of English, Michigan State University
ADVISORY EDITOR TO DODD, MEAD & COMPANY

WHITMAN'S "SONG OF MYSELF"—

ORIGIN, GROWTH, MEANING

Portrait of Whitman used in the 1855 edition of
Leaves of Grass opposite the opening of *Song of
Myself*. It is known as the "carpenter" portrait because Whitman is in carpenter's clothes. (From an
engraving by Samuel Hollyer after a daguerrotype
taken by Gabe Harrison of Brooklyn. Courtesy of
the New York Public Library.)

WHITMAN'S
"SONG OF MYSELF"–
ORIGIN, GROWTH, MEANING

Edited by JAMES E. MILLER, JR.

University of Chicago

DODD, MEAD & COMPANY, *New York, Toronto, 1964*

Printed in the United States of America

PREFACE

GRADUALLY twentieth century criticism has come to see that Walt Whitman's "Song of Myself" is perhaps the greatest of American poems, and among the great poems written in English. Yet it remains a poem full of mystery. There is mystery as to what, in the deepest sense, its sources are. And there is mystery still as to its many meanings.

This book is designed to bring together in convenient form the basic materials of the poem for a penetration in depth. It dictates no method and applies no formula. Instead, it invites exploration. The mysteries of poetry, and particularly of "Song of Myself," are of a singular nature yielding not to group detection but to individual involvement. Although much has been written and said about "Song of Myself," it remains a rich mine in which the reader may make exciting discoveries.

In the first part of the book, the poem itself is presented in two separate versions, reprinted from the first (1855) and last (1892) of the nine lifetime editions of *Leaves of Grass*. These versions are placed on facing pages to enable the reader to see at a glance the major changes the poet made in revising his poem over the years. In a following section appear early notebook versions of the poem, fragments which reveal Whitman in the process of creation. From these materials the reader may construct a biography of the poem and come to his own conclusions as to the sources of its life and its strength.

In the second part of the book, six critics present their views of the poem, seeing it as structure, as poetry, as mysticism, as comedy, as epic, as inspired prophecy. These are not contradictory views so much as varied perspectives, each taking the measure of a different dimension of "Song of Myself." No one of the essays by any means exhausts the poem; and jointly they provide stimulation for new ways of approaching it. The curious reader will discover much that the critics have left unsaid, and will come ultimately to see the poem with his own informed eyes.

James E. Miller, Jr.

University of Chicago
March, 1964

CONTENTS

I. ORIGIN AND GROWTH OF "SONG OF MYSELF"

SONG OF MYSELF, 1855

I celebrate myself,
And what I assume you shall assume,
For every atom belonging to me as good belongs to you.

I loafe and invite my soul,
5 I lean and loafe at my ease . . . . observing a spear of summer grass.

[2]

Houses and rooms are full of perfumes . . . . the shelves are crowded with
    perfumes,
I breathe the fragrance myself, and know it and like it,
The distillation would intoxicate me also, but I shall not let it.

The atmosphere is not a perfume . . . . it has no taste of the distillation . . . .
    it is odorless,
10 It is for my mouth forever . . . . I am in love with it,
I will go to the bank by the wood and become undisguised and naked,
I am mad for it to be in contact with me.

The 1855 version of "Song of Myself" was untitled and was not divided into numbered sections. For the sake of convenience, the numbering system Whitman finally settled on for the poem is inserted in brackets in this reprint of the 1855 version.

SONG OF MYSELF, 1892

1

I celebrate myself, and sing myself,
And what I assume you shall assume,
For every atom belonging to me as good belongs to you.

I loafe and invite my soul,
I lean and loafe at my ease observing a spear of summer grass. 5

My tongue, every atom of my blood, form'd from this soil, this air,
Born here of parents born here from parents the same, and their parents the same,
I, now thirty-seven years old in perfect health begin,
Hoping to cease not till death.

Creeds and schools in abeyance, 10
Retiring back a while sufficed at what they are, but never forgotten,
I harbor for good or bad, I permit to speak at every hazard.
Nature without check with original energy.

2

Houses and rooms are full of perfumes, the shelves are crowded with perfumes,
I breathe the fragrance myself and know it and like it, 15
The distillation would intoxicate me also, but I shall not let it.

The atmosphere is not a perfume, it has no taste of the distillation, it is odorless,
It is for my mouth forever, I am in love with it,
I will go to the bank by the wood and become undisguised and naked,
I am mad for it to be in contact with me. 20

The smoke of my own breath,
Echoes, ripples, and buzzed whispers . . . . loveroot, silkthread, crotch and vine,
My respiration and inspiration . . . . the beating of my heart . . . . the passing
15   of blood and air through my lungs,
The sniff of green leaves and dry leaves, and of the shore and darkcolored sea-
        rocks, and of hay in the barn,
The sound of the belched words of my voice . . . . words loosed to the eddies
        of the wind,
A few light kisses . . . . a few embraces . . . . a reaching around of arms,
The play of shine and shade on the trees as the supple boughs wag,
20 The delight alone or in the rush of the streets, or along the fields and hillsides,
The feeling of health . . . . the full-noon trill . . . . the song of me rising from
        bed and meeting the sun.

Have you reckoned a thousand acres much? Have you reckoned the earth much?
Have you practiced so long to learn to read?
Have you felt so proud to get at the meaning of poems?

25 Stop this day and night with me and you shall possess the origin of all poems,
You shall possess the good of the earth and sun . . . . there are millions of suns
        left,
You shall no longer take things at second or third hand . . . . nor look through
        the eyes of the dead . . . . nor feed on the spectres in books,
You shall not look through my eyes either, nor take things from me,
You shall listen to all sides and filter them from yourself.

[3]
I have heard what the talkers were talking . . . . the talk of the beginning and
30   the end,
But I do not talk of the beginning or the end.

There was never any more inception than there is now,
Nor any more youth or age than there is now;
And will never be any more perfection than there is now,
35 Nor any more heaven or hell than there is now.

Urge and urge and urge,
Always the procreant urge of the world.

Out of the dimness opposite equals advance . . . . Always substance and increase,
Always a knit of identity . . . . always distinction . . . . always a breed of life.

40 To elaborate is no avail . . . . Learned and unlearned feel that it is so.

The smoke of my own breath,
Echoes, ripples, buzz'd whispers, love-root, silk-thread, crotch and vine,
My respiration and inspiration, the beating of my heart, the passing of blood and
    air through my lungs,
The sniff of green leaves and dry leaves, and of the shore and dark-color'd sea-rocks,
    and of hay in the barn,
The sound of the belch'd words of my voice loos'd to the eddies of the wind,   25
A few light kisses, a few embraces, a reaching around of arms,
The play of shine and shade on the trees as the supple boughs wag,
The delight alone or in the rush of the streets, or along the fields and hill-sides,
The feeling of health, the full-moon trill, the song of me rising from bed and
    meeting the sun.

Have you reckon'd a thousand acres much? have you reckon'd the earth much?   30
Have you practis'd so long to learn to read?
Have you felt so proud to get at the meaning of poems?

Stop this day and night with me and you shall possess the origin of all poems,
You shall possess the good of the earth and sun, (there are millions of suns left,)
You shall no longer take things at second or third hand, nor look through the eyes
    of the dead, nor feed on the spectres in books,   35
You shall not look through my eyes either, nor take things from me,
You shall listen to all sides and filter them from your self.

3

I have heard what the talkers were talking, the talk of the beginning and the end,
But I do not talk of the beginning or the end.

There was never any more inception than there is now,   40
Nor any more youth or age than there is now,
And will never be any more perfection than there is now,
Nor any more heaven or hell than there is now.

Urge and urge and urge,
Always the procreant urge of the world.   45

Out of the dimness opposite equals advance, always substance and increase,
    always sex,
Always a knit of identity, always distinction, always a breed of life.

To elaborate is no avail, learn'd and unlearn'd feel that it is so.

Sure as the most certain sure . . . . plumb in the uprights, well entretied, braced
    in the beams,
Stout as a horse, affectionate, haughty, electrical,
I and this mystery here we stand.

Clear and sweet is my soul . . . . and clear and sweet is all that is not my soul.

45 Lack one lacks both . . . . and the unseen is proved by the seen,
Till that becomes unseen and receives proof in its turn.

Showing the best and dividing it from the worst, age vexes age,
Knowing the perfect fitness and equanimity of things, while they discuss I am
    silent, and go bathe and admire myself.

Welcome is every organ and attribute of me, and of any man hearty and clean,
Not an inch nor a particle of an inch is vile, and none shall be less familiar than
50   the rest.

I am satisfied . . . . I see, dance, laugh, sing;
As God comes a loving bedfellow and sleeps at my side all night and close on the
    peep of the day,
And leaves for me baskets covered with white towels bulging the house with their
    plenty,
Shall I postpone my acceptation and realization and scream at my eyes,
55 That they turn from gazing after and down the road,
And forthwith cipher and show me to a cent,
Exactly the contents of one, and exactly the contents of two, and which is ahead?

[4]

Trippers and askers surround me,
People I meet . . . . the effect upon me of my early life . . . . of the ward and
    city I live in . . . . of the nation,
60 The latest news . . . . discoveries, inventions, societies . . . . authors old and new,
My dinner, dress, associates, looks, business, compliments, dues,
The real or fancied indifference of some man or woman I love,
The sickness of one of my folks—or of myself . . . . or ill-doing . . . . or loss or
    lack of money . . . . or depressions or exaltations,
They come to me days and nights and go from me again,
65 But they are not the Me myself.

Apart from the pulling and hauling stands what I am,
Stands amused, complacent, compassionating, idle, unitary,
Looks down, is erect, bends an arm on an impalpable certain rest,

Sure as the most certain sure, plumb in the uprights, well entretied, braced
   in the beams,
Stout as a horse, affectionate, haughty, electrical,
I and this mystery here we stand.

Clear and sweet is my soul, and clear and sweet is all that is not my soul.

Lack one lacks both, and the unseen is proved by the seen,
Till that becomes unseen and receives proof in its turn.

Showing the best and dividing it from the worst age vexes age,
Knowing the perfect fitness and equanimity of things, while they discuss I am
   silent, and go bathe and admire myself.

Welcome is every organ and attribute of me, and of any man hearty and clean,
Not an inch nor a particle of an inch is vile, and none shall be less familiar
   than the rest.

I am satisfied—I see, dance, laugh, sing;
As the hugging and loving bed-fellow sleeps at my side through the night, and
   withdraws at the peep of the day with stealthy tread,
Leaving me baskets cover'd with white towels swelling the house with their plenty,
Shall I postpone my acceptation and realization and scream at my eyes,
That they turn from gazing after and down the road,
And forthwith cipher and show me to a cent,
Exactly the value of one and exactly the value of two, and which is ahead?

4

Trippers and askers surround me,
People I meet, the effect upon me of my early life or the ward and city I live in,
   or the nation,
The latest dates, discoveries, inventions, societies, authors old and new,
My dinner, dress, associates, looks, compliments, dues,
The real or fancied indifference of some man or woman I love,
The sickness of one of my folks or of myself, or ill-doing or loss or lack of money,
   or depressions or exaltations,
Battles, the horrors of fratricidal war, the fever of doubtful news, the fitful events;
These come to me days and nights and go from me again,
But they are not the Me myself.

Apart from the pulling and hauling stands what I am,
Stands amused, complacent, compassionating, idle, unitary,
Looks down, is erect, or bends an arm on an impalpable certain rest,

Looks with its sidecurved head curious what will come next,
70 Both in and out of the game, and watching and wondering at it.

Backward I see in my own days where I sweated through fog with linguists and
    contenders,
I have no mockings or arguments . . . . I witness and wait.

[5]

I believe in you my soul . . . . the other I am must not abase itself to you,
And you must not be abased to the other.

75 Loafe with me on the grass . . . . loose the stop from your throat,
Not words, not music or rhyme I want . . . . not custom or lecture, not even
    the best,
Only the lull I like, the hum of your valved voice.

I mind how we lay in June, such a transparent summer morning;
You settled your head athwart my hips and gently turned over upon me,
And parted the shirt from my bosom-bone, and plunged your tongue to my bare-
80   stript heart,
And reached till you felt my beard, and reached till you held my feet.

Swiftly arose and spread around me the peace and joy and knowledge that pass all
    the art and argument of the earth;
And I know that the hand of God is the elderhand of my own,
And I know that the spirit of God is the eldest brother of my own,
And that all the men ever born are also my brothers . . . . and the women my
85   sisters and lovers,
And that a kelson of the creation is love;
And limitless are leaves stiff or drooping in the fields,
And brown ants in the little wells beneath them,
And mossy scabs of the wormfence, and heaped stones, and elder and mullen and
    pokeweed.

[6]

90 A child said, What is the grass? fetching it to me with full hands;
How could I answer the child? . . . . I do not know what it is any more than he.

I guess it must be the flag of my disposition, out of hopeful green stuff woven.

Or I guess it is the handkerchief of the Lord,
A scented gift and remembrancer designedly dropped,
Bearing the owner's name someway in the corners, that we may see and remark,
95   and say Whose?

Looking with side-curved head curious what will come next,
Both in and out of the game and watching and wondering at it.

Backward I see in my own days where I sweated through fog with linguists and
    contenders,   80
I have no mockings or arguments, I witness and wait.

5

I believe in you my soul, the other I am must not abase itself to you,
And you must not be abased to the other.

Loafe with me on the grass, loose the stop from your throat,
Not words, not music or rhyme I want, not custom or lecture, not even the best,   85
Only the lull I like, the hum of your valvèd voice.

I mind how once we lay such a transparent summer morning,
How you settled your head athwart my hips and gently turn'd over upon me,
And parted the shirt from my bosom-bone, and plunged your tongue to my
    bare-stript heart,
And reach'd till you felt my beard, and reach'd till you held my feet.   90

Swiftly arose and spread around me the peace and knowledge that pass all the
    argument of the earth,
And I know that the hand of God is the promise of my own,
And I know that the spirit of God is the brother of my own,
And that all the men ever born are also my brothers, and the women my sisters
    and lovers,
And that a kelson of the creation is love,   95
And limitless are leaves stiff or drooping in the fields,
And brown ants in the little wells beneath them,
And mossy scabs of the worm fence, heap'd stones, elder, mullein and poke-weed.

6

A child said What is the grass? fetching it to me with full hands,
How could I answer the child? I do not know what it is any more than he.   100

I guess it must be the flag of my disposition, out of hopeful green stuff woven.

Or I guess it is the handkerchief of the Lord,
A scented gift and remembrancer designedly dropt,
Bearing the owner's name someway in the corners, that we may see and remark,
    and say Whose?

Or I guess the grass is itself a child . . . . the produced babe of the vegetation.

Or I guess it is a uniform hieroglyphic,
And it means, Sprouting alike in broad zones and narrow zones,
Growing among black folks as among white,
Kanuck, Tuckahoe, Congressman, Cuff, I give them the same, I receive them the
100   same.

And now it seems to me the beautiful uncut hair of graves.

Tenderly will I use you curling grass,
It may be you transpire from the breasts of young men,
It may be if I had known them I would have loved them;
It may be you are from old people and from women, and from offspring taken soon
105   out of their mothers' laps,
And here you are the mothers' laps.

This grass is very dark to be from the white heads of old mothers,
Darker than the colorless beards of old men,
Dark to come from under the faint red roofs of mouths.

110 O I perceive after all so many uttering tongues!
And I perceive they do not come from the roofs of mouths for nothing.

I wish I could translate the hints about the dead young men and women,
And the hints about old men and mothers, and the offspring taken soon out of
their laps.

What do you think has become of the young and old men?
115 And what do you think has become of the women and children?

They are alive and well somewhere;
The smallest sprout shows there is really no death,
And if ever there was it led forward life, and does not wait at the end to arrest it,
And ceased the moment life appeared.

120 All goes onward and outward . . . . and nothing collapses,
And to die is different from what any one supposed, and luckier.

[7]
Has any one supposed it lucky to be born?
I hasten to inform him or her it is just as lucky to die, and I know it.

I pass death with the dying, and birth with the new-washed babe . . . . and am not
contained between my hat and boots,

Or I guess the grass is itself a child, the produced babe of the vegetation.   105

Or I guess it is a uniform hieroglyphic,
And it means, Sprouting alike in broad zones and narrow zones,
Growing among black folks as among white,
Kanuck, Tuckahoe, Congressman, Cuff, I give them the same, I receive them
    the same.

And now it seems to me the beautiful uncut hair of graves.   110

Tenderly will I use you curling grass,
It may be you transpire from the breasts of young men,
It may be if I had known them I would have loved them,
It may be you are from old people, or from offspring taken soon out of their
    mothers' laps.
And here you are the mothers' laps.   115

This grass is very dark to be from the white heads of old mothers,
Darker than the colorless beards of old men,
Dark to come from under the faint red roofs of mouths.

O I perceive after all so many uttering tongues,
And I perceive they do not come from the roofs of mouths for nothing.   120

I wish I could translate the hints about the dead young men and women,
And the hints about old men and mothers, and the offspring taken soon out
    of their laps.

What do you think has become of the young and old men?
And what do you think has become of the women and children?

They are alive and well somewhere,   125
The smallest sprout shows there is really no death,
And if ever there was it led forward life, and does not wait at the end to arrest it,
And ceas'd the moment life appear'd.

All goes onward and outward, nothing collapses,
And to die is different from what any one supposed, and luckier.   130

7

Has any one supposed it lucky to be born?
I hasten to inform him or her it is just as lucky to die, and I know it.

I pass death with the dying and birth with the new-wash'd babe, and am not
    contain'd between my hat and boots,

125   And peruse manifold objects, no two alike, and every one good,
The earth good, and the stars good, and their adjuncts all good.

I am not an earth nor an adjunct of an earth,
I am the mate and companion of people, all just as immortal and fathomless as
      myself;
They do not know how immortal, but I know.

130   Every kind for itself and its own . . . . for me mine male and female,
For me all that have been boys and that love women,
For me the man that is proud and feels how it stings to be slighted,
For me the sweetheart and the old maid . . . . for me mothers and the mothers of
      mothers,
For me lips that have smiled, eyes that have shed tears,
135   For me children and the begetters of children.

Who need be afraid of the merge?
Undrape . . . . you are not guilty to me, nor stale nor discarded,
I see through the broadcloth and gingham whether or no,
And am around, tenacious, acquisitive, tireless . . . . and can never be shaken away.

[8]
140   The little one sleeps in its cradle,
I lift the gauze and look a long time, and silently brush away flies with my hand.

The youngster and the redfaced girl turn aside up the bushy hill,
I peeringly view them from the top.

The suicide sprawls on the bloody floor of the bedroom,
145   It is so . . . . I witnessed the corpse . . . . there the pistol had fallen.

The blab of the pave . . . . the tires of carts and sluff of bootsoles and talk of the
      promenaders,
The heavy omnibus, the driver with his interrogating thumb, the clank of the shod
      horses on the granite floor,
The carnival of sleighs, the clinking and shouted jokes and pelts of snowballs;
The hurrahs for popular favorites . . . . the fury of roused mobs,
150   The flap of the curtained litter—the sick man inside, borne to the hospital,
The meeting of enemies, the sudden oath, the blows and fall,
The excited crowd—the policeman with his star quickly working his passage to the
      centre of the crowd;
The impassive stones that receive and return so many echoes,
The souls moving along . . . . are they invisible while the least atom of the stones
      is visible?

And peruse manifold objects, no two alike and every one good,
The earth good and the stars good, and their adjuncts all good.   135

I am not an earth nor an adjunct of an earth,
I am the mate and companion of people, all just as immortal and fathomless
    as myself,
(They do not know how immortal, but I know.)

Every kind for itself and its own, for me mine male and female,
For me those that have been boys and that love women,   140
For me the man that is proud and feels how it stings to be slighted,
For me the sweet-heart and the old maid, for me mothers and the mothers
    of mothers,
For me lips that have smiled, eyes that have shed tears,
For me children and the begetters of children.

Undrape! you are not guilty to me, nor stale nor discarded,   145
I see through the broadcloth and gingham whether or no,
And am around, tenacious, acquisitive, tireless, and cannot be shaken away.

8

The little one sleeps in its cradle,
I lift the gauze and look a long time, and silently brush away flies with my hand.

The youngster and the red-faced girl turn aside up the bushy hill,   150
I peeringly view them from the top.

The suicide sprawls on the bloody floor of the bedroom,
I witness the corpse with its dabbled hair, I note where the pistol has fallen.

The blab of the pave, tires of carts, sluff of boot-soles, talk of the promenaders,
The heavy omnibus, the driver with his interrogating thumb, the clank of the
    shod horses on the granite floor,   155
The snow-sleighs, clinking, shouted jokes, pelts of snow-balls,
The hurrahs for popular favorites, the fury of rous'd mobs,
The flap of the curtain'd litter, a sick man inside borne to the hospital,
The meeting of enemies, the sudden oath, the blows and fall,
The excited crowd, the policeman with his star quickly working his passage to the
    centre of the crowd,   160
The impassive stones that receive and return so many echoes,

155 What groans of overfed or half-starved who fall on the flags sunstruck or in fits,
    What exclamations of women taken suddenly, who hurry home and give birth to
        babes,
    What living and buried speech is always vibrating here . . . . what howls restrained
        by decorum,
    Arrests of criminals, slights, adulterous offers made, acceptances, rejections with
        convex lips,
    I mind them or the resonance of them . . . . I come again and again.

[9]

160 The big doors of the country-barn stand open and ready,
    The dried grass of the harvest-time loads the slow-drawn wagon,
    The clear light plays on the brown gray and green intertinged,
    The armfuls are packed to the sagging mow:
    I am there . . . . I help . . . . I came stretched atop of the load,
165 I felt its soft jolts . . . . one leg reclined on the other,
    I jump from the crossbeams, and seize the clover and timothy,
    And roll head over heels, and tangle my hair full of wisps.

[10]

    Alone far in the wilds and mountains I hunt,
    Wandering amazed at my own lightness and glee,
170 In the late afternoon choosing a safe spot to pass the night,
    Kindling a fire and broiling the freshkilled game,
    Soundly falling asleep on the gathered leaves, my dog and gun by my side.

    The Yankee clipper is under her three skysails . . . . she cuts the sparkle and scud,
    My eyes settle the land . . . . I bend at her prow or shout joyously from the deck.

175 The boatmen and clamdiggers arose early and stopped for me,
    I tucked my trowser-ends in my boots and went and had a good time,
    You should have been with us that day round the chowder-kettle.

    I saw the marriage of the trapper in the open air in the far-west . . . . the bride
        was a red girl,
    Her father and his friends sat near by crosslegged and dumbly smoking . . . . they
        had moccasins to their feet and large thick blankets hanging from their
        shoulders;
    On a bank lounged the trapper . . . . he was dressed mostly in skins . . . . his
180   luxuriant beard and curls protected his neck,
    One hand rested on his rifle . . . . the other hand held firmly the wrist of the red
        girl,
    She had long eyelashes . . . . her head was bare . . . . her coarse straight locks
        descended upon her voluptuous limbs and reached to her feet.

What groans of over-fed or half-starv'd who fall sunstruck or in fits,
What exclamations of women taken suddenly who hurry home and give birth
    to babes,
What living and buried speech is always vibrating here, what howls restrain'd
    by decorum,
Arrests of criminals, slights, adulterous offers made, acceptances, rejections with
    convex lips,   165
I mind them or the show or resonance of them—I come and I depart.

9

The big doors of the country barn stand open and ready,
The dried grass of the harvest-time loads the slow-drawn wagon,
The clear light plays on the brown gray and green intertinged,
The armfuls are pack'd to the sagging mow.   170

I am there, I help, I came stretch'd atop of the load,
I felt its soft jolts, one leg reclined on the other,
I jump from the cross-beams and seize the clover and timothy,
And roll head over heels and tangle my hair full of wisps.

10

Alone far in the wilds and mountains I hunt,   175
Wandering amazed at my own lightness and glee,
In the late afternoon choosing a safe spot to pass the night,
Kindling a fire and broiling the fresh-kill'd game,
Falling asleep on the gather'd leaves with my dog and gun by my side.

The Yankee clipper is under her sky-sails, she cuts the sparkle and scud,   180
My eyes settle the land, I bend at her prow or shout joyously from the deck.

The boatmen and clam-diggers arose early and stopt for me,
I tuck'd my trowser-ends in my boots and went and had a good time;
You should have been with us that day round the chowder-kettle.

I saw the marriage of the trapper in the open air in the far west, the bride was
    a red girl,   185
Her father and his friends sat near cross-legged and dumbly smoking, they had
    moccasins to their feet and large thick blankets hanging from their shoulders,
On a bank lounged the trapper, he was drest mostly in skins, his luxuriant beard
    and curls protected his neck, he held his bride by the hand,
She had long eyelashes, her head was bare, her coarse straight locks descended
    upon her voluptuous limbs and reach'd to her feet.

The runaway slave came to my house and stopped outside,
I heard his motions crackling the twigs of the woodpile,
185   Through the swung half-door of the kitchen I saw him limpsey and weak,
And went where he sat on a log, and led him in and assured him,
And brought water and filled a tub for his sweated body and bruised feet,
And gave him a room that entered from my own, and gave him some coarse
    clean clothes,
And remember perfectly well his revolving eyes and his awkwardness,
190   And remember putting plasters on the galls of his neck and ankles;
He staid with me a week before he was recuperated and passed north,
I had him sit next me at table . . . . my firelock leaned in the corner.

[11]

Twenty-eight young men bathe by the shore,
Twenty-eight young men, and all so friendly,
195   Twenty-eight years of womanly life, and all so lonesome.

She owns the fine house by the rise of the bank,
She hides handsome and richly drest aft the blinds of the window.

Which of the young men does she like the best?
Ah the homeliest of them is beautiful to her.

200   Where are you off to, lady? for I see you,
You splash in the water there, yet stay stock still in your room.

Dancing and laughing along the beach came the twenty-ninth bather,
The rest did not see her, but she saw them and loved them.

The beards of the young men glistened with wet, it ran from their long hair,
205   Little streams passed all over their bodies.

An unseen hand also passed over their bodies,
It descended tremblingly from their temples and ribs.

The young men float on their backs, their white bellies swell to the sun . . . .
    they do not ask who seizes fast to them,
They do not know who puffs and declines with pendant and bending arch,
210   They do not think whom they souse with spray.

[12]

The butcher-boy puts off his killing-clothes, or sharpens his knife at the stall
    in the market,
I loiter enjoying his repartee and his shuffle and breakdown.

The runaway slave came to my house and stopt outside,
I heard his motions crackling the twigs of the woodpile, 190
Through the swung half-door of the kitchen I saw him, limpsy and weak,
And went where he sat on a log and led him in and assured him,
And brought water and fill'd a tub for his sweated body and bruis'd feet,
And gave him a room that enter'd from my own, and gave him some coarse
    clean clothes,
And remember perfectly well his revolving eyes and his awkwardness, 195
And remember putting plasters on the galls of his neck and ankles;
He staid with me a week before he was recuperated and pass'd north,
I had him sit next me at table, my fire-lock lean'd in the corner.

11

Twenty-eight young men bathe by the shore,
Twenty-eight young men and all so friendly; 200
Twenty-eight years of womanly life and all so lonesome.

She owns the fine house by the rise of the bank,
She hides handsome and richly drest aft the blinds of the window.

Which of the young men does she like the best?
Ah the homeliest of them is beautiful to her. 205

Where are you off to, lady? for I see you,
You splash in the water there, yet stay stock still in your room.

Dancing and laughing along the beach came the twenty-ninth bather,
The rest did not see her, but she saw them and loved them.

The beards of the young men glisten'd with wet, it ran from their long hair, 210
Little streams pass'd all over their bodies.

An unseen hand also pass'd over their bodies,
It descended tremblingly from their temples and ribs.

The young men float on their backs, their white bellies bulge to the sun, they do
    not ask who seizes fast to them,
They do not know who puffs and declines with pendant and bending arch, 215
They do not think whom they souse with spray.

12

The butcher-boy puts off his killing-clothes, or sharpens his knife at the stall
    in the market,
I loiter enjoying his repartee and his shuffle and break-down.

Blacksmiths with grimed and hairy chests environ the anvil,
Each has his main-sledge . . . . they are all out . . . . there is a great heat
    in the fire.

215 From the cinder-strewed threshold I follow their movements,
The lithe sheer of their waists plays even with their massive arms,
Overhand the hammers roll—overhand so slow—overhand so sure,
They do not hasten, each man hits in his place.

[13]
The negro holds firmly the reins of his four horses . . . . the block swags
    underneath on its tied-over chain,
The negro that drives the huge dray of the stoneyard . . . . steady and tall he
220   stands poised on one leg on the stringpiece,
His blue shirt exposes his ample neck and breast and loosens over his hipband,
His glance is calm and commanding . . . . he tosses the slouch of his hat
    away from his forehead,
The sun falls on his crispy hair and moustache . . . . falls on the black of his
    polish'd and perfect limbs.

I behold the picturesque giant and love him . . . . and I do not stop there,
225 I go with the team also.

In me the caresser of life wherever moving . . . . backward as well as
    forward slueing,
To niches aside and junior bending.

Oxen that rattle the yoke or halt in the shade, what is that you express in
    your eyes?
It seems to me more than all the print I have read in my life.

230 My tread scares the wood-drake and wood-duck on my distant and daylong ramble,
They rise together, they slowly circle around.
. . . . I believe in those winged purposes,
And acknowledge the red yellow and white playing within me,
And consider the green and violet and the tufted crown intentional;
235 And do not call the tortoise unworthy because she is not something else,
And the mockingbird in the swamp never studied the gamut, let trills
    pretty well to me,
And the look of the bay mare shames silliness out of me.

[14]
The wild gander leads his flock through the cool night,
Ya-honk! he says, and sounds it down to me like an invitation;

Blacksmiths with grimed and hairy chests environ the anvil,
Each has his main-sledge, they are all out, there is a great heat in the fire.   **220**

From the cinder-strew'd threshold I follow their movements,
The lithe sheer of their waists plays even with their massive arms,
Overhand the hammers swing, overhand so slow, overhand so sure,
They do not hasten, each man hits in his place.

13

The negro holds firmly the reins of his four horses, the block swags underneath
    on its tied-over chain,   **225**
The negro that drives the long dray of the stone-yard, steady and tall he stands
    pois'd on one leg on the string-piece,
His blue shirt exposes his ample neck and breast and loosens over his hip-band,
His glance is calm and commanding, he tosses the slouch of his hat away from
    his forehead,
The sun falls on his crispy hair and mustache, falls on the black of his polish'd
    and perfect limbs.

I behold the picturesque giant and love him, and I do not stop there,   **230**
I go with the team also.

In me the caresser of life wherever moving, backward as well as forward sluing,
To niches aside and junior bending, not a person or object missing,
Absorbing all to myself and for this song.

Oxen that rattle the yoke and chain or halt in the leafy shade, what is that you
    express in your eyes?   **235**
It seems to me more than all the print I have read in my life.

My tread scares the wood-drake and wood-duck on my distant and day-long
    ramble,
They rise together, they slowly circle around.

I believe in those wing'd purposes,
And acknowledge red, yellow, white, playing within me,   **240**
And consider green and violet and the tufted crown intentional,
And do not call the tortoise unworthy because she is not something else,
And the jay in the woods never studied the gamut, yet trills pretty well to me,
And the look of the bay mare shames silliness out of me.

14

The wild gander leads his flock through the cool night,   **245**
Ya-honk he says, and sounds it down to me like an invitation,

240 The pert may suppose it meaningless, but I listen closer,
I find its purpose and place up there toward the November sky.

The sharphoofed moose of the north, the cat on the housesill, the
chickadee, the prairie-dog,
The litter of the grunting sow as they tug at her teats,
The brood of the turkeyhen, and she with her halfspread wings,
245 I see in them and myself the same old law.

The press of my foot to the earth springs a hundred affections,
They scorn the best I can do to relate them.

I am enamoured of growing outdoors,
Of men that live among cattle or taste of the ocean or woods,
Of the builders and steerers of ships, of the wielders of axes and mauls, of the
250   drivers of horses,
I can eat and sleep with them week in and week out.

What is commonest and cheapest and nearest and easiest is Me,
Me going in for my chances, spending for vast returns,
Adorning myself to bestow myself on the first that will take me,
255 Not asking the sky to come down to my goodwill,
Scattering it freely forever.

[15]

The pure contralto sings in the organloft,
The carpenter dresses his plank . . . . the tongue of his foreplane whistles its
wild ascending lisp,
The married and unmarried children ride home to their thanksgiving dinner,
260 The pilot seizes the king-pin, he heaves down with a strong arm,
The mate stands braced in the whaleboat, lance and harpoon are ready,
The duck-shooter walks by silent and cautious stretches,
The deacons are ordained with crossed hands at the altar,
The spinning-girl retreats and advances to the hum of the big wheel,
265 The farmer stops by the bars of a Sunday and looks at the oats and rye,
day's sport.
The lunatic is carried at last to the asylum a confirmed case,
He will never sleep any more as he did in the cot in his mother's bedroom;
The jour printer with gray head and gaunt jaws works at his case,
He turns his quid of tobacco, his eyes get blurred with the manuscript;
270 The malformed limbs are tied to the anatomist's table,
What is removed drops horribly in a pail;
The quadroon girl is sold at the stand . . . . the drunkard nods by the
barroom stove,

The pert may suppose it meaningless, but I listening close,
Find its purpose and place up there toward the wintry sky.

The sharp-hoof'd moose of the north, the cat on the house-sill, the chickadee, the
    prairie-dog,
The litter of the grunting sow as they tug at her teats,   250
The brood of the turkey-hen and she with her half-spread wings,
I see in them and myself the same old law.

The press of my foot to the earth springs a hundred affections,
They scorn the best I can do to relate them.

I am enamour'd of growing out-doors,   255
Of men that live among cattle or taste of the ocean or woods,
Of the builders and steerers of ships and the wielders of axes and mauls, and
    the drivers of horses,
I can eat and sleep with them week in and week out.

What is commonest, cheapest, nearest, easiest, is Me,
Me going in for my chances, spending for vast returns,   260
Adorning myself to bestow myself on the first that will take me,
Not asking the sky to come down to my good will,
Scattering it freely forever.

15

The pure contralto sings in the organ loft,
The carpenter dresses his plank, the tongue of his foreplane whistles its wild
    ascending lisp,   265
The married and unmarried children ride home to their Thanksgiving dinner,
The pilot seizes the king-pin, he heaves down with a strong arm,
The mate stands braced in the whale-boat, lance and harpoon are ready,
The duck-shooter walks by silent and cautious stretches,
The deacons are ordain'd with cross'd hands at the altar,   270
The spinning-girl retreats and advances to the hum of the big wheel,
The farmer stops by the bars as he walks on a First-day loafe and looks at the
    oats and rye,
The lunatic is carried at last to the asylum a confirm'd case,
(He will never sleep any more as he did in the cot in his mother's bed-room;)
The jour printer with gray head and gaunt jaws works at his case,   275
He turns his quid of tobacco while his eyes blurr with the manuscript;
The malform'd limbs are tied to the surgeon's table,
What is removed drops horribly in a pail;
The quadroon girl is sold at the auction-stand, the drunkard nods by the
    bar-room stove,

The machinist rolls up his sleeves . . . . the policeman travels his beat . . . the
    gatekeeper marks who pass,
The young fellow drives the express-wagon . . . . I love him though I do not
    know him;
275 The half-breed straps on his light boots to compete in the race,
The western turkey-shooting draws old and young . . . . some lean on their
    rifles, some sit on logs,
Out from the crowd steps the marksman and takes his position and levels
    his piece;
The groups of newly-come immigrants cover the wharf or levee,
The woollypates hoe in the sugarfield, the overseer views them from his saddle;
The bugle calls in the ballroom, the gentlemen run for their partners, the dancers
280   bow to each other;
The youth lies awake in the cedar-roofed garret and harks to the musical rain,
The Wolverine sets traps on the creek that helps fill the Huron,
The reformer ascends the platform, he spouts with his mouth and nose,
The company returns from its excursion, the darkey brings up the rear and
    bears the well-riddled target,
The squaw wrapt in her yellow-hemmed cloth is offering moccasins and beadbags
285   for sale,
The connoisseur peers along the exhibition-gallery with halfshut eyes
    bent sideways,
The deckhands make fast the steamboat, the plank is thrown for the
    shoregoing passengers,
The young sister holds out the skein, the elder sister winds it off in a ball and
    stops now and then for the knots,
The one-year wife is recovering and happy, a week ago she bore her first child,
The cleanhaired Yankee girl works with her sewing-machine or in the factory
290   or mill,
The nine months' gone is in the parturition chamber, her faintness and pains
    are advancing;
The pavingman leans on his twohanded rammer—the reporter's lead flies swiftly
    over the notebook—the signpainter is lettering with red and gold,
The canal-boy trots on the towpath—the bookkeeper counts at his desk—the
    shoemaker waxes his thread,
The conductor beats time for the band and all the performers follow him,
295 The child is baptised—the convert is making the first professions,
The regatta is spread on the bay . . . . how the white sails sparkle!
The drover watches his drove, he sings out to them that would stray,
The pedlar sweats with his pack on his back—the purchaser higgles about the
    odd cent,
The camera and plate are prepared, the lady must sit for her daguerreotype,
300 The bride unrumples her white dress, the minutehand of the clock moves slowly,
The opium eater reclines with rigid head and just-opened lips,

The machinist rolls up his sleeves, the policeman travels his beat, the gate-keeper
    marks who pass,   280
The young fellow drives the express-wagon, (I love him, though I do not
    know him;)
The half-breed straps on his light boots to compete in the race,
The western turkey-shooting draws old and young, some lean on their rifles,
    some sit on logs,
Out from the crowd steps the marksman, takes his position, levels his piece,
The groups of newly-come immigrants cover the wharf or levee,   285
As the wooly-pates hoe in the sugar-field, the overseer views them from his saddle,
The bugle calls in the ball-room, the gentlemen run for their partners, the dancers
    bow to each other,
The youth lies awake in the cedar-roof'd garret and harks to the musical rain,
The Wolverine sets traps on the creek that helps fill the Huron,
The squaw wrapt in her yellow-hemm'd cloth is offering moccasins and bead-bags
    for sale,   290
The connoisseur peers along the exhibition-gallery with half-shut eyes bent
    sideways,
As the deck-hands make fast the steamboat the plank is thrown for the
    shore-going passengers,
The young sister holds out the skein while the elder sister winds it off in a ball,
    and stops now and then for the knots,
The one-year wife is recovering and happy having a week ago borne her first child,
The clean-hair'd Yankee girl works with her sewing-machine or in the factory
    or mill,   295
The paving-man leans on his two-handed rammer, the reporter's lead flies swiftly
    over the note-book, the sign-painter is lettering with blue and gold.
The canal boy trots on the tow-path, the book-keeper counts at his desk, the
    shoemaker waxes his thread,
The conductor beats time for the band and all the performers follow him,
The child is baptized, the convert is making his first professions,
The regatta is spread on the bay, the race is begun, (how the white sails sparkle!)   300
The drover watching his drove sings out to them that would stray,
The pedler sweats with his pack on his back, (the purchaser higgling about the
    odd cent;)
The bride unrumples her white-dress, the minute-hand of the clock moves slowly,
The opium-eater reclines with rigid head and just-open'd lips,

The prostitute draggles her shawl, her bonnet bobs on her tipsy and pimpled neck,
The crowd laughs at her blackguard oaths, the men jeer and wink to each other,
(Miserable! I do not laugh at your oaths nor jeer you,)
305 The President holds a cabinet council, he is surrounded by the great secretaries,
On the piazza walk five friendly matrons with twined arms;
The crew of the fish-smack pack repeated layers of halibut in the hold,
The Missourian crosses the plains toting his wares and his cattle,
The fare-collector goes through the train—he gives notice by the jingling of
    loose change,
The floormen are laying the floor—the tinners are tinning the roof—the masons
310   are calling for mortar,
In single file each shouldering his hod pass onward the laborers;
Seasons pursuing each other the indescribable crowd is gathered . . . . . it is the
    Fourth of July . . . . what salutes of cannon and small arms!
Seasons pursuing each other the plougher ploughs and the mower mows and the
    wintergrain falls in the ground;
Off on the lakes the pikefisher watches and waits by the hole in the frozen surface,
315 The stumps stand thick round the clearing, the squatter strikes deep with his axe,
The flatboatmen make fast toward dusk near the cottonwood or pekantrees,
The coon-seekers go now through the regions of the Red river, or through those
    drained by the Tennessee, or through those of the Arkansas,
The torches shine in the dark that hangs on the Chattahoochee or Altamahaw;
Patriarchs sit at supper with sons and grandsons and great grandsons around them,
320 In walls of abode [adobie], in canvass tents, rest hunters and trappers after their
    day's sport.
The city sleeps and the country sleeps,
The living sleep for their time . . . . the dead sleep for their time,
The old husband sleeps by his wife and the young husband sleeps by his wife;
And these one and all tend inward to me, and I tend outward to them,
325 And such as it is to be of these more or less I am.

[16]

I am of old and young, of the foolish as much as the wise,
Regardless of others, ever regardful of others,
Maternal as well as paternal, a child as well as a man,
Stuffed with the stuff that is coarse, and stuffed with the stuff that is fine,
One of the great nations, the nation of many nations—the smallest the same and
330   the largest the same,
A southerner soon as a northerner, a planter nonchalant and hospitable,
A Yankee bound my own way . . . . ready for trade . . . . my joints the limberest
    joints on earth and the sternest joints on earth,
A Kentuckian walking the vale of the Elkhorn in my deerskin leggings,
A boatman over the lakes or bays or along coasts . . . . a Hoosier, a Badger,
    a Buckeye,
335 A Louisianian or Georgian, a poke-easy from sandhills and pines,

The prostitute draggles her shawl, her bonnet bobs on her tipsy and pimpled neck,   305
The crowd laugh at her blackguard oaths, the men jeer and wink to each other,
(Miserable! I do not laugh at your oaths nor jeer you;)
The President holding a cabinet council is surrounded by the great Secretaries,
On the piazza walk three matrons stately and friendly with twined arms,
The crew of the fish-smack pack repeated layers of halibut in the hold,   310
The Missourian crosses the plains toting his wares and his cattle,
As the fare-collector goes through the train he gives notice by the jingling of
    loose change,
The floor-men are laying the floor, the tinners are tinning the roof, the masons
    are calling for mortar,
In single file each shouldering his hod pass onward the laborers;
Seasons pursuing each other the indescribable crowd is gather'd, it is the fourth
    of Seventh-month, (what salutes of cannon and small arms!)   315
Seasons pursuing each other the plougher ploughs, the mower mows, and the
    winter-grain falls in the ground;
Off on the lakes the pike-fisher watches and waits by the hole in the frozen
    surface,
The stumps stand thick round the clearing, the squatter strikes deep with his axe,
Flatboatmen make fast towards dusk near the cotton-wood or pecan-trees,
Coon-seekers go through the regions of the Red river or through those drain'd
    by the Tennessee, or through those of the Arkansas,   320
Torches shine in the dark that hangs on the Chattahooche or Altamahaw,
Patriarchs sit at supper with sons and grandsons and great-grandsons around them,
In walls of adobie, in canvas tents, rest hunters and trappers after their day's sport,
The city sleeps and the country sleeps,
The living sleep for their time, the dead sleep for their time,   325
The old husband sleeps by his wife and the young husband sleeps by his wife;
And these tend inward to me, and I tend outward to them,
And such as it is to be of these more or less I am,
And of these one and all I weave the song of myself.

16

I am of old and young, of the foolish as much as the wise,   330
Regardless of others, ever regardful of others,
Maternal as well as paternal, a child as well as a man,
Stuff'd with the stuff that is coarse and stuff'd with the stuff that is fine,
One of the Nation of many nations, the smallest the same and the largest the same,
A Southerner soon as a Northerner, a planter nonchalant and hospitable down
    by the Oconee I live,   335
A Yankee bound my own way ready for trade, my joints the limberest joints on
    earth and the sternest joints on earth,
A Kentuckian walking the vale of the Elkhorn in my deerskin leggings, a
    Louisianian or Georgian,
A boatman over lakes or bays or along coasts, a Hoosier, Badger, Buckeye;

At home on Canadian snowshoes or up in the bush, or with fishermen
    off Newfoundland,
At home in the fleet of iceboats, sailing with the rest and tacking,
At home on the hills of Vermont or in the woods of Maine or the Texan ranch,
Comrade of Californians . . . . comrade of free northwesterners, loving their
    big proportions,
Comrade of raftsmen and coalmen—comrade of all who shake hands and welcome
340   to drink and meat;
A learner with the simplest, a teacher of the thoughtfulest,
A novice beginning experient of myriads of seasons,
Of every hue and trade and rank, of every caste and religion,
Not merely of the New World but of Africa Europe or Asia . . . . a
    wandering savage,
345 A farmer, mechanic, or artist . . . . a gentleman, sailor, lover or quaker,
A prisoner, fancy-man, rowdy, lawyer, physician or priest.

I resist anything better than my own diversity,
And breathe the air and leave plenty after me,
And am not stuck up, and am in my place.

350 The moth and the fisheggs are in their place,
The suns I see and the suns I cannot see are in their place,
The palpable is in its place and the impalpable is in its place.

[17]

These are the thoughts of all men in all ages and lands, they are not original
    with me,
If they are not yours as much as mine they are nothing or next to nothing,
355 If they do not enclose everything they are next to nothing,
If they are not the riddle and the untying of the riddle they are nothing,
If they are not just as close as they are distant they are nothing.

This is the grass that grows wherever the land is and the water is,
This is the common air that bathes the globe.

360 This is the breath of laws and songs and behaviour,
This is the tasteless water of souls . . . . this is the true sustenance,
It is for the illiterate . . . . it is for the judges of the supreme court . . . it is
    for the federal capitol and the state capitols,
It is for the admirable communes of literary men and composers and singers and
    lecturers and engineers and savans,
It is for the endless races of working people and farmers and seamen.

At home on Kanadian snow-shoes or up in the bush, or with fishermen off
    Newfoundland,
At home in the fleet of ice-boats, sailing with the rest and tacking,   340
At home on the hills of Vermont or in the woods of Maine, or the Texan ranch,
Comrade of Californians, comrade of free North-Westerners, (loving their big
    proportions,)
Comrade of raftsmen and coalmen, comrade of all who shake hands and welcome
    to drink and meat,
A learner with the simplest, a teacher of the thoughtfullest,
A novice beginning yet experient of myriads of seasons,   345
Of every hue and caste am I, of every rank and religion,
A farmer, mechanic, artist, gentleman, sailor, quaker,
Prisoner, fancy-man, rowdy, lawyer, physician, priest.

I resist any thing better than my own diversity,
Breathe the air but leave plenty after me,   350
And am not stuck up, and am in my place.

(The moth and the fish-eggs are in their place,
The bright suns I see and the dark suns I cannot see are in their place,
The palpable is in its place and the impalpable in its place.)

17

These are really the thoughts of all men in all ages and lands, they are not
    original with me,   355
If they are not yours as much as mine they are nothing, or next to nothing.
If they are not the riddle and the untying of the riddle they are nothing,
If they are not just as close as they are distant they are nothing.

This is the grass that grows wherever the land is and the water is,
This the common air that bathes the globe.   360

[18]

This is the trill of a thousand clear cornets and scream of the octave flute and
865 strike of triangles.

I play not a march for victors only . . . . I play great marches for conquered and
slain persons.

Have you heard that it was good to gain the day?
I also say it is good to fall . . . . battles are lost in the same spirit in which they
are won.

I sound triumphal drums for the dead . . . . I fling through my embouchures
the loudest and gayest music to them,
Vivas to those who have failed, and to those whose war-vessels sank in the sea,
870 and those themselves who sank in the sea,
And to all generals that lost engagements, and all overcome heroes, and the
numberless unknown heroes equal to the greatest heroes known.

[19]

This is the meal pleasantly set . . . . this is the meat and drink for natural hunger,
It is for the wicked just the same as the righteous . . . . I make appointments
with all,
I will not have a single person slighted or left away,
The keptwoman and sponger and thief are hereby invited . . . . the heavy-lipped
875 slave is invited . . . the venerealee is invited,
There shall be no difference between them and the rest.

This is the press of a bashful hand . . . . this is the float and odor of hair,
This is the touch of my lips to yours . . . . this is the murmur of yearning,
This is the far-off depth and height reflecting my own face,
880 This is the thoughtful merge of myself and the outlet again.

Do you guess I have some intricate purpose?
Well I have . . . . for the April rain has, and the mica on the side of a rock has.

Do you take it I would astonish?
Does the daylight astonish? or the early redstart twittering through the woods?
885 Do I astonish more than they?

This hour I tell things in confidence,
I might not tell everybody but I will tell you.

[20]

Who goes there! hankering, gross, mystical, nude?
How is it I extract strength from the beef I eat?

18

With music strong I come, with my cornets and my drums,
I play not marches for accepted victors only, I play marches for conquer'd and
    slain persons.

Have you heard that it was good to gain the day?
I also say it is good to fall, battles are lost in the same spirit in which they are won.

I beat and pound for the dead,   365
I blow through my embouchures my loudest and gayest for them.

Vivas to those who have fail'd!
And to those whose war-vessels sank in the sea!
And to those themselves who sank in the sea!
And to all generals that lost engagements, and all overcome heroes!   370
And the numberless unkown heroes equal to the greatest heroes known!

19

This is the meal equally set, this the meat for natural hunger,
It is for the wicked just the same as the righteous, I make appointments with all,
I will not have a single person slighted or left away,
The kept-woman, sponger, thief, are hereby invited,   375
The heavy-lipp'd slave is invited, the venerealee is invited;
There shall be no difference between them and the rest.

This is the press of a bashful hand, this the float and odor of hair,
This the touch of my lips to yours, this the murmur of yearning,
This the far-off depth and height reflecting my own face,   380
This the thoughtful merge of myself, and the outlet again.

Do you guess I have some intricate purpose?
Well I have, for the Fourth-month showers have, and the mica on the side of a
    rock has.

Do you take it I would astonish?
Does the daylight astonish? does the early redstart twittering through the woods? 885
Do I astonish more than they?

This hour I tell things in confidence,
I might not tell everybody, but I will tell you.

20

Who goes there? hankering, gross, mystical, nude;
How is it I extract strength from the beef I eat?   890

390   What is a man anyhow? What am I? and what are you?
      All I mark as my own you shall offset it with your own,
      Else it were time lost listening to me.

      I do not snivel that snivel the world over,
      That months are vacuums and the ground but wallow and filth,
      That life is a suck and a sell, and nothing remains at the end but threadbare
395   crape and tears.

      Whimpering and truckling fold with powders for invalids . . . . conformity goes
         to the fourth-removed,
      I cock my hat as I please indoors or out.

      Shall I pray? Shall I venerate and be ceremonious?

      I have pried through the strata and analyzed to a hair,
      And counselled with doctors and calculated close and found no sweeter fat than
400   sticks to my own bones.

      In all people I see myself, none more and not one a barleycorn less,
      And the good or bad I say of myself I say of them.

      And I know I am solid and sound,
      To me the converging objects of the universe perpetually flow,
405   All are written to me, and I must get what the writing means.

      And I know I am deathless,
      I know this orbit of mine cannot be swept by a carpenter's compass,
      I know I shall not pass like a child's carlacue cut with a burnt stick at night.

      I know I am august,
410   I do not trouble my spirit to vindicate itself or be understood,
      I see that the elementary laws never apologize,
      I reckon I behave no prouder than the level I plant my house by after all.

      I exist as I am, that is enough,
      If no other in the world be aware I sit content,
415   And if each and all be aware I sit content.

      One world is aware, and by far the largest to me, and that is myself,
      And whether I come to my own today or in ten thousand or ten million years,
      I can cheerfully take it now, or with equal cheerfulness I can wait.

      My foothold is tenoned and mortised in granite,

What is a man anyhow? what am I? what are you?

All I mark as my own you shall offset it with your own,
Else it were time lost listening to me.

I do not snivel that snivel the world over,
The months are vacuums and the ground but wallow and filth.   395

Whimpering and truckling fold with powders for invalids, conformity goes to the
   fourth-remov'd,
I wear my hat as I please indoors or out.

Why should I pray? why should I venerate and be ceremonious?

Having pried through the strata, analyzed to a hair, counsel'd with doctors and
   calculated close,
I find no sweeter fat than sticks to my own bones.   400

In all people I see myself, none more and not one a barley-corn less,
And the good or bad I say of myself I say of them.

I know I am solid and sound,
To me the converging objects of the universe perpetually flow,
All are written to me, and I must get what the writing means.   405

I know I am deathless,
I know this orbit of mine cannot be swept by a carpenter's compass,
I know I shall not pass like a child's carlacue cut with a burnt stick at night.

I know I am august,
I do not trouble my spirit to vindicate itself or be understood,   410
I see that the elementary laws never apologize,
(I reckon I behave no prouder than the level I plant my house by, after all.)

I exist as I am, that is enough,
If no other in the world be aware I sit content,
And if each and all be aware I sit content.   415

One world is aware and by far the largest to me, and that is myself,
And whether I come to my own to-day or in ten thousand or ten million years,
I can cheerfully take it now, or with equal cheerfulness I can wait.

My foothold is tenon'd and mortis'd in granite,

420 I laugh at what you call dissolution,
    And I know the amplitude of time.

[21]

    I am the poet of the body,
    And I am the poet of the soul.

    The pleasures of heaven are with me, and the pains of hell are with me,
    The first I graft and increase upon myself . . . . the latter I translate into a
425   new tongue.

    I am the poet of the woman the same as the man,
    And I say it is as great to be a woman as to be a man,
    And I say there is nothing greater than the mother of men.

    I chant a new chant of dilation or pride,
430 We have had ducking and deprecating about enough,
    I show that size is only developement.

    Have you outstript the rest? Are you the President?
    It is a trifle . . . . they will more than arrive there every one, and still pass on.

    I am he that walks with the tender and growing night;
435 I call to the earth and sea half-held by the night.

    Press close barebosomed night! Press close magnetic nourishing night!
    Night of south winds! Night of the large few stars!
    Still nodding night! Mad naked summer night!

    Smile O voluptuous coolbreathed earth!
440 Earth of the slumbering and liquid trees!
    Earth of departed sunset! Earth of the mountains misty-topt!
    Earth of the vitreous pour of the full moon just tinged with blue!
    Earth of shine and dark mottling the tide of the river!
    Earth of the limpid gray of clouds brighter and clearer for my sake!
445 Far-swooping elbowed earth! Rich apple-blossomed earth!
    Smile, for your lover comes!

    Prodigal! you have given me love! . . . . therefore I to you give love!
    O unspeakable passionate love!

    Thruster holding me tight and that I hold tight!
450 We hurt each other as the bridegroom and the bride hurt each other.

I laugh at what you call dissolution,   420
And I know the amplitude of time.

21

I am the poet of the Body and I am the poet of the Soul,
The pleasures of heaven are with me and the pains of hell are with me,
The first I graft and increase upon myself, the latter I translate into a new tongue.

I am the poet of the woman the same as the man,   425
And I say it is as great to be a woman as to be a man,
And I say there is nothing greater than the mother of men.

I chant the chant of dilation or pride,
We have had ducking and deprecating about enough,
I show that size is only development.   430

Have you outstript the rest? are you the President?
It is a trifle, they will more than arrive there every one, and still pass on.

I am he that walks with the tender and growing night,
I call to the earth and sea half-held by the night.

Press close bare-bosom'd night—press close magnetic nourishing night!   435
Night of south winds—night of the large few stars!
Still nodding night—mad naked summer night.

Smile O voluptuous cool-breath'd earth!
Earth of the slumbering and liquid trees!
Earth of departed sunset—earth of the mountains misty-topt!   440
Earth of the vitreous pour of the full moon just tinged with blue!
Earth of shine and dark mottling the tide of the river!
Earth of the limpid gray of clouds brighter and clearer for my sake!
Far-swooping elbow'd earth—rich apple-blossom'd earth!
Smile, for your lover comes.   445

Prodigal, you have given me love—therefore I to you give love!
O unspeakable passionate love.

[22]

You sea! I resign myself to you also . . . . I guess what you mean,
I behold from the beach your crooked inviting fingers,
I believe you refuse to go back without feeling of me;
We must have a turn together . . . . I undress . . . . hurry me out of sight of
  the land,
455 Cushion me soft . . . . rock me in billowy drowse,
Dash me with amorous wet . . . . I can repay you.

Sea of stretched ground-swells!
Sea breathing broad and convulsive breaths!
Sea of the brine of life! Sea of unshovelled and always-ready graves!
460 Howler and scooper of storms! Capricious and dainty sea!
I am integral with you . . . . I too am of one phase and of all phases.

Partaker of influx and efflux . . . . extoler of hate and conciliation,
Extoler of amies and those that sleep in each others' arms.

I am he attesting sympathy;
465 Shall I make my list of things in the house and skip the house that supports them?

I am the poet of commonsense and of the demonstrable and of immortality;
And am not the poet of goodness only . . . . I do not decline to be the poet of
  wickedness also.

Washes and razors for foofoos . . . . for me freckles and a bristling beard.

What blurt is it about virtue and about vice?
470 Evil propels me, and reform of evil propels me . . . . I stand indifferent,
My gait is no faultfinder's or rejecter's gait,
I moisten the roots of all that has grown.

Did you fear some scrofula out of the unflagging pregnancy?
Did you guess the celestial laws are yet to be worked over and rectified?

I step up to say that what we do is right and what we affirm is right . . . . and
475   some is only the ore of right,
Witnesses of us . . . . one side a balance and the antipodal side a balance,
Soft doctrine as steady help as stable doctrine,
Thoughts and deeds of the present our rouse and early start.

This minute that comes to me over the past decillions,
480 There is no better than it and now.

22

You sea! I resign myself to you also—I guess what you mean,
I behold from the beach your crooked inviting fingers,
I believe you refuse to go back without feeling of me,   450
We must have a turn together, I undress, hurry me out of sight of the land,
Cushion me soft, rock me in billowy drowse,
Dash me with amorous wet, I can repay you.

Sea of stretch'd ground-swells,
Sea breathing broad and convulsive breaths,   455
Sea of the brine of life and of unshovell'd yet always-ready graves,
Howler and scooper of storms, capricious and dainty sea,
I am integral with you, I too am of one phase and of all phases.

Partaker of influx and efflux I, extoller of hate and conciliation,
Extoller of amies and those that sleep in each others' arms,   460

I am he attesting sympathy,
(Shall I make my list of things in the house and skip the house that supports them?)

I am not the poet of goodness only, I do not decline to be the poet of
    wickedness also.

What blurt is this about virtue and about vice?
Evil propels me and reform of evil propels me, I stand indifferent,   465
My gait is no fault-finder's or rejecter's gait,
I moisten the roots of all that has grown.

Did you fear some scrofula out of the unflagging pregnancy?
Did you guess the celestial laws are yet to be work'd over and rectified?

I find one side a balance and the antipodal side a balance,   470
Soft doctrine as steady help as stable doctrine,
Thoughts and deeds of the present our rouse and early start.

This minute that comes to me over the past decillions,
There is no better than it and now.

What behaved well in the past or behaves well today is not such a wonder,
The wonder is always and always how there can be a mean man or an infidel.

[23]

Endless unfolding of words of ages!
And mine a word of the modern . . . . a word en masse.

485 A word of the faith that never balks,
One time as good as another time. . . . here or henceforward it is all the same
     to me.

A word of reality . . . . materialism first and last imbueing.

Hurrah for positive science! Long live exact demonstration!
Fetch stonecrop and mix it with cedar and branches of lilac;
This is the lexicographer or chemist . . . . this made a grammar of the
490   old cartouches,
These mariners put the ship through dangerous unknown seas,
This is the geologist, and this works with the scalpel, and this is a mathematician.

Gentlemen I receive you, and attach and clasp hands with you,
The facts are useful and real . . . . they are not my dwelling . . . . I enter by
     them to an area of the dwelling.

495 I am less the reminder of property or qualities, and more the reminder of life,
And go on the square for my own sake and for others' sake,
And make short account of neuters and geldings, and favor men and women
     fully equipped,
And beat the gong of revolt, and stop with fugitives and them that plot and
     conspire.

[24]

Walt Whitman, an American, one of the roughs, a kosmos,
500 Disorderly fleshy and sensual . . . . eating drinking and breeding,
No sentimentalist . . . . no stander above men and women or apart from
     them . . . . no more modest than immodest.

Unscrew the locks from the doors!
Unscrew the doors themselves from their jambs!

Whoever degrades another degrades me . . . . and whatever is done or said
     returns at last to me,
505 And whatever I do or say I also return.

What behaved well in the past or behaves well to-day is not such a wonder,   475
The wonder is always and always how there can be a mean man or an infidel.

23

Endless unfolding of words of ages!
And mine a word of the modern, the word En-Masse.

A word of the faith that never balks,
Here or henceforward it is all the same to me, I accept Time absolutely.   480

It alone is without flaw, it alone rounds and completes all,
That mystic baffling wonder alone completes all.

I accept Reality and dare not question it,
Materialism first and last imbuing.

Hurrah for positive science! long live exact demonstration!   485
Fetch stonecrop mixt with cedar and branches of lilac,
This is the lexicographer, this the chemist, this made a grammar of the old
    cartouches,
These mariners put the ship through dangerous unknown seas,
This is the geologist, this works with the scalpel, and this is a mathematician.

Gentlemen, to you the first honors always!   490
Your facts are useful, and yet they are not my dwelling,
I but enter by them to an area of my dwelling.

Less the reminders of properties told my words,
And more the reminders they of life untold, and of freedom and extrication,
And make short account of neuters and geldings, and favor men and women
    fully equipt,   495
And beat the gong of revolt, and stop with fugitives and them that plot and
    conspire.

24

Walt Whitman, a kosmos, of Manhattan the son,
Turbulent, fleshy, sensual, eating, drinking and breeding,
No sentimentalist, no stander above men and women or apart from them,
No more modest than immodest.   500

Unscrew the locks from the doors!
Unscrew the doors themselves from their jambs!

Whoever degrades another degrades me,
And whatever is done or said returns at last to me.

Through me the afflatus surging and surging . . . . through me the current
    and index.

I speak the password primeval . . . . I give the sign of democracy;
By God! I will accept nothing which all cannot have their counterpart of on the
    same terms.

Through me many long dumb voices,
510 Voices of the interminable generations of slaves,
Voices of prostitutes and of deformed persons,
Voices of the diseased and despairing, and of thieves and dwarfs,
Voices of cycles of preparation and accretion,
And of the threads that connect the stars—and of wombs, and of the fatherstuff,
515 And of the rights of them the others are down upon,
Of the trivial and flat and foolish and despised,
Of fog in the air and beetles rolling balls of dung.

Through me forbidden voices,
Voices of sexes and lusts . . . . voices veiled, and I remove the veil,
520 Voices indecent by me clarified and transfigured.

I do not press my finger across my mouth,
I keep as delicate around the bowels as around the head and heart,
Copulation is no more rank to me than death is.

I believe in the flesh and the appetites,
525 Seeing hearing and feeling are miracles, and each part and tag of me is a miracle.

Divine am I inside and out, and I make holy whatever I touch or am
    touched from;
The scent of these arm-pits is aroma finer than prayer,
This head is more than churches or bibles or creeds.

If I worship any particular thing it shall be some of the spread of my body;
530 Translucent mould of me it shall be you,
Shaded ledges and rests, firm masculine coulter, it shall be you,

Whatever goes to the tilth of me it shall be you,
You my rich blood, your milky stream pale strippings of my life;
Breast that presses against other breasts it shall be you,
535 My brain it shall be your occult convolutions,
Root of washed sweet-flag, timorous pond-snipe, nest of guarded duplicate eggs,
    it shall be you,
Mixed tussled hay of head and beard and brawn it shall be you,

Through me the afflatus surging and surging, through me the current and ind

I speak the pass-word primeval, I give the sign of democracy,
By God! I will accept nothing which all cannot have their counterpart of on the
    same terms.

Through me many long dumb voices,
Voices of the interminable generations of prisoners and slaves,
Voices of the diseas'd and despairing and of thieves and dwarfs,   510
Voices of cycles of preparation and accretion,
And of the threads that connect the stars, and of wombs and of the father-stuff,
And of the rights of them the others are down upon,
Of the deform'd, trivial, flat, foolish, despised,
Fog in the air, beetles rolling balls of dung.   515

Through me forbidden voices,
Voices of sexes and lusts, voices veil'd and I remove the veil,
Voices indecent by me clarified and transfigur'd.

I do not press my fingers across my mouth,
I keep as delicate around the bowels as around the head and heart,   520
Copulation is no more rank to me than death is.

I believe in the flesh and the appetites,
Seeing, hearing, feeling, are miracles, and each part and tag of me is a miracle.

Divine am I inside and out, and I make holy whatever I touch or am touch'd from,
The scent of these arm-pits aroma finer than prayer,   525
This head more than churches, bibles, and all the creeds.

If I worship one thing more than another it shall be the spread of my own body,
    or any part of it,
Translucent mould of me it shall be you!
Shaded ledges and rests it shall be you!
Firm masculine colter it shall be you!   530
Whatever goes to the tilth of me it shall be you!
You my rich blood! your milky stream pale strippings of my life!
Breast that presses against other breasts it shall be you!
My brain it shall be your occult convolutions!
Root of wash'd sweet-flag! timorous pond-snipe! nest of guarded duplicate eggs!
    it shall be you!   535
Mix'd tussled hay of head, beard, brawn, it shall be you!

Trickling sap of maple, fibre of manly wheat, it shall be you;
Sun so generous it shall be you,
540 Vapors lighting and shading my face it shall be you,
You sweaty brooks and dews it shall be you,
Winds whose soft-tickling genitals rub against me it shall be you,
Broad muscular fields, branches of liveoak, loving lounger in my winding paths,
    it shall be you,
Hands I have taken, face I have kissed, mortal I have ever touched, it shall be you.

545 I dote on myself . . . . there is that lot of me, and all so luscious,
Each moment and whatever happens thrills me with joy.

I cannot tell how my ankles bend . . . . nor whence the cause of my faintest wish,
Nor the cause of the friendship I emit . . . . nor the cause of the friendship
    I take again.

To walk up my stoop is unaccountable . . . . I pause to consider if it really be,
550 That I eat and drink is spectacle enough for the great authors and schools,
A morning-glory at my window satisfies me more than the metaphysics of books.

To behold the daybreak!
The little light fades the immense and diaphanous shadows,
The air tastes good to my palate.

555 Hefts of the moving world at innocent gambols, silently rising, freshly exuding,
Scooting obliquely high and low.

Something I cannot see puts upward libidinous prongs,
Seas of bright juice suffuse heaven.

The earth by the sky staid with . . . . the daily close of their junction,
560 The heaved challenge from the east that moment over my head,
The mocking taunt, See then whether you shall be master!

[25]

Dazzling and tremendous how quick the sunrise would kill me,
If I could not now and always send sunrise out of me.

We also ascend dazzling and tremendous as the sun,
565 We found our own my soul in the calm and cool of the daybreak.

My voice goes after what my eyes cannot reach,
With the twirl of my tongue I encompass worlds and volumes of worlds.

Trickling sap of maple, fibre of manly wheat, it shall be you!
Sun so generous it shall be you!
Vapors lighting and shading my face it shall be you!
You sweaty brooks and dews it shall be you!   540
Winds whose soft-tickling genitals rub against me it shall be you!
Broad muscular fields, branches of live oak, loving lounger in my winding paths,
    it shall be you!
Hands I have taken, face I have kiss'd, mortal I have ever touch'd, it shall be you.

I dote on myself, there is that lot of me and all so luscious,
Each moment and whatever happens thrills me with joy,   545
I cannot tell how my ankles bend, nor whence the cause of my faintest wish,
Nor the cause of the friendship I emit, nor the cause of the friendship I take again.

That I walk up my stoop, I pause to consider if it really be,
A morning-glory at my window satisfies me more than the metaphysics of books.

To behold the day-break!   550
The little light fades the immense and diaphanous shadows,
The air tastes good to my palate.

Hefts of the moving world at innocent gambols silently rising, freshly exuding,
Scooting obliquely high and low.

Something I cannot see puts upward libidinous prongs,   555
Seas of bright juice suffuse heaven.

The earth by the sky staid with, the daily close of their junction,
The heav'd challenge from the east that moment over my head,
The mocking taunt, See then whether you shall be master!

25

Dazzling and tremendous how quick the sun-rise would kill me,   560
If I could not now and always send sun-rise out of me.

We also ascend dazzling and tremendous as the sun,
We found our own O my soul in the calm and cool of the daybreak.

My voice goes after what my eyes cannot reach,
With the twirl of my tongue I encompass worlds and volumes of worlds.   565

Speech is the twin of my vision . . . . it is unequal to measure itself.

It provokes me forever,
It says sarcastically, Walt, you understand enough . . . . why don't you let it
570   out then?

Come now I will not be tantalized . . . . you conceive too much of articulation.

Do you not know how the buds beneath are folded?
Waiting in gloom protected by frost,
The dirt receding before my prophetical screams,
575 I underlying causes to balance them at last,
My knowledge my live parts . . . . it keeping tally with the meaning of things,
Happiness . . . . which whoever hears me let him or her set out in search of
        this day.

My final merit I refuse you . . . . I refuse putting from me the best I am.

Encompass worlds but never try to encompass me,
580 I crowd your noisiest talk by looking toward you.

Writing and talk do not prove me,
I carry the plenum of proof and every thing else in my face,
With the hush of my lips I confound the topmost skeptic.

[26]

I think I will do nothing for a long time but listen,
585 And accrue what I hear unto myself . . . . and let sounds contribute toward me.

I hear the bravuras of birds . . . . the bustle of growing wheat . . . . gossip of
        flames . . . . clack of sticks cooking my meals.

I hear the sound of the human voice . . . . a sound I love,
I hear all sounds as they are tuned to their uses . . . . sounds of the city and
        sounds out of the city . . . . sounds of the day and night;
Talkative young ones to those that like them . . . . the recitative of fish-pedlars
        and fruit-pedlars . . . . the loud laugh of workpeople at their meals,
590 The angry base of disjointed friendship . . . . the faint tones of the sick,
The judge with hands tight to the desk, his shaky lips pronouncing a
        death-sentence,
The heave'e'yo of stevedores unlading ships by the wharves . . . . the refrain
        of the anchor-lifters;
The ring of alarm-bells . . . . the cry of fire . . . . the whirr of swift-streaking
        engines and hose-carts with premonitory tinkles and colored lights,

Speech is the twin of my vision, it is unequal to measure itself,
It provokes me forever, it says sarcastically,
Walt you contain enough, why don't you let it out then?

Come now I will not be tantalized, you conceive too much of articulation,
Do you not know O speech how the buds beneath you are folded?   570
Waiting in gloom, protected by frost,
The dirt receding before my prophetical screams,
I underlying causes to balance them at last,
My knowledge my live parts, it keeping tally with the meaning of all things,
Happiness, (which whoever hears me let him or her set out in search of this day.)   575

My final merit I refuse you, I refuse putting from me what I really am,
Encompass worlds, but never try to encompass me,
I crowd your sleekest and best by simply looking toward you.

Writing and talk do not prove me,
I carry the plenum of proof and every thing else in my face,   580
With the hush of my lips I wholly confound the skeptic.

26

Now I will do nothing but listen,
To accrue what I hear into this song, to let sounds contribute toward it.

I hear bravuras of birds, bustle of growing wheat, gossip of flames, clack of sticks
    cooking my meals,
I hear the sound I love, the sound of the human voice,   585
I hear all sounds running together, combined, fused or following,
Sounds of the city and sounds out of the city, sounds of the day and night,
Talkative young ones to those that like them, the loud laugh of work-people
    at their meals,
The angry base of disjointed friendship, the faint tones of the sick,
The judge with hands tight to the desk, his pallid lips pronouncing a
    death-sentence,   590
The heave'e'yo of stevedores unlading ships by the wharves, the refrain of the
    anchor-lifters,
The ring of alarm-bells, the cry of fire, the whirr of swift-streaking engines and
    hose-carts with premonitory tinkles and color'd lights,

The steam-whistle . . . . the solid roll of the train of approaching cars;
595 The slow-march played at night at the head of the association,
They go to guard some corpse . . . . the flag-tops are draped with black muslin.

I hear the violincello or man's heart's complaint,
And hear the keyed cornet or else the echo of sunset.

I hear the chorus . . . . it is a grand-opera . . . . this indeed is music!

600 A tenor large and fresh as the creation fills me,
The orbic flex of his mouth is pouring and filling me full.

I hear the trained soprano . . . . she convulses me like the climax of my
        love-grip;
The orchestra whirls me wider than Uranus flies,
It wrenches unnamable ardors from my breast,
605 It throbs me to gulps of the farthest down horror,
It sails me . . . . I dab with bare feet . . . . they are licked by the indolent waves,
I am exposed . . . . cut by bitter and poisoned hail,
Steeped amid honeyed morphine . . . my windpipe squeezed in the fakes of death,
Let up again to feel the puzzle of puzzles,
610 And that we call Being.

[27]

To be in any form, what is that?
If nothing lay more developed the quahaug and its callous shell were enough.

Mine is no callous shell,
I have instant conductors all over me whether I pass or stop,
615 They seize every object and lead it harmlessly through me.

I merely stir, press, feel with my fingers, and am happy,
To touch my person to some one else's is about as much as I can stand.

[28]

Is this then a touch? . . . . quivering me to a new identity,
Flames and ether making a rush for my veins,
620 Treacherous tip of me reaching and crowding to help them,
My flesh and blood playing out lightning, to strike what is hardly different
        from myself,
On all sides prurient provokers stiffening my limbs,
Straining the udder of my heart for its withheld drip,
Behaving licentious toward me, taking no denial,

The steam-whistle, the solid roll of the train of approaching cars,
The slow march play'd at the head of the association marching two and two,
(They go to guard some corpse, the flag-tops are draped with black muslin.)   595

I hear the violoncello, ('tis the young man's heart's complaint,)
I hear the key'd cornet, it glides quickly in through my ears,
It shakes mad-sweet pangs through my belly and breast.

I hear the chorus, it is a grand opera,
Ah this indeed is music—this suits me.   600

A tenor large and fresh as the creation fills me,
The orbic flex of his mouth is pouring and filling me full.

I hear the train'd soprano (what work with hers is this?)
The orchestra whirls me wider than Uranus flies,
It wrenches such ardors from me I did not know I possess'd them,   605
It sails me, I dab with bare feet, they are lick'd by the indolent waves,
I am cut by bitter and angry hail, I lose my breath,
Steep'd amid honey'd morphine, my windpipe throttled in fakes of death,
At length let up again to feel the puzzle of puzzles,
And that we call Being.   610

27

To be in any form, what is that?
(Round and round we go, all of us, and ever come back thither,)
If nothing lay more develop'd the quahaug in its callous shell were enough.

Mine is no callous shell,
I have instant conductors all over me whether I pass or stop,   615
They seize every object and lead it harmlessly through me.

I merely stir, press, feel with my fingers, and am happy,
To touch my person to some one else's is about as much as I can stand.

28

Is this then a touch? quivering me to a new identity,
Flames and ether making a rush for my veins,   620
Treacherous tip of me reaching and crowding to help them,
My flesh and blood playing out lightning to strike what is hardly different
    from myself,
On all sides prurient provokers stiffening my limbs,
Straining the udder of my heart for its withheld drip,
Behaving licentious toward me, taking no denial,   625

625 Depriving me of my best as for a purpose,
Unbuttoning my clothes and holding me by the bare waist,
Deluding my confusion with the calm of the sunlight and pasture fields,
Immodestly sliding the fellow-senses away,
They bribed to swap off with touch, and go and graze at the edges of me,
630 No consideration, no regard for my draining strength or my anger,
Fetching the rest of the herd around to enjoy them awhile,
Then all uniting to stand on a headland and worry me.

The sentries desert every other part of me,
They have left me helpless to a red marauder,
635 They all come to the headland to witness and assist against me.

I am given up by traitors;
I talk wildly . . . . I have lost my wits . . . . I and nobody else am the
greatest traitor,
I went myself first to the headland . . . . my own hands carried me there.

You villain touch! what are you doing? . . . . my breath is tight in its throat;
640 Unclench your floodgates! you are too much for me.

[29]
Blind loving wrestling touch! Sheathed hooded sharptoothed touch!
Did it make you ache so leaving me?

Parting tracked by arriving . . . . perpetual payment of the perpetual loan,
Rich showering rain, and recompense richer afterward.

645 Sprouts take and accumulate . . . . stand by the curb prolific and vital,
Landscapes projected masculine full-sized and golden.

[30]
All truths wait in all things,
They neither hasten their own delivery nor resist it,
They do not need the obstetric forceps of the surgeon,
650 The insignificant is as big to me as any,
What is less or more than a touch?

Logic and sermons never convince,
The damp of the night drives deeper into my soul.

Only what proves itself to every man and woman is so,
655 Only what nobody denies is so.

Depriving me of my best as for a purpose,
Unbuttoning my clothes, holding me by the bare waist,
Deluding my confusion with the calm of the sunlight and pasture-fields,
Immodestly sliding the fellow-senses away,
They bribed to swap off with touch and go and graze at the edges of me,   630
No consideration, no regard for my draining strength or my anger,
Fetching the rest of the herd around to enjoy them a while,
Then all uniting to stand on a headland and worry me.

The sentries desert every other part of me,
They have left me helpless to a red marauder,   635
They all come to the headland to witness and assist against me.

I am given up by traitors,
I talk wildly, I have lost my wits, I and nobody else am the greatest traitor,
I went myself first to the headland, my own hands carried me there.

You villain touch! what are you doing? my breath is tight in its throat,   640
Unclench your floodgates, you are too much for me.

29

Blind loving wrestling touch, sheath'd hooded sharp-tooth'd touch!
Did it make you ache so, leaving me?

Parting track'd by arriving, perpetual payment of perpetual loan,
Rich showering rain, and recompense richer afterward.   645

Sprouts take and accumulate, stand by the curb prolific and vital,
Landscapes projected masculine, full-sized and golden.

30

All truths wait in all things,
They neither hasten their own delivery nor resist it,
They do not need the obstetric forceps of the surgeon,   650
The insignificant is as big to me as any,
(What is less or more than a touch?)

Logic and sermons never convince,
The damp of the night drives deeper into my soul.

(Only what proves itself to every man and woman is so,   655
Only what nobody denies is so.)

A minute and a drop of me settle my brain;
I believe the soggy clods shall become lovers and lamps,
And a compend of compends is the meat of a man or woman,
And a summit and flower there is the feeling they have for each other,
660 And they are to branch boundlessly out of that lesson until it becomes omnific,
And until every one shall delight us, and we them.

[31]

I believe a leaf of grass is no less than the journeywork of the stars,
And the pismire is equally perfect, and a grain of sand, and the egg of the wren,
And the tree-toad is a chef-d'œuvre for the highest,
665 And the running blackberry would adorn the parlors of heaven,
And the narrowest hinge in my hand puts to scorn all machinery,
And the cow crunching with depressed head surpasses any statue,
And a mouse is miracle enough to stagger sextillions of infidels,
And I could come every afternoon of my life to look at the farmer's girl boiling
    her iron tea-kettle and baking shortcake.

I find I incorporate gneiss and coal and long-threaded moss and fruits and grains
670   and esculent roots,
And am stucco'd with quadrupeds and birds all over,
And have distanced what is behind me for good reasons,
And call any thing close again when I desire it.

In vain the speeding or shyness,
675 In vain the plutonic rocks send their old heat against my approach,
In vain the mastodon retreats beneath its own powdered bones,
In vain objects stand leagues off and assume manifold shapes,
In vain the ocean settling in hollows and the great monsters lying low,
In vain the buzzard houses herself with the sky,
680 In vain the snake slides through the creepers and logs,
In vain the elk takes to the inner passes of the woods,
In vain the razorbilled auk sails far north to Labrador,
I follow quickly . . . . I ascend to the nest in the fissure of the cliff.

[32]

I think I could turn and live awhile with the animals . . . . they are so placid
    and self-contained,
685 I stand and look at them sometimes half the day long.

They do not sweat and whine about their condition,
They do not lie awake in the dark and weep for their sins,
They do not make me sick discussing their duty to God,

A minute and a drop of me settle my brain,
I believe the soggy clods shall become lovers and lamps,
And a compend of compends is the meat of a man or woman,
And a summit and flower there is the feeling they have for each other,
And they are to branch boundlessly out of that lesson until it becomes
And until one and all shall delight us, and we them.

31

I believe a leaf of grass is no less than the journey-work of the stars,
And the pismire is equally perfect, and a grain of sand, and the egg of the wren,
And the tree-toad is a chef-d'œuvre for the highest,   665
And the running blackberry would adorn the parlors of heaven,
And the narrowest hinge in my hand puts to scorn all machinery,
And the cow crunching with depress'd head surpasses any statue,
And a mouse is miracle enough to stagger sextillions of infidels.

I find I incorporate gneiss, coal, long-threaded moss, fruits, grains, esculent roots,   670
And am stucco'd with quadrupeds and birds all over,
And have distanced what is behind me for good reasons,
But call any thing back again when I desire it.

In vain the speeding or shyness,
In vain the plutonic rocks send their old heat against my approach,   675
In vain the mastodon retreats beneath its own powder'd bones,
In vain objects stand leagues off and assume manifold shapes,
In vain the ocean settling in hollows and the great monsters lying low,
In vain the buzzard houses herself with the sky,
In vain the snake slides through the creepers and logs,   680
In vain the elk takes to the inner passes of the woods,
In vain the razor-bill'd auk sails far north to Labrador,
I follow quickly, I ascend to the nest in the fissure of the cliff.

32

I think I could turn and live with animals, they're so placid and self-contain'd,
I stand and look at them long and long.   685

They do not sweat and whine about their condition,
They do not lie awake in the dark and weep for their sins,
They do not make me sick discussing their duty to God,

Not one is dissatisfied . . . . not one is demented with the mania of
    owning things,
690 Not one kneels to another nor to his kind that lived thousands of years ago,
Not one is respectable or industrious over the whole earth.

So they show their relations to me and I accept them;
They bring me tokens of myself . . . . they evince them plainly in their
    possession.

I do not know where they got those tokens,
695 I must have passed that way untold times ago and negligently dropt them,
Myself moving forward then and now and forever,
Gathering and showing more always and with velocity,
Infinite and omnigenous and the like of these among them;
Not too exclusive toward the reachers of my remembrancers,
700 Picking out here one that shall be my amie,
Choosing to go with him on brotherly terms.

A gigantic beauty of a stallion, fresh and responsive to my caresses,
Head high in the forehead and wide between the ears,
Limbs glossy and supple, tail dusting the ground,
Eyes well apart and full of sparkling wickedness . . . . ears finely cut and
705   flexibly moving.

His nostrils dilate . . . . my heels embrace him . . . . his well built limbs
    tremble with pleasure . . . . we speed around and return.

I but use you a moment and then I resign you stallion . . . . and do not need
    your paces, and outgallop them,
And myself as I stand or sit pass faster than you.

[33]
Swift wind! Space! My Soul! Now I know it is true what I guessed at;
710 What I guessed when I loafed on the grass,
What I guessed while I lay alone in my bed . . . . and again as I walked the
    beach under the paling stars of the morning.

My ties and ballasts leave me . . . . I travel . . . . I sail . . . . my elbows rest
    in the sea-gaps,
I skirt the sierras . . . . my palms cover continents,
I am afoot with my vision.

715 By the city's quadrangular houses . . . . in log-huts, or camping with lumbermen,
Along the ruts of the turnpike . . . . along the dry gulch and rivulet bed,

Not one is dissatisfied, not one is demented with the mania of owning things,
Not one kneels to another, nor to his kind that lived thousands of years ago,   690
Not one is respectable or unhappy over the whole earth.

So they show their relations to me and I accept them,
They bring me tokens of myself, they evince them plainly in their possession.

I wonder where they get those tokens,
Did I pass that way huge times ago and negligently drop them?   695

Myself moving forward then and now and forever,
Gathering and showing more always and with velocity,
Infinite and omnigenous, and the like of these among them,
Not too exclusive toward the reachers of my remembrancers,
Picking out here one that I love, and now go with him on brotherly terms.   700

A gigantic beauty of a stallion, fresh and responsive to my caresses,
Head high in the forehead, wide between the ears,
Limbs glossy and supple, tail dusting the ground,
Eyes full of sparkling wickedness, ears finely cut, flexibly moving.

His nostrils dilate as my heels embrace him,   705
His well-built limbs tremble with pleasure as we race around and return.

I but use you a minute, then I resign you, stallion,
Why do I need your paces when I myself out-gallop them?
Even as I stand or sit passing faster than you.

33

Space and Time! now I see it is true, what I guess'd at,   710
What I guess'd when I loaf'd on the grass,
What I guess'd while I lay alone in my bed,
And again as I walk'd the beach under the paling stars of the morning.

My ties and ballasts leave me, my elbows rest in sea-gaps,
I skirt sierras, my palms cover continents,   715
I am afoot with my vision.

By the city's quadrangular houses—in log huts, camping with lumbermen,
Along the ruts of the turnpike, along the dry gulch and rivulet bed,

Hoeing my onion-patch, and rows of carrots and parsnips . . . . crossing
    savannas . . . . trailing in forests,
Prospecting . . . . gold-digging . . . . girdling the trees of a new purchase,
Scorched ankle-deep by the hot sand . . . . hauling my boat down the
    shallow river;
Where the panther walks to and fro on a limb overhead . . . . where the buck
720   turns furiously at the hunter,
Where the rattlesnake suns his flabby length on a rock . . . . where the otter
    is feeding on fish,
Where the alligator in his tough pimples sleeps by the bayou,
Where the black bear is searching for roots or honey . . . . where the beaver
    pats the mud with his paddle-tail;
Over the growing sugar . . . . . over the cottonplant . . . . over the rice in its
    low moist field;
Over the sharp-peaked farmhouse with its scalloped scum and slender shoots from
725   the gutters;
Over the western persimmon . . . . over the longleaved corn and the delicate
    blue-flowered flax;
Over the white and brown buckwheat, a hummer and a buzzer there with
    the rest,
Over the dusky green of the rye as it ripples and shades in the breeze;
Scaling mountains . . . . pulling myself cautiously up . . . . holding on by low
    scragged limbs,
730 Walking the path worn in the grass and beat through the leaves of the brush;
Where the quail is whistling betwixt the woods and the wheatlot,
Where the bat flies in the July eve . . . . where the great goldbug drops through
    the dark;
Where the flails keep time on the barn floor,
Where the brook puts out of the roots of the old tree and flows to the meadow,
Where cattle stand and shake away flies with the tremulous shuddering of
735   their hides,
Where the cheese-cloth hangs in the kitchen, and andirons straddle the
    hearth-slab, and cobwebs fall in festoons from the rafters;
Where triphammers crash . . . . where the press is whirling its cylinders;
Wherever the human heart beats with terrible throes out of its ribs;
Where the pear-shaped balloon is floating aloft . . . . floating in it myself and
    looking composedly down;
Where the life-car is drawn on the slipnoose . . . . where the heat hatches
740   pale-green eggs in the dented sand,
Where the she-whale swims with her calves and never forsakes them,
Where the steamship trails hindways its long pennant of smoke,
Where the ground-shark's fin cuts like a black chip out of the water,
Where the half-burned brig is riding on unknown currents,
745 Where shells grow to her slimy deck, and the dead are corrupting below;

Weeding my onion-patch or hoeing rows of carrots and parsnips, crossing savannas,
    trailing in forests,
Prospecting, gold-digging, girdling the trees of a new purchase,   720
Scorch'd ankle-deep by the hot sand, hauling my boat down the shallow river,
Where the panther walks to and fro on a limb overhead, where the buck turns
    furiously at the hunter,
Where the rattlesnake suns his flabby length on a rock, where the otter is
    feeding on fish,
Where the alligator in his tough pimples sleeps by the bayou,
Where the black bear is searching for roots or honey, where the beaver pats the
    mud with his paddle-shaped tail;   725
Over the growing sugar, over the yellow-flower'd cotton plant, over the rice in its
    low moist field,
Over the sharp-peak'd farm house, with its scallop'd scum and slender shoots from
    the gutters,
Over the western persimmon, over the long-leav'd corn, over the delicate blue-
    flower flax,
Over the white and brown buckwheat, a hummer and buzzer there with the rest,
Over the dusky green of the rye as it ripples and shades in the breeze;   730
Scaling mountains, pulling myself cautiously up, holding on by low scragged limbs,
Walking the path worn in the grass and beat through the leaves of the brush,
Where the quail is whistling betwixt the woods and the wheat-lot,
Where the bat flies in the Seventh-month eve, where the great gold-bug drops
    through the dark,
Where the brook puts out of the roots of the old tree and flows to the meadow,   735
Where cattle stand and shake away flies with the tremulous shuddering of
    their hides,
Where the cheese-cloth hangs in the kitchen, where andirons straddle the hearth-
    slab, where cobwebs fall in festoons from the rafters;
Where trip-hammers crash, where the press is whirling its cylinders,
Where the human heart beats with terrible throes under its ribs,
Where the pear-shaped balloon is floating aloft, (floating in it myself and looking
    composedly down,)   740
Where the life-car is drawn on the slip-noose, where the heat hatches pale-green eggs
    in the dented sand,
Where the she-whale swims with her calf and never forsakes it,
Where the steam-ship trails hind-ways its long pennant of smoke,
Where the fin of the shark cuts like a black chip out of the water,
Where the half-burn'd brig is riding on unknown currents,   745
Where shells grow to her slimy deck, where the dead are corrupting below;

Where the striped and starred flag is borne at the head of the regiments;
Approaching Manhattan, up by the long-stretching island,
Under Niagara, the cataract falling like a veil over my countenance;
Upon a door-step . . . . upon the horse-block of hard wood outside,
750 Upon the race-course, or enjoying pic-nics or jigs or a good game of base-ball,
At he-festivals with blackguard jibes and ironical license and bull-dances and
    drinking and laughter,
At the cider-mill, tasting the sweet of the brown sqush . . . . sucking the juice
    through a straw,
At apple-pealings, wanting kisses for all the red fruit I find,
At musters and beach-parties and friendly bees and huskings and house-raisings;
Where the mockingbird sounds his delicious gurgles, and cackles and screams
755   and weeps,
Where the hay-rick stands in the barnyard, and the dry-stalks are scattered, and
    the brood cow waits in the hovel,
Where the bull advances to do his masculine work, and the stud to the mare,
    and the cock is treading the hen,
Where the heifers browse, and the geese nip their food with short jerks;
Where the sundown shadows lengthen over the limitless and lonesome prairie,
Where the herds of buffalo make a crawling spread of the square miles far
760   and near;
Where the hummingbird shimmers . . . . where the neck of the longlived swan
    is curving and winding;
Where the laughing-gull scoots by the slappy shore and laughs her near-human
    laugh;
Where beehives range on a gray bench in the garden half-hid by the high weeds;
Where the band-necked partridges roost in a ring on the ground with their
    heads out;
765 Where burial coaches enter the arched gates of a cemetery;
Where winter wolves bark amid wastes of snow and icicled trees;
Where the yellow-crowned heron comes to the edge of the marsh at night and
    feeds upon small crabs;
Where the splash of swimmers and divers cools the warm noon;
Where the katydid works her chromatic reed on the walnut-tree over the well;
770 Through patches of citrons and cucumbers with silver-wired leaves,
Through the salt-lick or orange glade . . . . or under conical furs;
Through the gymnasium . . . . through the curtained saloon . . . through the
    office or public hall;
Pleased with the native and pleased with the foreign . . . . pleased with the
    new and old,
Pleased with women, the homely as well as the handsome,
775 Pleased with the quakeress as she puts off her bonnet and talks melodiously,
Pleased with the primitive tunes of the choir of the whitewashed church,
Pleased with the earnest words of the sweating Methodist preacher, or any
    preacher . . . . looking seriously at the camp-meeting;

Where the dense-starr'd flag is borne at the head of the regiments,
Approaching Manhattan up by the long-stretching island,
Under Niagara, the cataract falling like a veil over my countenance,
Upon a door-step, upon the horse-block of hard wood outside,   750
Upon the race-course, or enjoying picnics or jigs or a good game of base-ball,
At he-festivals, with blackguard jibes, ironical license, bull-dances, drinking, laughter,
At the cider-mill tasting the sweets of the brown mash, sucking the juice through a
 straw,
At apple-peelings wanting kisses for all the red fruit I find,
At musters, beach-parties, friendly bees, huskings, house-raisings,   755
Where the mocking-bird sounds his delicious gurgles, cackles, screams, weeps,
Where the hay-rick stands in the barn-yard, where the dry-stalks are scatter'd, where
 the brood-cow waits in the hovel,
Where the bull advances to do his masculine work, where the stud to the mare,
 where the cock is treading the hen,
Where the heifers browse, where geese nip their food with short jerks,
Where sun-down shadows lengthen over the limitless and lonesome prairie,   760
Where herds of buffalo make a crawling spread of the square miles far and near,
Where the humming-bird shimmers, where the neck of the long-lived swan is curving
 and winding,
Where the laughing-gull scoots by the shore, where she laughs her near-human laugh,
Where bee-hives range on a gray bench in the garden half hid by the high weeds,
Where band-neck'd partridges roost in a ring on the ground with their heads out,   765
Where burial coaches enter the arch'd gates of a cemetery,
Where winter wolves bark amid wastes of snow and icicled trees,
Where the yellow-crown'd heron comes to the edge of the marsh at night and feeds
 upon small crabs,
Where the splash of swimmers and divers cools the warm noon,
Where the katy-did works her chromatic reed on the walnut-tree over the well,   770
Through patches of citrons and cucumbers with silver-wired leaves,
Through the salt-lick or orange glade, or under conical firs,
Through the gymnasium, through the curtain'd saloon, through the office or
 public hall;
Pleas'd with the native and pleas'd with the foreign, pleas'd with the new and old,
Pleas'd with the homely woman as well as the handsome,   775
Pleas'd with the quakeress as she puts off her bonnet and talks melodiously,
Pleas'd with the tune of the choir of the whitewash'd church,
Pleas'd with the earnest words of the sweating Methodist preacher, impress'd
 seriously at the camp-meeting;

Looking in at the shop-windows in Broadway the whole forenoon . . . . pressing
the flesh of my nose to the thick plate-glass,
Wandering the same afternoon with my face turned up to the clouds;
780 My right and left arms round the sides of two friends and I in the middle;
Coming home with the bearded and dark-cheeked bush-boy . . . . riding behind
him at the drape of the day;
Far from the settlements studying the print of animals' feet, or the moccasin print;
By the cot in the hospital reaching lemonade to a feverish patient,
By the coffined corpse when all is still, examining with a candle;
785 Voyaging to every port to dicker and adventure;
Hurrying with the modern crowd, as eager and fickle as any,
Hot toward one I hate, ready in my madness to knife him;
Solitary at midnight in my back yard, my thoughts gone from me a long while,
Walking the old hills of Judea with the beautiful gentle god by my side;
790 Speeding through space . . . . speeding through heaven and the stars,
Speeding amid the seven satellites and the broad ring and the diameter of
eighty thousand miles,
Speeding with tailed meteors . . . . throwing fire-balls like the rest,
Carrying the crescent child that carries its own full mother in its belly:
Storming enjoying planning loving cautioning,
795 Backing and filling, appearing and disappearing,
I tread day and night such roads.

I visit the orchards of God and look at the spheric product,
And look at quintillions ripened, and look at quintillions green.

I fly the flight of the fluid and swallowing soul,
800 My course runs below the soundings of plummets.

I help myself to material and immaterial,
No guard can shut me off, no law can prevent me.

I anchor my ship for a little while only,
My messengers continually cruise away or bring their returns to me.

I go hunting polar furs and the seal . . . . leaping chasms with a pike-pointed
805   staff . . . . clinging to topples of brittle and blue.

I ascend to the foretruck . . . . I take my place late at night in the crow's nest
. . . . we sail through the arctic sea . . . . it is plenty light enough,
Through the clear atmosphere I stretch around on the wonderful beauty,
The enormous masses of ice pass me and I pass them . . . . the scenery is plain
in all directions,

Looking in at the shop-windows of Broadway the whole forenoon, flatting the flesh
    of my nose on the thick plate glass,
Wandering the same afternoon with my face turn'd up to the clouds, or down a
    lane or along the beach,   780
My right and left arms round the sides of two friends, and I in the middle;
Coming home with the silent and dark-cheek'd bush-boy, (behind me he rides at the
    drape of the day,)
Far from the settlements studying the print of animals' feet, or the moccasin print,
By the cot in the hospital reaching lemonade to a feverish patient,
Nigh the coffin'd corpse when all is still, examining with a candle;   785
Voyaging to every port to dicker and adventure,
Hurrying with the modern crowd as eager and fickle as any,
Hot toward one I hate, ready in my madness to knife him,
Solitary at midnight in my back yard, my thoughts gone from me a long while,
Walking the old hills of Judæa with the beautiful gentle God by my side,   790
Speeding through space, speeding through heaven and the stars,
Speeding amid the seven satellites and the broad ring, and the diameter of eighty
    thousand miles,
Speeding with tail'd meteors, throwing fire-balls like the rest,
Carrying the crescent child that carries its own full mother in its belly,
Storming, enjoying, planning, loving, cautioning,   795
Backing and filling, appearing and disappearing,
I tread day and night such roads.

I visit the orchards of spheres and look at the product,
And look at quintillions ripen'd and look at quintillions green.

I fly those flights of a fluid and swallowing soul,   800
My course runs below the soundings of plummets.

I help myself to material and immaterial,
No guard can shut me off, no law prevent me.

I anchor my ship for a little while only,
My messengers continually cruise away or bring their returns to me.   805

I go hunting polar furs and the seal, leaping chasms with a pike-pointed staff,
    clinging to topples of brittle and blue.

I ascend to the foretruck,
I take my place late at night in the crow's-nest,
We sail the arctic sea, it is plenty light enough,
Through the clear atmosphere I stretch around on the wonderful beauty,   810
The enormous masses of ice pass me and I pass them, the scenery is plain in all
    directions,

The white-topped mountains point up in the distance . . . . I fling out my fancies
    toward them;
We are about approaching some great battlefield in which we are soon to
810   be engaged,
We pass the colossal outposts of the encampment . . . . we pass with still feet
    and caution;
Or we are entering by the suburbs some vast and ruined city . . . . the blocks
    and fallen architecture more than all the living cities of the globe.

I am a free companion . . . . I bivouac by invading watchfires.

I turn the bridegroom out of bed and stay with the bride myself,
815 And tighten her all night to my thighs and lips.

My voice is the wife's voice, the screech by the rail of the stairs,
They fetch my man's body up dripping and drowned.

I understand the large hearts of heroes,
The courage of present times and all times;
How the skipper saw the crowded and rudderless wreck of the steamship, and death
820   chasing it up and down the storm,
How he knuckled tight and gave not back one inch, and was faithful of days and
    faithful of nights,
And chalked in large letters on a board, Be of good cheer, We will not desert you;
How he saved the drifting company at last,
How the lank loose-gowned women looked when boated from the side of their
    prepared graves,
How the silent old-faced infants, and the lifted sick, and the sharp-lipped
825   unshaved men;
All this I swallow and it tastes good . . . . I like it well, and it becomes mine,
I am the man . . . . I suffered . . . . I was there.

The disdain and calmness of martyrs,
The mother condemned for a witch and burnt with dry wood, and her children
    gazing on;
The hounded slave that flags in the race and leans by the fence, blowing and
830   covered with sweat,
The twinges that sting like needles his legs and neck,
The murderous buckshot and the bullets,
All these I feel or am.

I am the hounded slave . . . . I wince at the bite of the dogs,
835 Hell and despair are upon me . . . . crack and again crack the marksmen,

The white-topt mountains show in the distance, I fling out my fancies toward them,
We are approaching some great battle-field in which we are soon to be engaged,
We pass the colossal outposts of the encampment, we pass with still feet and
    caution,
Or we are entering by the suburbs some vast and ruin'd city,   815
The blocks and fallen architecture more than all the living cities of the globe.

I am a free companion, I bivouac by invading watchfires,
I turn the bridegroom out of bed and stay with the bride myself,
I tighten her all night to my thighs and lips.

My voice is the wife's voice, the screech by the rail of the stairs,   820
They fetch my man's body up dripping and drown'd.

I understand the large hearts of heroes,
The courage of present times and all times,
How the skipper saw the crowded and ruddlerless wreck of the steam-ship, and
    Death chasing it up and down the storm,
How he knuckled tight and gave not back an inch, and was faithful of days and
    faithful of nights,   825
And chalk'd in large letters on a board, *Be of good cheer, we will not desert you;*
How he follow'd with them and tack'd with them three days and would not give
    it up,
How he saved the drifting company at last,
How the lank loose-gown'd women look'd when boated from the side of their
    prepared graves,
How the silent old-faced infants and the lifted sick, and the sharp-lipp'd
    unshaved men;   830
All this I swallow, it tastes good, I like it well, it becomes mine,
I am the man, I suffer'd, I was there.

The disdain and calmness of martyrs,
The mother of old, condemn'd for a witch, burnt with dry wood, her children
    gazing on,
The hounded slave that flags in the race, leans by the fence, blowing, cover'd
    with sweat,   835
The twinges that sting like needles his legs and neck, the murderous buckshot and
    the bullets,
All these I feel or am.

I am the hounded slave, I wince at the bite of the dogs,
Hell and despair are upon me, crack and again crack the marksmen,

I clutch the rails of the fence . . . . my gore dribs thinned with the ooze of
    my skin,
I fall on the weeds and stones,
The riders spur their unwilling horses and haul close,
They taunt my dizzy ears . . . . they beat me violently over the head with
    their whip-stocks.

840 Agonies are one of my changes of garments;
I do not ask the wounded person how he feels . . . . I myself become the
    wounded person,
My hurt turns livid upon me as I lean on a cane and observe.

I am the mashed fireman with breastbone broken . . . . tumbling walls buried me
    in their debris,
Heat and smoke I inspired . . . . I heard the yelling shouts of my comrades,
845 I heard the distant click of their picks and shovels;
They have cleared the beams away . . . . they tenderly lift me forth.

I lie in the night air in my red shirt . . . . the pervading hush is for my sake,
Painless after all I lie, exhausted but not so unhappy,
White and beautiful are the faces around me . . . . the heads are bared of
    their fire-caps,
850 The kneeling crowd fades with the light of the torches.

Distant and dead resuscitate,
They show as the dial or move as the hands of me . . . . and I am the clock myself.

I am an old artillerist, and tell of some fort's bombardment . . . . and am
    there again.

Again the reveille of drummers . . . . again the attacking cannon and mortars
    and howitzers,
855 Again the attacked send their cannon responsive.

I take part . . . . I see and hear the whole,
The cries and curses and roar . . . . the plaudits for well aimed shots,
The ambulanza slowly passing and trailing its red drip,
Workmen searching after damages and to make indispensable repairs,
860 The fall of grenades through the rent roof . . . . the fan-shaped explosion,
The whizz of limbs heads stone wood and iron high in the air.

Again gurgles the mouth of my dying general . . . . he furiously waves with
    his hand,
He gasps through the clot . . . . Mind not me . . . . mind . . . . the entrenchments.

I clutch the rails of the fence, my gore dribs, thinn'd with the ooze of my skin,   840
I fall on the weeds and stones,
The riders spur their unwilling horses, haul close,
Taunt my dizzy ears and beat me violently over the head with whip-stocks.

Agonies are one of my changes of garments.
I do not ask the wounded person how he feels, I myself become the wounded
    person,   845
My hurts turn livid upon me as I lean on a cane and observe.

I am the mash'd fireman with breast-bone broken,
Tumbling walls buried me in their debris,
Heat and smoke I inspired, I heard the yelling shouts of my comrades,
I heard the distant click of their picks and shovels,   850
They have clear'd the beams away, they tenderly lift me forth.

I lie in the night air in my red shirt, the pervading hush is for my sake,
Painless after all I lie exhausted but not so unhappy,
White and beautiful are the faces around me, the heads are bared of their
    fire-caps,
The kneeling crowd fades with the light of the torches.   855

Distant and dead resuscitate,
They show me as the dial or move as the hands of me, I am the clock myself.

I am an old artillerist, I tell of my fort's bombardment,
I am there again.

Again the long roll of the drummers,   860
Again the attacking cannon, mortars,
Again to my listening ears the cannon responsive.

I take part, I see and hear the whole,
The cries, curses, roar, the plaudits for well-aim'd shots,
The ambulanza slowly passing trailing its red drip,   865
Workmen searching after damages, making indispensable repairs,
The fall of grenades through the rent roof, the fan-shaped explosion,
The whizz of limbs, heads, stone, wood, iron, high in the air.

Again gurgles the mouth of my dying general, he furiously waves with his hand,
He gasps through the clot *Mind not me—mind—the entrenchments.*   870

[34]

I tell not the fall of Alamo . . . . not one escaped to tell the fall of Alamo,
865 The hundred and fifty are dumb yet at Alamo.

Hear now the tale of a jetblack sunrise,
Hear of the murder in cold blood of four hundred and twelve young men.

Retreating they had formed in a hollow square with their baggage for breastworks,
Nine hundred lives out of the surrounding enemy's nine times their number was
  the price they took in advance,
870 Their colonel was wounded and their ammunition gone,
They treated for an honorable capitulation, received writing and seal, gave up their
  arms, and marched back prisoners of war.

They were the glory of the race of rangers,
Matchless with a horse, a rifle, a song, a supper or a courtship,
Large, turbulent, brave, handsome, generous, proud and affectionate,
875 Bearded, sunburnt, dressed in the free costume of hunters,
Not a single one over thirty years of age.

The second Sunday morning they were brought out in squads and massacred
  . . . . it was beautiful early summer,
The work commenced about five o'clock and was over by eight.

None obeyed the command to kneel,
880 Some made a mad and helpless rush . . . . some stood stark and straight,
A few fell at once, shot in the temple or heart . . . . the living and dead lay
  together,
The maimed and mangled dug in the dirt . . . . the new-comers saw them there;
Some half-killed attempted to crawl away,
These were dispatched with bayonets or battered with the blunts of muskets;
A youth not seventeen years old seized his assassin till two more came to
885 release him,
The three were all torn, and covered with the boy's blood.

At eleven o'clock began the burning of the bodies;
And that is the tale of the murder of the four hundred and twelve young men,
And that was a jetblack sunrise.

[35]

890 Did you read in the seabooks of the oldfashioned frigate-fight?
Did you learn who won by the light of the moon and stars?

Our foe was no skulk in his ship, I tell you,

34

Now I tell what I knew in Texas in my early youth,
(I tell not the fall of Alamo,
Not one escaped to tell the fall of Alamo,
The hundred and fifty are dumb yet at Alamo,)
'Tis the tale of the murder in cold blood of four hundred and twelve young men.   875

Retreating they had form'd in a hollow square with their baggage for breastworks,
Nine hundred lives out of the surrounding enemy's, nine times their number, was
    the price they took in advance,
Their colonel was wounded and their ammunition gone,
They treated for an honorable capitulation, receiv'd writing and seal, gave up their
    arms and march'd back prisoners of war.

They were the glory of the race of rangers,   880
Matchless with horse, rifle, song, supper, courtship,
Large, turbulent, generous, handsome, proud, and affectionate,
Bearded, sunburnt, drest in the free costume of hunters,
Not a single one over thirty years of age.

The second First-day morning they were brought out in squads and massacred,
    it was beautiful early summer,   885
The work commenced about five o'clock and was over by eight.

None obey'd the command to kneel,
Some made a mad and helpless rush, some stood stark and straight,
A few fell at once, shot in the temple or heart, the living and dead lay together,
The maim'd and mangled dug in the dirt, the new-comers saw them there,   890
Some half-kill'd attempted to crawl away,
These were despatch'd with bayonets or batter'd with the blunts of muskets,
A youth not seventeen years old seiz'd his assassin till two more came to
    release him,
The three were all torn and cover'd with the boy's blood.

At eleven o'clock began the burning of the bodies;   895
This is the tale of the murder of the four hundred and twelve young men.

35

Would you hear of an old-time sea-fight?
Would you learn who won by the light of the moon and stars?
List to the yarn, as my grandmother's father the sailor told it to me.

Our foe was no skulk in his ship I tell you, (said he,)   900

His was the English pluck, and there is no tougher or truer, and never was,
     and never will be;
Along the lowered eve he came, horribly raking us.

895   We closed with him . . . . the yards entangled . . . . the cannon touched,
My captain lashed fast with his own hands.

We had received some eighteen-pound shots under the water,
On our lower-gun-deck two large pieces had burst at the first fire, killing all around
     and blowing up overhead.

Ten o'clock at night, and the full moon shining and the leaks on the gain, and
     five feet of water reported,
The master-at-arms loosing the prisoners confined in the after-hold to give them a
900   chance for themselves.

The transit to and from the magazine was now stopped by the sentinels,
They saw so many strange faces they did not know whom to trust.

Our frigate was afire . . . . the other asked if we demanded quarters? if our colors
     were struck and the fighting done?

I laughed content when I heard the voice of my little captain,
We have not struck, he composedly cried, We have just begun our part of the
905   fighting.

Only three guns were in use,
One was directed by the captain himself against the enemy's mainmast,
Two well-served with grape and canister silenced his musketry and cleared his decks.

The tops alone seconded the fire of this little battery, especially the maintop,
910   They all held out bravely during the whole of the action.

Not a moment's cease,
The leaks gained fast on the pumps . . . . the fire eat toward the powder-magazine,
One of the pumps was shot away . . . . it was generally thought we were sinking.

Serene stood the little captain,
915   He was not hurried . . . . his voice was neither high nor low,
His eyes gave more light to us than our battle-lanterns.

Toward twelve at night, there in the beams of the moon they surrendered to us.

His was the surly English pluck, and there is no tougher or truer, and never was,
     and never will be;
Along the lower'd eve he came horribly raking us.

We closed with him, the yards entangled, the cannon touch'd,
My captain lash'd fast with his own hands.

We had receiv'd some eighteen pound shots under the water,   905
On our lower-gun-deck two large pieces had burst at the first fire, killing all around
     and blowing up overhead.

Fighting at sun-down, fighting at dark,
Ten o'clock at night, the full moon well up, our leaks on the gain, and five feet
     of water reported,
The master-at-arms loosing the prisoners confined in the after-hold to give them
     a chance for themselves.

The transit to and from the magazine is now stopt by the sentinels,   910
They see so many strange faces they do not know whom to trust.

Our frigate takes fire,
The other asks if we demand quarter?
If our colors are struck and the fighting done?

Now I laugh content, for I hear the voice of my little captain,   915
We have not struck, he composedly cries, we have just begun our part of
     the fighting.

Only three guns are in use,
One is directed by the captain himself against the enemy's main-mast,
Two well serv'd with grape and canister silence his musketry and clear his decks.

The tops alone second the fire of this little battery, especially the main-top,   920
They hold out bravely during the whole of the action.

Not a moment's cease,
The leaks gain fast on the pumps, the fire eats toward the powder-magazine.

One of the pumps has been shot away, it is generally thought we are sinking.

Serene stands the little captain,   925
He is not hurried, his voice is neither high nor low,
His eyes give more light to us than our battle-lanterns.

Toward twelve there in the beams of the moon they surrender to us.

[36]

Stretched and still lay the midnight,
Two great hulls motionless on the breast of the darkness,
Our vessel riddled and slowly sinking . . . . preparations to pass to the one we
920   had conquered,
The captain on the quarter deck coldly giving his orders through a countenance
white as a sheet,
Near by the corpse of the child that served in the cabin,
The dead face of an old salt with long white hair and carefully curled whiskers,
The flames spite of all that could be done flickering aloft and below,
925 The husky voices of the two or three officers yet fit for duty,
Formless stacks of bodies and bodies by themselves . . . . dabs of flesh upon the
masts and spars,
The cut of cordage and dangle of rigging . . . . the slight shock of the soothe
of waves,
Black and impassive guns, and litter of powder-parcels, and the strong scent,
Delicate sniffs of the seabreeze . . . . smells of sedgy grass and fields by the shore
. . . . death-messages given in charge to survivors,
930 The hiss of the surgeon's knife and the gnawing teeth of his saw,
The wheeze, the cluck, the swash of falling blood . . . . the short wild scream,
the long dull tapering groan,
These so . . . . these irretrievable.

[37]

O Christ! My fit is mastering me!
What the rebel said gaily adjusting his throat to the rope-noose,
What the savage at the stump, his eye-sockets empty, his mouth spirting whoops
935   and defiance,
What stills the traveler come to the vault at Mount Vernon,
What sobers the Brooklyn boy as he looks down the shores of the Wallabout and
remembers the prison ships,
What burnt the gums of the redcoat at Saratoga when he surrendered his brigades,
These become mine and me every one, and they are but little,
940 I become as much more as I like.

I become any presence or truth of humanity here,
And see myself in prison shaped like another man,
And feel the dull unintermitted pain.

For me the keepers of convicts shoulder their carbines and keep watch,
945 It is I let out in the morning and barred at night.

Not a mutineer walks handcuffed to the jail, but I am handcuffed to him and
walk by his side,

36

Stretch'd and still lies the midnight,
Two great hulls motionless on the breast of the darkness, 930
Our vessel riddled and slowly sinking, preparations to pass to the one we have
    conquer'd,
The captain on the quarter-deck coldly giving his orders through a countenance
    white as a sheet,
Near by the corpse of the child that serv'd in the cabin,
The dead face of an old salt with long white hair and carefully curl'd whiskers,
The flames spite of all that can be done flickering aloft and below, 935
The husky voices of the two or three officers yet fit for duty,
Formless stacks of bodies and bodies by themselves, dabs of flesh upon the masts
    and spars,
Cut of cordage, dangle of rigging, slight shock of the soothe of waves,
Black and impassive guns, litter of powder-parcels, strong scent,
A few large stars overhead, silent and mournful shining, 940
Delicate sniffs of sea-breeze, smells of sedgy grass and fields by the shore,
    death-messages given in charge to survivors,
The hiss of the surgeon's knife, the gnawing teeth of his saw,
Wheeze, cluck, swash of falling blood, short wild scream, and long, dull,
    tapering groan,
These so, these irretrievable.

37

You laggards there on guard! look to your arms! 945
In at the conquer'd doors they crowd! I am possess'd!
Embody all presences outlaw'd or suffering,
See myself in prison shaped like another man,
And feel the dull unintermitted pain.

For me the keepers of convicts shoulder their carbines and keep watch, 950
It is I let out in the morning and barr'd at night.

Not a mutineer walks handcuff'd to jail but I am handcuff'd to him and walk
    by his side,

I am less the jolly one there, and more the silent one with sweat on my
    twitching lips.

Not a youngster is taken for larceny, but I go too and am tried and sentenced.

Not a cholera patient lies at the last gasp, but I also lie at the last gasp,
950 My face is ash-colored, my sinews gnarl . . . . away from me people retreat.

Askers embody themselves in me, and I am embodied in them,
I project my hat and sit shamefaced and beg.

[38]

I rise extatic through all, and sweep with the true gravitation,
The whirling and whirling is elemental within me.

955 Somehow I have been stunned. Stand back!
Give me a little time beyond my cuffed head and slumbers and dreams and gaping,
I discover myself on a verge of the usual mistake.

That I could forget the mockers and insults!
That I could forget the trickling tears and the blows of the bludgeons and
    hammers!
960 That I could look with a separate look on my own crucifixion and bloody crowning!

I remember . . . . I resume the overstaid fraction,
The grave of rock multiplies what has been confided to it . . . . or to any graves,
The corpses rise . . . . the gashes heal . . . . the fastenings roll away.

I troop forth replenished with supreme power, one of an average unending
    procession,
We walk the roads of Ohio and Massachusetts and Virginia and Wisconsin and
    New York and New Orleans and Texas and Montreal and San Francisco and
965   Charleston and Savannah and Mexico,
Inland and by the seacoast and boundary lines . . . . and we pass the boundary
    lines.

Our swift ordinances are on their way over the whole earth,
The blossoms we wear in our hats are the growth of two thousand years.

Eleves I salute you,
I see the approach of your numberless gangs . . . . I see you understand yourselves
970   and me,
And know that they who have eyes are divine, and the blind and lame are
    equally divine,

(I am less the jolly one there, and more the silent one with sweat on my
    twitching lips.)

Not a youngster is taken for larceny but I go up too, and am tried and
    sentenced.

Not a cholera patient lies at the last gasp but I also lie at the last gasp,   955
My face is ash-color'd, my sinews gnarl, away from me people retreat.

Askers embody themselves in me and I am embodied in them,
I project my hat, sit shame-faced, and beg.

38

Enough! enough! enough!
Somehow I have been stunn'd. Stand back!   960
Give me a little time beyond my cuff'd head, slumbers, dreams, gaping,
I discover myself on the verge of a usual mistake.

That I could forget the mockers and insults!
That I could forget the trickling tears and the blows of the bludgeons and
    hammers!
That I could look with a separate look on my own crucifixion and bloody
    crowning!   965

I remember now,
I resume the overstaid fraction,
The grave of rock multiplies what has been confided to it, or to any graves,
Corpses rise, gashes heal, fastenings roll from me.

I troop forth replenish'd with supreme power, one of an average unending
    procession,   970
Inland and sea-coast we go, and pass all boundary lines,
Our swift ordinances on their way over the whole earth,
The blossoms we wear in our hats the growth of thousands of years.

Eleves, I salute you! come forward!
Continue your annotations, continue your questionings.   975

And that my steps drag behind yours yet go before them,
And are aware how I am with you no more than I am with everybody.

[39]
The friendly and flowing savage . . . . Who is he?
975 Is he waiting for civilization or past it and mastering it?

Is he some southwesterner raised outdoors? Is he Canadian?
Is he from the Mississippi country? or from Iowa, Oregon or California? or from
   the mountains? or prairie life or bush-life? or from the sea?

Wherever he goes men and women accept and desire him,
They desire he should like them and touch them and speak to them and
   stay with them.

Behaviour lawless as snow-flakes . . . . words simple as grass . . . . uncombed
980   head and laughter and naivete;
Slowstepping feet and the common features, and the common modes and
   emanations,
They descend in new forms from the tips of his fingers,
They are wafted with the odor of his body or breath . . . . they fly out of the
   glance of his eyes.

[40]
Flaunt of the sunshine I need not your bask . . . . lie over,
985 You light surfaces only . . . . I force the surfaces and the depths also.

Earth! you seem to look for something at my hands,
Say old topknot! what do you want?

Man or woman! I might tell how I like you, but cannot,
And might tell what it is in me and what it is in you, but cannot,
990 And might tell the pinings I have . . . . the pulse of my nights and days.

Behold I do not give lectures or a little charity,
What I give I give out of myself.

You there, impotent, loose in the knees, open your scarfed chops till I blow grit
   within you,
Spread your palms and lift the flaps of your pockets,
995 I am not to be denied . . . . I compel . . . . I have stores plenty and to spare,
And any thing I have I bestow.

I do not ask who you are . . . . that is not important to me,

39

The friendly and flowing savage, who is he?
Is he waiting for civilization, or past it and mastering it?

Is he some Southwesterner rais'd out-doors? is he Kanadian?
Is he from the Mississippi country? Iowa, Oregon, California?
The mountains? prairie-life, bush-life? or sailor from the sea?   980

Wherever he goes men and women accept and desire him,
They desire he should like them, touch them, speak to them, stay with them.

Behavior lawless as snow-flakes, words simple as grass, uncomb'd head, laughter,
    and naivetè,
Slow-stepping feet, common features, common modes and emanations,
They descend in new forms from the tips of his fingers,   985
They are wafted with the odor of his body or breath, they fly out of the glance
    of his eyes.

40

Flaunt of the sunshine I need not your bask—lie over!
You light surfaces only, I force surfaces and depths also.

Earth! you seem to look for something at my hands,
Say, old top-knot, what do you want?   990

Man or woman, I might tell how I like you, but cannot,
And might tell what it is in me and what it is in you, but cannot,
And might tell that pining I have, that pulse of my nights and days.

Behold, I do not give lectures or a little charity,
When I give I give myself.   995

You there, impotent, loose in the knees,
Open your scarf'd chops till I blow grit within you,
Spread your palms and lift the flaps of your pockets,
I am not to be denied, I compel, I have stores plenty and to spare,
And any thing I have I bestow.   1000

I do not ask who you are, that is not important to me,

You can do nothing and be nothing but what I will infold you.

To a drudge of the cottonfields or emptier of privies I lean . . . . on his right
    cheek I put the family kiss,
1000 And in my soul I swear I never will deny him.

On women fit for conception I start bigger and nimbler babes,
This day I am jetting the stuff of far more arrogant republics.

To any one dying . . . . thither I speed and twist the knob of the door,
Turn the bedclothes toward the foot of the bed,
1005 Let the physician and the priest go home.

I seize the descending man . . . . I raise him with resistless will.

O despairer, here is my neck,
By God! you shall not go down! Hang your whole weight upon me.

I dilate you with tremendous breath . . . . I buoy you up;
Every room of the house do I fill with an armed force . . . . lovers of me,
1010   bafflers of graves:
Sleep! I and they keep guard all night;
Not doubt, not decease shall dare to lay finger upon you,
I have embraced you, and henceforth possess you to myself,
And when you rise in the morning you will find what I tell you is so.

[41]
1015 I am he bringing help for the sick as they pant on their backs,
And for strong upright men I bring yet more needed help.

I heard what was said of the universe,
Heard it and heard of several thousand years;
It is middling well as far as it goes . . . . but is that all?

1020 Magnifying and applying come I,
Outbidding at the start the old cautious hucksters,
The most they offer for mankind and eternity less than a spirt of my own
    seminal wet,
Taking myself the exact dimensions of Jehovah and laying them away,
Lithographing Kronos and Zeus his son, and Hercules his grandson,
1025 Buying drafts of Osiris and Isis and Belus and Brahma and Adonai,
In my portfolio placing Manito loose, and Allah on a leaf, and the crucifix engraved,
With Odin, and the hideous-faced Mexitli, and all idols and images,
Honestly taking them all for what they are worth, and not a cent more,

You can do nothing and be nothing but what I will infold you.

To cotton-field drudge or cleaner of privies I lean,
On his right cheek I put the family kiss,
And in my soul I swear I never will deny him.   1005

On women fit for conception I start bigger and nimbler babes,
(This day I am jetting the stuff of far more arrogant republics.)

To any one dying, thither I speed and twist the knob of the door,
Turn the bed-clothes toward the foot of the bed,
Let the physician and the priest go home.   1010

I seize the descending man and raise him with resistless will,
O despairer, here is my neck,
By God, you shall not go down! hang your whole weight upon me.

I dilate you with tremendous breath, I buoy you up,
Every room of the house do I fill with an arm'd force,   1015
Lovers of me, bafflers of graves.

Sleep—I and they keep guard all night,
Not doubt, not decease shall dare to lay finger upon you,
I have embraced you, and henceforth possess you to myself,
And when you rise in the morning you will find what I tell you is so.   1020

41

I am he bringing help for the sick as they pant on their backs,
And for strong upright men I bring yet more needed help.

I heard what was said of the universe,
Heard it and heard it of several thousand years;
It is middling well as far as it goes—but is that all?   1025

Magnifying and applying come I,
Outbidding at the start the old cautious hucksters,
Taking myself the exact dimensions of Jehovah,
Lithographing Kronos, Zeus his son, and Hercules his grandson,
Buying drafts of Osiris, Isis, Belus, Brahma, Buddha,   1030
In my portfolio placing Manito loose, Allah on a leaf, the crucifix engraved,
With Odin and the hideous-faced Mexitli and every idol and image,
Taking them all for what they are worth and not a cent more,

Admitting they were alive and did the work of their day,

Admitting they bore mites as for unfledged birds who have now to rise and fly
1030   and sing for themselves,

Accepting the rough deific sketches to fill out better in myself . . . . bestowing
them freely on each man and woman I see,

Discovering as much or more in a framer framing a house,

Putting higher claims for him there with his rolled-up sleeves, driving the mallet
and chisel;

Not objecting to special revelations . . . . considering a curl of smoke or a hair
on the back of my hand as curious as any revelation;

Those ahold of fire-engines and hook-and-ladder ropes more to me than the gods
1035   of the antique wars,

Minding their voices peal through the crash of destruction,

Their brawny limbs passing safe over charred laths . . . . their white foreheads
whole and unhurt out of the flames;

By the mechanic's wife with her babe at her nipple interceding for every person
born;

Three scythes at harvest whizzing in a row from three lusty angels with shirts
bagged out at their waists;

1040 The snag-toothed hostler with red hair redeeming sins past and to come,

Selling all he possesses and traveling on foot to fee lawyers for his brother and
sit by him while he is tried for forgery:

What was strewn in the amplest strewing the square rod about me, and not
filling the square rod then;

The bull and the bug never worshipped half enough,

Dung and dirt more admirable than was dreamed,

The supernatural of no account . . . . myself waiting my time to be one of the
1045   supremes,

The day getting ready for me when I shall do as much good as the best, and be
as prodigious,

Guessing when I am it will not tickle me much to receive puffs out of pulpit
or print;

By my life-lumps! becoming already a creator!

Putting myself here and now to the ambushed womb of the shadows!

[42]

1050 . . . . A call in the midst of the crowd,

My own voice, orotund sweeping and final.

Come my children,

Come my boys and girls, and my women and household and intimates,

Now the performer launches his nerve . . . . he has passed his prelude on the
reeds within.

Admitting they were alive and did the work of their days,
(They bore mites as for unfledg'd birds who have now to rise and fly and sing
    for themselves.)   1035
Accepting the rough deific sketches to fill out better in myself, bestowing them
    freely on each man and woman I see,
Discovering as much or more in a framer framing a house,
Putting higher claims for him there with his roll'd-up sleeves driving the mallet
    and chisel,
Not objecting to special revelations, considering a curl of smoke or a hair on the
    back of my hand just as curious as any revelation,
Lads ahold of fire-engines and hook-and-ladder ropes no less to me than the gods
    of the antique wars,   1040
Minding their voices peal through the crash of destruction,
Their brawny limbs passing safe over charr'd laths, their white foreheads whole
    and unhurt out of the flames;
By the mechanic's wife with her babe at her nipple interceding for every
    person born,
Three scythes at harvest whizzing in a row from three lusty angels with shirts
    bagg'd out at their waists,
The snag-tooth'd hostler with red hair redeeming sins past and to come,   1045
Selling all he possesses, traveling on foot to fee lawyers for his brother and sit
    by him while he is tried for forgery;
What was strewn in the amplest strewing the square rod about me, and not filling
    the square rod then,
The bull and the bug never worshipp'd half enough,
Dung and dirt more admirable than was dream'd,
The supernatural of no account, myself waiting my time to be one of the supremes,   1050
The day getting ready for me when I shall do as much good as the best, and be
    as prodigious;
By my life-lumps! becoming already a creator,
Putting myself here and now to the ambush'd womb of the shadows.

42

A call in the midst of the crowd,
My own voice, orotund sweeping and final.   1055

Come my children,
Come my boys and girls, my women, household and intimates,
Now the performer launches his nerve, he has pass'd his prelude on the
    reeds within.

1055 Easily written loosefingered chords! I feel the thrum of their climax and close.

My head evolves on my neck,
Music rolls, but not from the organ . . . . folks are around me, but they are no
    household of mine.

Ever the hard and unsunk ground,
Ever the eaters and drinkers . . . . ever the upward and downward sun . . . .
    ever the air and the ceaseless tides,
1060 Ever myself and my neighbors, refreshing and wicked and real,
Ever the old inexplicable query . . . . ever that thorned thumb—that breath of
    itches and thirsts,
Ever the vexer's hoot! hoot! till we find where the sly one hides and bring
    him forth;
Ever love . . . . ever the sobbing liquid of life,
Ever the bandage under the chin . . . . ever the tressles of death.

1065 Here and there with dimes on the eyes walking,
To feed the greed of the belly the brains liberally spooning,
Tickets buying or taking or selling, but in to the feast never once going;
Many sweating and ploughing and thrashing, and then the chaff for payment
    receiving,
A few idly owning, and they the wheat continually claiming.

1070 This is the city . . . . and I am one of the citizens;
Whatever interests the rest interests me . . . . politics, churches, newspapers,
    schools,
Benevolent societies, improvements, banks, tariffs, steamships, factories, markets,
Stocks and stores and real estate and personal estate.

They who piddle and patter here in collars and tailed coats . . . . I am aware who
    they are . . . . and that they are not worms or fleas,
I acknowledge the duplicates of myself under all the scrape-lipped and pipe-legged
1075   concealments.

The weakest and shallowest is deathless with me,
What I do and say the same waits for them,
Every thought that flounders in me the same flounders in them.

I know perfectly well my own egotism,
1080 And know my omnivorous words, and cannot say any less,
And would fetch you whoever you are flush with myself.

My words are words of a questioning, and to indicate reality;

Easily written loose-finger'd chords—I feel the thrum of your climax and close.

My head slues round on my neck, 1060
Music rolls, but not from the organ,
Folks are around me, but they are no household of mine.

Ever the hard unsunk ground,
Ever the eaters and drinkers, ever the upward and downward sun, ever the air
    and the ceaseless tides,
Ever myself and my neighbors, refreshing, wicked, real, 1065
Ever the old inexplicable query, ever that thorn'd thumb, that breath of itches
    and thirsts,
Ever the vexer's *hoot! hoot!* till we find where the sly one hides and bring
    him forth,
Ever love, ever the sobbing liquid of life,
Ever the bandage under the chin, ever the trestles of death.

Here and there with dimes on the eyes walking, 1070
To feed the greed of the belly the brains liberally spooning,
Tickets buying, taking, selling, but in to the feast never once going,
Many sweating, ploughing, thrashing, and then the chaff for payment receiving,
A few idly owning, and they the wheat continually claiming.

This is the city and I am one of the citizens, 1075
Whatever interests the rest interests me, politics, wars, markets, newspapers,
    schools,
The mayor and councils, banks, tariffs, steamships, factories, stocks, stores, real
    estate and personal estate,

The little plentiful manikins skipping around in collars and tail'd coats,
I am aware who they are, (they are positively not worms or fleas,)
I acknowledge the duplicates of myself, the weakest and shallowest is deathless
    with me, 1080
What I do and say the same waits for them,
Every thought that flounders in me the same flounders in them.

I know perfectly well my own egotism,
Know my omnivorous lines and must not write any less,
And would fetch you whoever you are flush with myself. 1085

Not words of routine this song of mine,
But abruptly to question, to leap beyond yet nearer bring;

This printed and bound book . . . . but the printer and the printing-office boy?
The marriage estate and settlement . . . . but the body and mind of the
    bridegroom? also those of the bride?
1085 The panorama of the sea . . . . but the sea itself?
The well-taken photographs . . . . but your wife or friend close and solid in
    your arms?
The fleet of ships of the line and all the modern improvements . . . . but the
    craft and pluck of the admiral?
The dishes and fare and furniture . . . . but the host and hostess, and the look
    out of their eyes?
The sky up there . . . . yet here or next door or across the way?
1090 The saints and sages in history . . . . but you yourself?
Sermons and creeds and theology . . . . but the human brain, and what is called
    reason, and what is called love, and what is called life?

[43]

I do not despise you priests;
My faith is the greatest of faiths and the least of faiths,
Enclosing all worship ancient and modern, and all between ancient and modern,
1095 Believing I shall come again upon the earth after five thousand years,
Waiting responses from oracles . . . . honoring the gods . . . . saluting the sun,
Making a fetish of the first rock or stump . . . . powowing with sticks in the
    circle of obis,
Helping the lama or brahmin as he trims the lamps of the idols,
Dancing yet through the streets in a phallic procession . . . . rapt and austere
    in the woods, a gymnosophist,
Drinking mead from the skull-cup . . . . to shasta and vedas admirant . . . .
1100   minding the koran,
Walking the teokallis, spotted with gore from the stone and knife—beating the
    serpent-skin drum;
Accepting the gospels, accepting him that was crucified, knowing assuredly that
    he is divine,
To the mass kneeling—to the puritan's prayer rising—sitting patiently in a pew,
Ranting and frothing in my insane crisis—waiting dead-like till my spirit
    arouses me;
1105 Looking forth on pavement and land, and outside of pavement and land,
Belonging to the winders of the circuit of circuits.

One of that centripetal and centrifugal gang,
I turn and talk like a man leaving charges before a journey.

Down-hearted doubters, dull and excluded,
1110 Frivolous sullen moping angry affected disheartened atheistical,
I know every one of you, and know the unspoken interrogatories,
By experience I know them.

This printed and bound book—but the printer and the printing-office boy?
The well-taken photographs—but your wife or friend close and solid in your arms?
The black ship mail'd with iron, her mighty guns in her turrets—but the pluck of
    the captain and engineers?   1090
In the houses the dishes and fare and furniture—but the host and hostess, and the
    look out of their eyes?
The sky up there—yet here or next door, or across the way?
The saints and sages in history—but you yourself?
Sermons, creeds, theology—but the fathomless human brain,
And what is reason? and what is love? and what is life?   1095

43

I do not despise you priests, all time, the world over,
My faith is the greatest of faiths and the least of faiths,
Enclosing worship ancient and modern and all between ancient and modern,
Believing I shall come again upon the earth after five thousand years,
Waiting responses from oracles, honoring the gods, saluting the sun,   1100
Making a fetich of the first rock or stump, powowing with sticks in the circle
    of obis,
Helping the llama or brahmin as he trims the lamps of the idols,
Dancing yet through the streets in a phallic procession, rapt and austere in the
    woods a gymnosophist,
Drinking mead from the skull-cup, to Shastas and Vedas admirant, minding
    the Koran,
Walking the teokallis, spotted with gore from the stone and knife, beating the
    serpent-skin drum,   1105
Accepting the Gospels, accepting him that was crucified, knowing assuredly that he
    is divine,
To the mass kneeling or the puritan's prayer rising, or sitting patiently in a pew,
Ranting and frothing in my insane crisis, or waiting dead-like till my spirit
    arouses me,
Looking forth on pavement and land, or outside of pavement and land,
Belonging to the winders of the circuit of circuits.   1110

One of that centripetal and centrifugal gang I turn and talk like a man leaving
    charges before a journey.

Down-hearted doubters, dull and excluded,
Frivolous, sullen, moping, angry, affected, dishearten'd, atheistical,
I know every one of you, I know the sea of torment, doubt, despair and unbelief.

How the flukes splash!
How they contort rapid as lightning, with spasms and spouts of blood!

1115 Be at peace bloody flukes of doubters and sullen mopers,
I take my place among you as much as among any;
The past is the push of you and me and all precisely the same,
And the day and night are for you and me and all,
And what is yet untried and afterward is for you and me and all.

1120 I do not know what is untried and afterward,
But I know it is sure and alive and sufficient.

Each who passes is considered, and each who stops is considered, and not a single
one can it fail.

It cannot fail the young man who died and was buried,
Nor the young woman who died and was put by his side,
Nor the little child that peeped in at the door and then drew back and was
1125 never seen again,
Nor the old man who has lived without purpose, and feels it with bitterness
worse than gall,
Nor him in the poorhouse tubercled by rum and the bad disorder,
Nor the numberless slaughtered and wrecked . . . . nor the brutish koboo, called
the ordure of humanity,
Nor the sacs merely floating with open mouths for food to slip in,
1130 Nor any thing in the earth, or down in the oldest graves of the earth,
Nor any thing in the myriads of spheres, nor one of the myriads of myriads that
inhabit them,
Nor the present, nor the least wisp that is known.

[44]
It is time to explain myself . . . . let us stand up.

What is known I strip away . . . . I launch all men and women forward with me
into the unknown.

1135 The clock indicates the moment . . . . but what does eternity indicate?

Eternity lies in bottomless reservoirs . . . . its buckets are rising forever and ever,
They pour and they pour and they exhale away.

We have thus far exhausted trillions of winters and summers;
There are trillions ahead, and trillions ahead of them.

How the flukes splash!
How they contort rapid as lightning, with spasms and spouts of blood!

Be at peace bloody flukes of doubters and sullen mopers,
I take my place among you as much as among any,
The past is the push of you, me, all, precisely the same,
And what is yet untried and afterward is for you, me, all precisely the same.   1120

I do not know what is untried and afterward,
But I know it will in its turn prove sufficient, and cannot fail.

Each who passes is consider'd, each who stops is consider'd, not a single one
      can it fail.

It cannot fail the young man who died and was buried,
Nor the young woman who died and was put by his side,   1125
Nor the little child that peep'd in at the door, and then drew back and was never
      seen again,
Nor the old man who has lived without purpose, and feels it with bitterness worse
      than gall,
Nor him in the poor house tubercled by rum and the bad disorder,
Nor the numberless slaughter'd and wreck'd, nor the brutish koboo call'd the
      ordure of humanity,
Nor the sacs merely floating with open mouths for food to slip in,   1130
Nor any thing in the earth, or down in the oldest graves of the earth,
Nor any thing in the myriads of spheres, nor the myriads of myriads that
      inhabit them,
Nor the present, nor the least wisp that is known.

44

It is time to explain myself—let us stand up.

What is known I strip away,   1135
I launch all men and women forward with me into the Unknown.

The clock indicates the moment—but what does eternity indicate?

We have thus far exhausted trillions of winters and summers,
There are trillions ahead, and trillions ahead of them.

1140 Births have brought us richness and variety,
And other births will bring us richness and variety.

I do not call one greater and one smaller,
That which fills its period and place is equal to any.

Were mankind murderous or jealous upon you my brother or my sister?
1145 I am sorry for you . . . . they are not murderous or jealous upon me;
All has been gentle with me . . . . I keep no account with lamentation;
What have I to do with lamentation?

I am an acme of things accomplished, and I an encloser of things to be.

My feet strike an apex of the apices of the stairs,
1150 On every step bunches of ages, and larger bunches between the steps,
All below duly traveled—and still I mount and mount.

Rise after rise bow the phantoms behind me,
Afar down I see the huge first Nothing, the vapor from the nostrils of death,
I know I was even there . . . . I waited unseen and always,
1155 And slept while God carried me through the lethargic mist,
And took my time . . . . and took no hurt from the fœtid carbon.

Long I was hugged close . . . . long and long.

Immense have been the preparations for me,
Faithful and friendly the arms that have helped me.

1160 Cycles ferried my cradle, rowing and rowing like cheerful boatmen;
For room to me stars kept aside in their own rings,
They sent influences to look after what was to hold me.

Before I was born out of my mother generations guided me,
My embryo has never been torpid . . . . nothing could overlay it;
For it the nebula cohered to an orb . . . . the long slow strata piled to rest it on
1165   . . . . vast vegetables gave it sustenance,
Monstrous sauroids transported it in their mouths and deposited it with care.

All forces have been steadily employed to complete and delight me,
Now I stand on this spot with my soul.

[45]
Span of youth! Ever-pushed elasticity! Manhood balanced and florid and full!

Births have brought us richness and variety,   1140
And other births will bring us richness and variety.

I do not call one greater and one smaller,
That which fills its period and place is equal to any.

Were mankind murderous or jealous upon you, my brother, my sister?
I am sorry for you, they are not murderous or jealous upon me,   1145
All has been gentle with me, I keep no account with lamentation,
(What have I to do with lamentation?)

I am an acme of things accomplish'd, and I an encloser of things to be.

My feet strike an apex of the apices of the stairs,
On every step bunches of ages, and larger bunches between the steps,   1150
All below duly travel'd, and still I mount and mount.

Rise after rise bow the phantoms behind me,
Afar down I see the huge first Nothing, I know I was even there,
I waited unseen and always, and slept through the lethargic mist,
And took my time, and took no hurt from the fetid carbon.   1155

Long I was hugg'd close—long and long.

Immense have been the preparations for me,
Faithful and friendly the arms that have help'd me.

Cycles ferried my cradle, rowing and rowing like cheerful boatmen,
For room to me stars kept aside in their own rings,   1160
They sent influences to look after what was to hold me.

Before I was born out of my mother generations guided me,
My embryo has never been torpid, nothing could overlay it.

For it the nebula cohered to an orb,
The long slow strata piled to rest it on,   1165
Vast vegetables gave it sustenance,
Monstrous sauroids transported it in their mouths and deposited it with care.

All forces have been steadily employ'd to complete and delight me,
Now on this spot I stand with my robust soul.

45

O span of youth! ever-push'd elasticity!   1170
O manhood, balanced, florid and full.

1170 My lovers suffocate me!
Crowding my lips, and thick in the pores of my skin,
Jostling me through streets and public halls . . . . coming naked to me at night,
Crying by day Ahoy from the rocks of the river . . . . swinging and chirping
    over my head,
Calling my name from flowerbeds or vines or tangled underbrush,
Or while I swim in the bath . . . . or drink from the pump at the corner . . . .
    or the curtain is down at the opera . . . . or I glimpse at a woman's face
1175   in the railroad car;
Lighting on every moment of my life,
Bussing my body with soft and balsamic busses,
Noiselessly passing handfuls out of their hearts and giving them to be mine.

Old age superbly rising! Ineffable grace of dying days!

Every condition promulges not only itself . . . . it promulges what grows
1180   after and out of itself,
And the dark hush promulges as much as any.

I open my scuttle at night and see the far-sprinkled systems,
And all I see, multiplied as high as I can cipher, edge but the rim of the
    farther systems.

Wider and wider they spread, expanding and always expanding,
1185 Outward and outward and forever outward.

My sun has his sun, and round him obediently wheels,
He joins with his partners a group of superior circuit,
And greater sets follow, making specks of the greatest inside them.

There is no stoppage, and never can be stoppage;
If I and you and the worlds and all beneath or upon their surfaces, and all
    the palpable life, were this moment reduced back to a pallid float, it
1190   would not avail in the long run,
We should surely bring up again where we now stand,
And as surely go as much farther, and then farther and farther.

A few quadrillions of eras, a few octillions of cubic leagues, do not hazard the
    span, or make it impatient,
They are but parts . . . . any thing is but a part.

1195 See ever so far . . . . there is limitless space outside of that,
Count ever so much . . . . there is limitless time around that.

Our rendezvous is fitly appointed . . . . God will be there and wait till we come.

My lovers suffocate me,
Crowding my lips, thick in the pores of my skin,
Jostling me through streets and public halls, coming naked to me at night,
Crying by day *Ahoy!* from the rocks of the river, swinging and chirping over
    my head,   1175
Calling my name from flower-beds, vines, tangled underbrush,
Lighting on every moment of my life,
Bussing my body with soft balsamic busses,
Noiselessly passing handfuls out of their hearts and giving them to be mine.

Old age superbly rising! O welcome, ineffable grace of dying days!   1180

Every condition promulges not only itself, it promulges what grows after and out
    of itself,
And the dark hush promulges as much as any.

I open my scuttle at night and see the far-sprinkled systems,
And all I see multiplied as high as I can cipher edge but the rim of the farther
    systems.

Wider and wider they spread, expanding, always expanding,   1185
Outward and outward and forever outward.

My sun has his sun and round him obediently wheels,
He joins with his partners a group of superior circuit,
And greater sets follow, making specks of the greatest inside them.

There is no stoppage and never can be stoppage,   1190
If I, you, and the worlds, and all beneath or upon their surfaces, were this moment
    reduced back to a pallid float, it would not avail in the long run,
We should surely bring up again where we now stand,
And surely go as much farther, and then farther and farther.

A few quadrillions of eras, a few octillions of cubic leagues, do not hazard the span
    or make it impatient,
They are but parts, any thing is but a part.   1195

See ever so far, there is limitless space outside of that,
Count ever so much, there is limitless time around that.

My rendezvous is appointed, it is certain,
The Lord will be there and wait till I come on perfect terms,
The great Camerado, the lover true for whom I pine will be there.   1200

[46]

I know I have the best of time and space—and that I was never measured, and
never will be measured.

I tramp a perpetual journey,
1200 My signs are a rain-proof coat and good shoes and a staff cut from the woods;
No friend of mine takes his ease in my chair,
I have no chair, nor church nor philosophy;
I lead no man to a dinner-table or library or exchange,
But each man and each woman of you I lead upon a knoll,
1205 My left hand hooks you round the waist,
My right hand points to landscapes of continents, and a plain public road.

Not I, not any one else can travel that road for you,
You must travel it for yourself.

It is not far . . . . it is within reach,
1210 Perhaps you have been on it since you were born, and did not know,
Perhaps it is every where on water and on land.

Shoulder your duds, and I will mine, and let us hasten forth;
Wonderful cities and free nations we shall fetch as we go.

If you tire, give me both burdens, and rest the chuff of your hand on my hip,
1215 And in due time you shall repay the same service to me;
For after we start we never lie by again.

This day before dawn I ascended a hill and looked at the crowded heaven,
And I said to my spirit, When we become the enfolders of those orbs and the
pleasure and knowledge of every thing in them, shall we be filled and
satisfied then?
And my spirit said No, we level that lift to pass and continue beyond.

1220 You are also asking me questions, and I hear you;
I answer that I cannot answer . . . . you must find out for yourself.

Sit awhile wayfarer,
Here are biscuits to eat and here is milk to drink,
But as soon as you sleep and renew yourself in sweet clothes I will certainly kiss
you with my goodbye kiss and open the gate for your egress hence.

1225 Long enough have you dreamed contemptible dreams,
Now I wash the gum from your eyes,

46

I know I have the best of time and space, and was never measured and never will
　　be measured.

I tramp a perpetual journey, (come listen all!)
My signs are a rain-proof coat, good shoes, and a staff cut from the woods,
No friend of mine takes his ease in my chair,
I have no chair, no church, no philosophy,   1205
I lead no man to a dinner-table, library, exchange,
But each man and each woman of you I lead upon a knoll,
My left hand hooking you round the waist,
My right hand pointing to landscapes of continents and the public road.

Not I, not any one else can travel that road for you,   1210
You must travel it for yourself.

It is not far, it is within reach,
Perhaps you have been on it since you were born and did not know,
Perhaps it is everywhere on water and on land.

Shoulder your duds dear son, and I will mine, and let us hasten forth,   1215
Wonderful cities and free nations we shall fetch as we go.

If you tire, give me both burdens, and rest the chuff of your hand on my hip,
And in due time you shall repay the same service to me,
For after we start we never lie by again.

This day before dawn I ascended a hill and look'd at the crowded heaven,   1220
And I said to my spirit *When we become the enfolders of those orbs, and the
　　pleasure and knowledge of every thing in them, shall we be fill'd and
　　satisfied then?*
And my spirit said *No, we but level that lift to pass and continue beyond.*

You are also asking me questions and I hear you,
I answer that I cannot answer, you must find out for yourself.

Sit a while dear son,   1225
Here are biscuits to eat and here is milk to drink,
But as soon as you sleep and renew yourself in sweet clothes, I kiss you with a
　　good-by kiss and open the gate for your egress hence.

Long enough have you dream'd contemptible dreams,
Now I wash the gum from your eyes,

You must habit yourself to the dazzle of the light and of every moment
    of your life.

Long have you timidly waded, holding a plank by the shore,
Now I will you to be a bold swimmer,
To jump off in the midst of the sea, and rise again and nod to me and shout,
1230   and laughingly dash with your hair.

[47]

I am the teacher of athletes,
He that by me spreads a wider breast than my own proves the width of my own,
He most honors my style who learns under it to destroy the teacher.

The boy I love, the same becomes a man not through derived power but in his
    own right,
1235 Wicked, rather than virtuous out of conformity or fear,
Fond of his sweetheart, relishing well his steak,
Unrequited love or a slight cutting him worse than a wound cuts,
First rate to ride, to fight, to hit the bull's eye, to sail a skiff, to sing a song
    or play on the banjo,
Preferring scars and faces pitted with smallpox over all latherers and those that
    keep out of the sun.

1240 I teach straying from me, yet who can stray from me?
I follow you whoever you are from the present hour;
My words itch at your ears till you understand them.

I do not say these things for a dollar, or to fill up the time while I wait for
    a boat;
It is you talking just as much as myself . . . . I act as the tongue of you,
1245 It was tied in your mouth . . . . in mine it begins to be loosened.

I swear I will never mention love or death inside a house,
And I swear I never will translate myself at all, only to him or her who
    privately stays with me in the open air.

If you would understand me go to the heights or water-shore,
The nearest gnat is an explanation and a drop or the motion of waves a key,
1250 The maul the oar and the handsaw second my words.

No shuttered room or school can commune with me,
But roughs and little children better than they.

The young mechanic is closest to me . . . . he knows me pretty well,

You must habit yourself to the dazzle of the light and of every moment of
    your life.   1230

Long have you timidly waded holding a plank by the shore,
Now I will you to be a bold swimmer,
To jump off in the midst of the sea, rise again, nod to me, shout, and laughingly
    dash with your hair.

47

I am the teacher of athletes,
He that by me spreads a wider breast than my own proves the width of my own,   1235
He most honors my style who learns under it to destroy the teacher.

The boy I love, the same becomes a man not through derived power, but in his
    own right,
Wicked rather than virtuous out of conformity or fear,
Fond of his sweetheart, relishing well his steak,
Unrequited love or a slight cutting him worse than sharp steel cuts,   1240
First-rate to ride, to fight, to hit the bull's eye, to sail a skiff, to sing a song or play
    on the banjo,
Preferring scars and the beard and faces pitted with small-pox over all latherers,
And those well-tann'd to those that keep out of the sun.

I teach straying from me, yet who can stray from me?
I follow you whoever you are from the present hour,   1245
My words itch at your ears till you understand them.

I do not say these things for a dollar or to fill up the time while I wait for a boat,
(It is you talking just as much as myself, I act as the tongue of you,
Tied in your mouth, in mine it begins to be loosen'd.)

I swear I will never again mention love or death inside a house,   1250
And I swear I will never translate myself at all, only to him or her who privately
    stays with me in the open air.

If you would understand me go to the heights or water-shore,
The nearest gnat is an explanation, and a drop or motion of waves a key,
The maul, the oar, the hand-saw, second my words.

No shutter'd room or school can commune with me,   1255
But roughs and little children better than they.

The young mechanic is closest to me, he knows me well,

The woodman that takes his axe and jug with him shall take me with him
    all day,
1255 The farmboy ploughing in the field feels good at the sound of my voice,
In vessels that sail my words must sail . . . . I go with fishermen and seamen,
    and love them,
My face rubs to the hunter's face when he lies down alone in his blanket,
The driver thinking of me does not mind the jolt of his wagon,
The young mother and old mother shall comprehend me,
1260 The girl and the wife rest the needle a moment and forget where they are,
They and all would resume what I have told them.

[48]

I have said that the soul is not more than the body,
And I have said that the body is not more than the soul,
And nothing, not God, is greater to one than one's-self is,
And whoever walks a furlong without sympathy walks to his own funeral, dressed
1265   in his shroud,
And I or you pocketless of a dime may purchase the pick of the earth,
And to glance with an eye or show a bean in its pod confounds the learning
    of all times,
And there is no trade or employment but the young man following it may
    become a hero,
And there is no object so soft but it makes a hub for the wheeled universe,
1270 And any man or woman shall stand cool and supercilious before a million universes.

And I call to mankind, Be not curious about God,
For I who am curious about each am not curious about God,
No array of terms can say how much I am at peace about God and about death.

I hear and behold God in every object, yet I understand God not in the least,
1275 Nor do I understand who there can be more wonderful than myself.

Why should I wish to see God better than this day?
I see something of God each hour of the twenty-four, and each moment then,
In the faces of men and women I see God, and in my own face in the glass;
I find letters from God dropped in the street, and every one is signed
    by God's name,
And I leave them where they are, for I know that others will punctually
1280   come forever and ever.

[49]

And as to you death, and you bitter hug of mortality . . . . it is idle to try
    to alarm me.

The woodman that takes his axe and jug with him shall take me with him all day,
The farm-boy ploughing in the field feels good at the sound of my voice,
In vessels that sail my words sail, I go with fishermen and seamen and love them.   1260

The soldier camp'd or upon the march is mine,
On the night ere the pending battle many seek me, and I do not fail them,
On that solemn night (it may be their last) those that know me seek me.

My face rubs to the hunter's face when he lies down alone in his blanket,
The driver thinking of me does not mind the jolt of his wagon,   1265
The young mother and old mother comprehend me,
The girl and the wife rest the needle a moment and forget where they are,
They and all would resume what I have told them.

48

I have said that the soul is not more than the body,
And I have said that the body is not more than the soul,   1270
And nothing, not God, is greater to one than one's self is,
And whoever walks a furlong without sympathy walks to his own funeral drest
    in his shroud,
And I or you pocketless of a dime may purchase the pick of the earth,
And to glance with an eye or show a bean in its pod confounds the learning
    of all times,
And there is no trade or employment but the young man following it may become
    a hero,   1275
And there is no object so soft but it makes a hub for the wheel'd universe,
And I say to any man or woman, Let your soul stand cool and composed before
    a million universes.

And I say to mankind, Be not curious about God,
For I who am curious about each am not curious about God,
(No array of terms can say how much I am at peace about God and about death.)   1280

I hear and behold God in every object, yet understand God not in the least,
Nor do I understand who there can be more wonderful than myself.

Why should I wish to see God better than this day?
I see something of God each hour of the twenty-four, and each moment then,
In the faces of men and women I see God, and in my own face in the glass,   1285
I find letters from God dropt in the street, and every one is sign'd by God's name,
And I leave them where they are, for I know that wheresoe'er I go
Others will punctually come for ever and ever.

49

And as to you Death, and you bitter hug of mortality, it is idle to try to
    alarm me.

To work without flinching the accoucheur comes,
I see the elderhand pressing receiving supporting,
I recline by the sills of the exquisite flexible doors . . . . and mark the outlet,
    and mark the relief and escape.

1285 And as to you corpse I think you are good manure, but that does not offend me,
I smell the white roses sweetscented and growing,
I reach to the leafy lips . . . . I reach to the polished breasts of melons.

And as to you life, I reckon you are the leavings of many deaths,
No doubt I have died myself ten thousand times before.

1290 I hear you whispering there O stars of heaven,
O suns . . . . O grass of graves . . . . O perpetual transfers and promotions . . . .
    if you do not say anything how can I say anything?

Of the turbid pool that lies in the autumn forest,
Of the moon that descends the steeps of the soughing twilight,
Toss, sparkles of day and dusk . . . . toss on the black stems that decay
    in the muck,
1295 Toss to the moaning gibberish of the dry limbs.

I ascend from the moon . . . . I ascend from the night,
And perceive of the ghastly glitter the sunbeams reflected,
And debouch to the steady and central from the offspring great or small.

[50]
There is that in me . . . . I do not know what it is . . . . but I know it is
    in me.

1300 Wrenched and sweaty . . . . calm and cool then my body becomes;
I sleep . . . . I sleep long.

I do not know it . . . . it is without name . . . . it is a word unsaid,
It is not in any dictionary or utterance or symbol.

Something it swings on more than the earth I swing on,
1305 To it the creation is the friend whose embracing awakes me.

Perhaps I might tell more . . . . Outlines! I plead for my brothers and sisters.

Do you see O my brothers and sisters?
It is not chaos or death . . . . it is form and union and plan . . . . it is eternal
    life . . . . it is happiness.

To his work without flinching the accoucheur comes, 1290
I see the elder-hand pressing receiving supporting,
I recline by the sills of the exquisite flexible doors,
And mark the outlet, and mark the relief and escape.

And as to you Corpse I think you are good manure, but that does not
     offend me,
I smell the white roses sweet-scented and growing, 1295
I reach to the leafy lips, I reach to the polish'd breasts of melons.

And as to you Life I reckon you are the leavings of many deaths,
(No doubt I have died myself ten thousand times before.)

I hear you whispering there O stars of heaven,
O suns—O grass of graves—O perpetual transfers and promotions, 1300
If you do not say any thing how can I say any thing?

Of the turbid pool that lies in the autumn forest,
Of the moon that descends the steeps of the soughing twilight,
Toss, sparkles of day and dusk—toss on the black stems that decay in the muck,
Toss to the moaning gibberish of the dry limbs. 1305

I ascend from the moon, I ascend from the night,
I perceive that the ghastly glimmer is noonday sunbeams reflected,
And debouch to the steady and central from the offspring great or small.

50

There is that in me—I do not know what it is—but I know it is in me.

Wrench'd and sweaty—calm and cool then my body becomes, 1310
I sleep—I sleep long.

I do not know it—it is without name—it is a word unsaid,
It is not in any dictionary, utterance, symbol.

Something it swings on more than the earth I swing on,
To it the creation is the friend whose embracing awakes me. 1315

Perhaps I might tell more. Outlines! I plead for my brothers and sisters.

Do you see O my brothers and sisters?
It is not chaos or death—it is form, union, plan—it is eternal life—it is Happiness.

[51]

The past and present wilt . . . . I have filled them and emptied them,
1810 And proceed to fill my next fold of the future.

Listener up there! Here you . . . . what have you to confide to me?
Look in my face while I snuff the sidle of evening,
Talk honestly, for no one else hears you, and I stay only a minute longer.

Do I contradict myself?
1815 Very well then . . . . I contradict myself;
I am large . . . . I contain multitudes.

I concentrate toward them that are nigh . . . . I wait on the door-slab.

Who has done his day's work and will soonest be through with his supper?
Who wishes to walk with me?

1320 Will you speak before I am gone? Will you prove already too late?

[52]

The spotted hawk swoops by and accuses me . . . . he complains of my gab
and my loitering.

I too am not a bit tamed . . . . I too am untranslatable,
I sound my barbaric yawp over the roofs of the world.

The last scud of day holds back for me.
1325 It flings my likeness after the rest and true as any on the shadowed wilds,
It coaxes me to the vapor and the dusk.

I depart as air . . . . I shake my white locks at the runaway sun,
I effuse my flesh in eddies and drift it in lacy jags.

I bequeath myself to the dirt to grow from the grass I love,
1330 If you want me again look for me under your bootsoles.

You will hardly know who I am or what I mean,
But I shall be good health to you nevertheless,
And filter and fibre your blood.

Failing to fetch me at first keep encouraged,
1335 Missing me one place search another,
I stop some where waiting for you[.]

51

The past and present wilt—I have fill'd them, emptied them,
And proceed to fill my next fold of the future.   1320

Listener up there! what have you to confide to me?
Look in my face while I snuff the sidle of evening,
(Talk honestly, no one else hears you, and I stay only a minute longer.)

Do I contradict myself?
Very well then I contradict myself,   1325
(I am large, I contain multitudes.)

I concentrate toward them that are nigh, I wait on the door-slab.

Who has done his day's work? who will soonest be through with his supper?
Who wishes to walk with me?

Will you speak before I am gone? will you prove already too late?   1330

52

The spotted hawk swoops by and accuses me, he complains of my gab and
    my loitering.

I too am not a bit tamed, I too am untranslatable,
I sound my barbaric yawp over the roofs of the world.

The last scud of day holds back for me,
It flings my likeness after the rest and true as any on the shadow'd wilds,   1335
It coaxes me to the vapor and the dusk.

I depart as air, I shake my white locks at the runaway sun,
I effuse my flesh in eddies, and drift it in lacy jags.

I bequeath myself to the dirt to grow from the grass I love,
If you want me again look for me under your boot-soles.   1340

You will hardly know who I am or what I mean,
But I shall be good health to you nevertheless,
And filter and fibre your blood.

Failing to fetch me at first keep encouraged,
Missing me one place search another,   1345
I stop somewhere waiting for you.

EMERGENCE OF "SONG OF MYSELF"

Early Notebook Versions

THE HISTORY of the creative process can never be complete: the poet never sets down on paper many of the earliest ideas or images that float restlessly about in his mind, seeking imaginative fusion or form. But the early "trial" jottings of a poet can provide glimpses of the creative process at that crucial stage—the birth of the poem. "Song of Myself" was not constructed: it *emerged* from the creative depths of the poet. Or at least so it would seem from a glance at the early random pieces and fragments left by Whitman in various notebooks. These lines taken together give the impression of a poet listening to inner voices, sometimes clear, sometimes obscure, forcing their way into his consciousness. The lines appear at times to be early versions of specific sections of the poem, at other times the source of several widely scattered passages.

The lines assembled here are linked to specific sections of "Song of Myself": the exploring reader will find other connections and relationships. No attempt has been made to gather every line and fragment which may have gone into the making of "Song of Myself"—but rather a sampling of the more significant passages. Two sources were used: the variorum readings compiled by Oscar Lovell Triggs for the 1902 *Complete Writings of Walt Whitman,* now most readily accessible in the *Inclusive Edition: Leaves of Grass* (Doubleday, Page & Co., 1926), edited by Emory Holloway (below, quotations have been transcribed from the 1902 *Complete Writings;* but the *Inclusive Edition* has been cited because it is more widely available). The other source is a series of Whitman notebooks reprinted in volume two of *The Uncollected Poetry and Prose of Walt Whitman* (Doubleday, Page & Co.), also edited by Holloway.[1] The source of each fragment reprinted here is identified by page number in *Inclusive Edition* or *Uncollected Poetry and Prose.*

SECTION 1
(These lines appear to be an early version of the opening lines of "Song of Myself," but they seem also to turn up in part in Sections 21 and 47.)

> I am your voice—It was tied in you—In me it begins to talk.
> I celebrate myself to celebrate every man and woman alive;

[1] Fragments from *The Uncollected Poetry and Prose of Walt Whitman,* edited by Emory Holloway (copyright 1921 by Emory Holloway), are reprinted by permission of Doubleday & Company, Inc.

I loosen the tongue that was tied in them,
It begins to talk out of my mouth.

I celebrate myself to celebrate you:
I say the same word for every man and woman alive.
And I say that the soul is not greater than the body,
And I say that the body is not greater than the soul.

                                    (*Inclusive Edition*, 550)

SECTION 2

I call back blunderers;
I give strong meat in place of panada;
I expose what ties loads on the soul.
Are you so poor that you are always miserly, Priests?
Will you prize a round trifle like a saucer, done in red and yellow paint?

I offer men no painted saucer—I make every one a present of the sun;
I have plenty more—I have millions of suns left.

                                    (*Inclusive Edition*, 550)

SECTION 3

When I see where the east is greater than the west,—where the sound man's part
of the child is greater than the sound woman's part—or where a father is more
needful than a mother to produce me—then I guess I shall see how spirit is greater
than matter.—Here the run of poets and the learned always strike, and here shoots
the ballast of many a grand head.—My life is a miracle and my body which lives is
a miracle; but of what I can nibble at the edges of the limitless and delicious wonder
I know that I cannot separate them, and call one superior and the other inferior,
any more than I can say my sight is greater than my eyes.—
You have been told that mind is greater than matter
I cannot understand the mystery, but I am always conscious of myself as two—
as my soul and I: and I reckon it is the same with all men and women.—
I know that my body will [decay]

                                    (*Uncollected Poetry and Prose*, 66)

I ask nobody's faith . . . I am very little concerned about that.
You doubt not the east and the west,
You doubt not your desires or your fingernails,
You doubt not metal or acid or steam. . . .

Do I not prove myself?
I but show a scarlet tomato, or a sprig of parsley, or a paving stone or some seaweed,
All acknowledge and admire—Savans and Synods as much as the rest.

I meet not one heretic or unbeliever,
Could I do as well with the love of the pulpit? the whole or any part of it?

Whatever I say of myself you shall apply to yourself,
If you do not it were time lost listening to me.

I think there will never be any more heaven or hell than there is now,
Nor any more youth nor age than there is now,
Nor any more inception than there is now,
Nor any more perfection than there is now.

(Inclusive Edition, 550–51)

SECTION 7

> Have you supposed it beautiful to be born?
> I tell you I know it is just as beautiful to die;
> For I take my death with the dying
> And my birth with the new-born babe.

(Uncollected Poetry and Prose, 71)

SECTION 8

> The suicide went to a lonesome place with a pistol and killed himself,
> I came that way and stumbled upon him.

(Inclusive Edition, 552)

SECTION 13
(See also Sections 21 and 31)
All tends to the soul,
As materials so the soul,
As procreation, so the soul—if procreation is impure, all is impure.

As the shadow concurs with the body and comes not unless of the body, so the soul
   concurs with the body and comes not unless of the body,
As materials are so the soul,
As experiences, childhood, maturity, suffering, so the soul,
As craft, lies, thefts, adulteries, sarcasm, greed, denial, avarice, hatred, gluttony, so
   the soul,
As the types set up by the printers are faithfully returned by their impression, what
   they are for, so a man's life and a woman's life is returned in the soul before
   death and interminably after death.

And to me each minute of the night and day is vital and visible,
And I say the stars are not echoes,
And I perceive that the sedgy weed has refreshing odors;
And potatoes and milk afford a dinner of state,

And I guess the chipping bird sings as well as I, although she never learned the
    gamut;
And to shake my friendly right hand, governors and millionaires shall stand all day
    waiting their turns.

And to me each acre of the land and sea exhibits marvellous pictures;
They fill the worm-fence and lie on the heaped stones, and are hooked to the elder
    and poke weed;
And to me the cow crunching with depressed head is a statue perfect and plumb.

(Inclusive Edition, 553)

SECTION 17

These are the thoughts of all men in all ages and lands—
They are not original with me—they are mine—they are yours just the same
If these thoughts are not for all they are nothing
If they do not enclose everything they are nothing
If they are not the school of all the physical, moral and mental they are nothing

(Uncollected Poetry and Prose, 74–75)

SECTION 19

> This is the common air . . . it is for the heroes and
>   sages . . .
>   it is for the workingmen and farmers . . . it is
>   for the wicked just the same as the righteous.
> I will not have a single person left out . . . I will have
>   the prostitute and the thief invited . . . I will
>   make no difference between them and the rest.

(Uncollected Poetry and Prose, 75)

SECTION 21

Night of south winds—night of the large few stars!
Still slumberous night—mad, naked summer night!

Smile, O voluptuous procreant earth!
Earth of the nodding and liquid trees!
Earth of the mountains, misty-top't!
Earth of departed sunset—Earth of shine and dark, mottling the tide of the river!
Earth of the vitreous fall of the full moon just tinged with blue!
Earth of the limpid gray of clouds purer and clearer for my sake!
Earth of far arms—rich, apple-blossomed earth!
Smile, for your lover comes!

Spread round me earth! Spread with your curtained hours;
Take me as many a time you've taken;
Till springing up in . . . .

Prodigal, you have given me love;
Sustenance, happiness, health have given;
Therefore, I to you give love;
O, unspeakable, passionate love!

(*Inclusive Edition*, 556–557)

SECTION 23

I am the poet of reality
I say the earth is not an echo
Nor man an apparition;
But that all the things seen are real,
The witness and albic dawn of things equally real
I have split the earth and the hard coal and rocks and the solid bed of the sea
And went down to reconnoitre there a long time,
And bring back a report,
And I understand that those are positive and dense every one
And that what they seem to the child they are
[And the world is no joke,
Nor any part of it a sham]

(*Uncollected Poetry and Prose*, 69–70)

I am the poet of Reality,
And I say the stars are not echoes,
And I say that space is no apparition;
But all the things seen or demonstrated are so;
Witnesses and albic dawns of things equally great, yet not seen.

I announce myself the Poet of Materials and exact demonstration;
Say that Materials are just as eternal as growth, the semen of God that swims the
    entire creation.

Hurrah for Positive Science!
Bring honey-clover and branches of lilac!
These are the Philosophers of Nature,
Every one admirable and serene,
Traveling, sailing, measuring space,
Botanizing, dissecting, or making machines.

(*Inclusive Edition*, 558)

SECTION 26

I want that tenor, large and fresh as the creation, the orbed parting of whose mouth shall lift over my head the sluices of all the delight yet discovered for our race.—I want the soprano that lithely overleaps the stars, and convulses me like the love-grips of her in whose arms I lay last night.—I want an infinite chorus and orchestrium, wide as the orbit of Uranus, true as the hours of the day, and filling my capacities to receive, as thoroughly as the sea fills its scooped out sands.—I want the chanted Hymn whose tremendous sentiment shall uncage in my breast a thousand wide-winged strengths and unknown ardors and terrible ecstasies—putting me through the flights of all the passions—dilating me beyond time and air—startling me with the overture of some unnamable horror—calmly sailing me all day on a bright river with lazy slapping waves—stabbing my heart with myriads of forked distractions more furious than hail or lightning—lulling me drowsily with honeyed morphine—tightening the fakes of death about my throat, and awakening me again to know by that comparison, the most positive wonder in the world, and that's what we call life.

(Uncollected Poetry and Prose, 85)

A soprano heard at intervals over the immense waves,
Audible these from the underlying chorus,
Occupants and joyous vibraters of space.

Never fails the combination,
An underlying chorus, occupant and joyous vibrater of space.
A clear transparent base that lusciously shudders the universe,
A tenor strong and ascending, with glad notes of morning—with power and health.

(Inclusive Edition, 560)

SECTIONS 28 and 29

One touch of a tug of me has unhaltered all my senses but feeling
That pleases the rest so, they have given up to it in submission
They are all emulous to swap themselves off for what it can do to them.
Every one must be a touch
Or else she will abdicate and nibble only at the edges of feeling.

They move caressingly up and down my body
They leave themselves and come with bribes to whatever part of me touches.—
To my lips, to the palms of my hands, and whatever my hands hold.
Each brings the best she has,
For each is in love with touch.
I do not wonder that one feeling now does so much for me,
He is free of all the rest,—and swiftly begets offspring of them, better than the dams.
A touch now reads me a library of knowledge in an instant.
It smells for me the fragrance of wine and lemon-blows.

It tastes for me ripe strawberries and mellons,—
It talks for me with a tongue of its own,
It finds an ear wherever [wherein?] it rests or taps.

It brings the rest around it, and they all stand on a headland and mock me
They have left me to touch, and taken their place on a headland.
The sentries have deserted every other part of me
They have left me helpless to the torrent of touch
They have all come to the headland to witness and assist against me.—
I roam about drunk and stagger
I am given up by traitors,
I talk wildly I am surely out of my head,
I am myself the greatest traitor.
I went myself first to the headland

Unloose me, touch, you are taking the breath from my throat!
Unbar your gates you are too much for me
Fierce Wrestler! do you keep your heaviest grip for the last?
Will you sting me most even at parting?
Will you struggle even at the threshold with spasms more delicious than all before?
Does it make you to ache so to leave me?
Do you wish to show me that even what you did before was nothing to what you
   can do?
Or have you and all the rest combined to see how much I can endure (?)
Pass as you will; take drops of my life, if that is what you are after
Only pass to some one else, for I can contain you no longer
I held more than I thought
I did not think I was big enough for so much ecstasy
Or that a touch could take it all out of me.

(*Uncollected Poetry and Prose*, 72–73)

My hand will not hurt what it holds and yet will devour it,
It must remain perfect before me though I enclose and divide it.

Only one minute, only two or three sheathed touches,
Yet they gather all of me and my spirit into a knot,
They hold us long enough there to show us what we can be,
And that our flesh, and even a part of our flesh, seems more than senses and life.

What has become of my senses?
Touch has jolted down all of them but feeling;
He pleases the rest so every one would swap off and go with him,
Or else she will abdicate and nibble at the edges of me.

(*Inclusive Edition*, 560–561)

You villain touch! What are you doing?
Unloose me, the breath is leaving my throat;
Open your floodgates! You are too much for me.

Grip'd wrestler! do you keep the heaviest pull for the last?
Must you bite with your teeth at parting?

Will you struggle worst? I plunge you from the threshold.

Does it make you ache so to leave me!

Take what you like, I can resist you;
Take the tears of my soul if that is what you are after.

Pass to some one else;
Little as your mouth, it has drained me dry of my strength.

It is no miracle now that we are to live always.

Touch is the miracle!
What is it to be lost, or change our dresses, or sleep long, when . . .

A minute, a touch and a drop of us can launch immortality;
Little henceforth are proof and argument needful,
Eternity has no time for death, each inch of existence is so . . .
And that to pass existence is supreme over all, and what we thought death is but life
    brought to a firmer parturition.

(*Inclusive Edition*, 561)

Section 30

    All truths lie waiting in all things.—They neither urge the opening of themselves
nor resist it. For their birth you need not the obstetric forceps of the surgeon. They
unfold to you and emit themselves more fragrant than roses from living buds, whenever you fetch the spring sunshine moistened with summer rain.—But it must be
in yourself.—It shall come from your soul.—It shall be love. (The heart of man
alone is the one unbalanced and restless thing in the world)

(*Uncollected Poetry and Prose*, 80)

There can be nothing small or useless in the universe;
The insignificant is as big as the noble;
What is less than a touch?

All truths wait in all places,
They wait with inclined heads and arms folded over their breasts;

They neither urge their own birth nor resist it;
They do not need the obstetric forceps of the surgeon;
They enclose to those who ever fetches the warmth of the light and the moisture of
    rain.

Logic and sermons never convince;
The dew of the night drives deeper into the soul.

A test of anything!
It proves itself to the experience and senses of men and women!
Bring it to folk and you will see whether they doubt;
They do not doubt contact or hunger or love;
They do not doubt iron or steam;
We do not doubt the mystery of life;
We do not doubt the east and the west;
We do not doubt sight.

(Inclusive Edition, 561–562)

SECTION 31

Afar in the sky was a nest,
And my soul flew thither and squat, and looked out
And saw the journeywork of suns and systems of suns,
And that a leaf of grass is not less than they
And that the pismire is equally perfect, and all grains of sand, and every egg of the
    wren,
And the tree-toad is a chef' douvre for the highest,
And the running blackberry would adorn the parlors of Heaven
And the cow crunching with depressed neck surpasses every statue,
And pictures great and small crowd the rail-fence, and hang on its heaped stones
    and elder and poke-weed,
And a mouse is miracle enough to stagger trillions of infidels.
And I cannot put my toe anywhere to the ground,
But it must touch numberless and curious books
Each one scorning all that schools and science can do fully to translate them.
And the salt marsh and creek have delicious odor,
And potato and ear of maize make a fat breakfast,
And huckleberrys from the woods distill joyous deliriums.

(Uncollected Poetry and Prose, 70)

The crowds naked in the bath,
Can your sight behold them as with oyster's eyes?
Do you take the attraction of gravity for nothing?
Does the negress bear no children?
Are they never handsome? Do they not thrive?

Will cabinet officers become blue or yellow from excessive gin?

Shall I receive the great things of the spirit on easier terms than I do a note of hand?

Who examines the philosophies in the market less than a basket of peaches or barrels of salt fish?

Who accepts chemistry on tradition?

The light picks out a bishop or pope no more than the rest.

A mouse is miracle enough to stagger billions of infidels.

(Inclusive Edition, 562)

SECTION 32

I stand and look at them sometimes half the day long.

They do not sweat and whine about their condition,

They do not lie awake in the dark and weep for their sins,

They do not make me sick discussing their duty to God;

Not one is dissatisfied. . . . Not one takes medicine or is demented with the mania of owning things.

(Inclusive Edition, 562)

SECTION 33

The Poet

All the large hearts of heroes

All the courage of olden time and new

How spied the captain and sailors the great wreck with its drifting hundreds,

How they waited, their craft shooting like an arrow up and down the storm.

How they gripped close with Death there on the sea and gave him not one inch, and held on day and night

And chalked on a board, *Be of good cheer, we will not desert you,* and held it up and did it;

How the lank white faced women looked when ferried safely as from the sides their prepared graves

How the children and the lifted sick, and the sharp-lipped, unshaven men;

All this [he drinks] I swallow in [his] my soul, and it becomes [his] mine, and I like it well.

I am the man; I suffered, I was there:

All the beautiful disdain and calmness of martyrs

The old woman that was chained and burnt with dry wood, and her children looking on.

The great queens that walked serenely to the block.

The hunted slave who flags in the race at last, and leans up by the fence, blowing and covered with sweat,

And the twinges that sting like needles his breast and neck

The murderous buck-shot and the bullets,

All this I not only feel and see but am.
I am the hunted slave,
Damnation and despair are close upon me
I clutch the rail of the fence
My gore presently trickles thinned with the [plentiful sweat salt] ooze of my skin
     as I fall on the reddened grass and stones
And the hunters haul up close with their unwilling horses,
Till taunt and oath swim away from my dim and dizzy ears.

What the rebel felt gaily adjusting his neck to the rope noose,
[What Lucifer cursed when tumbling from Heaven]
What the savage, lashed to the stump, spirting yells and laughter at every foe
What rage of hell urged the lips and hands of the victors.—
How fared the young captain pale and flat on his own bloody deck
The pangs of defeat sharper than the green edged wounds of his side.
What choked the throat of the general when he surrendered his army,
What heightless dread falls in the click of a moment

                     (*Uncollected Poetry and Prose,* 81–82)

Where the little musk ox carries his perfumed bag at his navel,
Where the life car is drawn on its slip noose,
At dinner on a dish of huckleberries or rye bread and a round white pot cheese.

                     (*Inclusive Edition,* 565)

SECTION 37
     The fester of defeat sharper than the bayonet holes in his side;
     What choked the throat of the brigadier when he gave up his brigade;
     These become mine and me, every one;
     And I become much more when I like.
                     (*Inclusive Edition,* 566)

SECTION 38
     In vain were nails driven through my hands.
     I remember my crucifixion and bloody coronation
     I remember the mockers and the buffeting insults
     The sepulchre and the white linen have yielded me up
     I am alive in New York and San Francisco,
     Again I tread the streets after two thousand years.
     Not all the traditions can put vitality in churches
     They are not alive, they are cold mortar and brick,
     I can easily build as good, and so can you:—
     Books are not men—

                     (*Uncollected Poetry and Prose,* 74)

SECTION 40

> Strength
> Where is one abortive, mangy, cold
> Starved of his masculine lustiness?
> Without core and loose in the knees?
> Clutch fast to me, my ungrown brother,
> That I infuse you with grit and jets of life
> I am not to be scorned (?):—I Compel;
> It is quite indifferent to me who [you] are.
> I have stores plenty and to spare
> And of whatsoever I have I bestow upon you.
> And first I bestow of my love.

> *(Uncollected Poetry and Prose, 71–72)*

I am the poet of Strength and Hope
Where is the house of any one dying?
Thither I speed and turn the knob of the door,
Let the physician and the priest timidly withdraw.
That I seize on the ghastly man and raise him with resistless will.
O despairer! I tell you you shall not go down,
Here is my arm, press your whole weight upon me.
With tremendous breath I force him to dilate.
Sleep! for I and this stand guard this night,
And when you rise in the morning you find that what I told you is so.
Every room of your house do I fill with armed men
Lovers of me, bafflers of hell,
Not doubt not fear not death shall lay finger   you
And you are mine all to myself

> *(Uncollected Poetry and Prose, 69)*

> I dilate you with tremendous breath,
> I buoy you up,
> Every room of your house do I fill with armed men
> Lovers of me, bafflers of hell.
> Sleep! for I and they stand guard this night
> Not doubt, not fear, not Death shall lay finger upon you
> I have embraced you, and henceforth possess you all to myself,
> And when you rise in the morning you shall find it is so—
> God and I are now (?) here (?)
> Speak! what would you have (?) of us?

> *(Uncollected Poetry and Prose, 70–71)*

SECTION 41

I know as well as you that Bibles are divine revelations,
I say that each leaf of grass and each hair of my breast and beard is also a revelation
just as divine.
But do you stop there? Have you no more faith than that?

I live in no such infinitesimal meanness as that
Would you bribe the Lord with some stray change?

I outbid you shallow hucksters!
All you pile up is not august enough to dent the partition in my nose;
I say that all the churches now standing were well employed in orisons to a sprig of
parsley;
I tell you that all your caste have said about Belus, Osirus, and Jehovah is a shallow
description.

I claim for one of those framers over the way framing a house,
The young man there with rolled-up sleeves and sweat on his superb face,
More than your craft three thousand years ago, Kronos, or Zeus his son, or Hercules
his grandson.

. . . foot to fee lawyers for his brother and sit by him while he was tried for forgery.
Fables, traditions and formulas are not animate things;
Brick and mortar do not procreate like men;
In all of them and all existing creeds grows not so much of God as I grow in my
moustache;
I am myself waiting my time to be a God;
I think I shall do as much good and be as pure and prodigious as any,
And when I am do you suppose it will please me to receive puffs from pulpit or print?

Doctrine gets empty consent or mocking politeness,
It wriggles through mankind, it is never loved or believed.
The throat is not safe that speaks it aloud.
I will take a sprig of parsley and a budding rose and go through the whole earth.
You shall see I will not find one heretic against them.
Can you say as much of all the lore of the priesthood?

(*Inclusive Edition,* 568)

SECTION 42

And their voices, clearer than the valved cornet—they cry hoot! hoot! to us all our
lives till we seek where they hide and bring the sly ones forth!

(*Inclusive Edition,* 569)

SECTIONS 44 and 45

Amelioration is the blood that runs through the body of the universe.—I do not lag—I do not hasten—[it appears to say] I bide my hour over billions of billions of years—I exist in the

void that takes uncounted time and coheres to a nebula, and in further time cohering to an orb, marches gladly round, a beautiful tangible creature, in his place in the processions of God, where new comers have been falling in the ranks for ever, and will be so always—I could be balked no how, not if all the worlds and living beings were this minute reduced back into the impalpable film of chaos—I should surely bring up again where we now stand and go on as much further and thence on and on—My right hand is time, and my left hand is space—both are ample—a few quintillions of cycles, a few sextillions of cubic leagues, are not of importance to me—what I shall attain to I can never tell, for there is something that underlies me, of whom I am a part and instrument.

(*Uncollected Poetry and Prose*, 79–80)

My spirit sped back to the times when the earth was burning mist,
And peered aft and could see Concord beyond the aft, forming the mist,
And brings word that Dilation or Pride is a father of Causes,
And a mother of Causes is Goodness or Love—
And they are the Parents yet, and witness and register their Amours eternally;
And devise themselves to These States this hour.
And my spirit travelled ahead and pierced the stern hem of life and went fearlessly
    through,
And came back from the grave with serene face,
And said, It is well, I am satisfied, I behold the causes yet.—
I beheld Dilation just the same afterwards.
I beheld Love and Concord also in the darkness afterwards.

(*Inclusive Edition*, 570)

SECTION 46

I will not be a great philosopher, and found any school, and build it with iron pillars, and gather the young men around me, and make them my disciples, that new superior churches and politics shall come.—But I will take each man and woman of you to the window and open the shutters and the sash, and my left arm shall hook you round the waist, and my right shall point you to the endless and beginningless road along whose sides are crowded the rich cities of all living philosophy, and oval gates that pass you in to fields of clover and landscapes clumped with sassafras, and orchards of good apples, and every breath through your mouth shall be of a new perfumed and elastic air, which is love.—Not I—not God—can travel this road for you.—It is not far, it is within the stretch of your thumb; perhaps you shall find you are on it already and did not know.—Perhaps you shall find it every where over the ocean and over the land, when you once have the vision to behold it.—

(Uncollected Poetry and Prose, 66–67)

SECTION 48

Not even God, [that dread?] is so great to me as Myself is great to me.—Who knows but I too shall in time be a God as pure and prodigious as any of them?— Now I stand here in the Universe, a personality perfect and sound; all things and all other beings as an audience at the play-house perpetually and perpetually calling me out from behind my curtain.—

(Uncollected Poetry and Prose, 83)

SECTION 49

There is no word in any tongue,
No array, no form of symbol,
To tell his infatuation
Who would define the scope and purpose of **God.**

Mostly this we have of God; we have **man.**
Lo, the Sun;
Its glory floods the moon,
Which of a night shines in some turbid pool,
Shaken by soughing winds;
And there are sparkles mad and tossed and **broken,**
And their archetype is the sun.

Of God I know not;
But this I know;
I can comprehend no being more wonderful than man;
Man, before the rage of whose passions the storms of Heaven are but a breath;
Before whose caprices the lightning is slow and less fatal;
Man, microcosm of all Creation's wildness, terror, beauty and power,
And whose folly and wickedness are in nothing else existent.

O dirt, you corpse, I reckon you are good manure—but that I do not smell—
I smell your beautiful white roses—
I kiss your leafy lips—I slide my hands for the brown melons of your breasts.

(Inclusive Edition, 572)

SECTION 50

We know that sympathy or love is the law over all laws, because in nothing else but love is the soul conscious of pure happiness, which appears to be the ultimate resting place, and point of all things.—

(Uncollected Poetry and Prose, 81)

SECTION 52

> The spotted hawk salutes the approaching night;
> He sweeps by me and rebukes me hoarsely with his invitation;
> He complains with sarcastic voice of my lagging.
>
> I feel apt to clip it and go;
> I am not half tamed yet.
>
> (Inclusive Edition, 572–573)

II. VARIED CRITICAL PERSPECTIVES ON "SONG OF MYSELF"

"SONG OF MYSELF" AS STRUCTURE

THE STRUCTURE OF WALT WHITMAN'S
"SONG OF MYSELF"

by Carl F. Strauch

GOETHE said that a distinguishing mark of the great poet is his ability to build. Architectonics is the word he used. This ability a minor poet does not have; Edgar Allan Poe, for example, can write an exquisite song like "To One in Paradise," but he cannot create a fairly long poem and give it that articulation, that symmetry, that final shaping which elicit our admiration and praise. The difference is brought out never so well as when we set side by side a magnificent success like *Samson Agonistes* and a failure, however glorious in some reaches, like *Endymion*. The one has the finality of solid structure; the other throws up brilliant skyrockets of phrase and image, pyrotechnics that pale into the empyrean. Critics of the Romantic persuasion have not sufficiently remarked the aesthetic pleasure derived from the recognition of structure. They have been too much occupied with the verbal felicity and the glowing aura of short poems like the best of Keats and Shelley. Critics of the Romantic persuasion have been too easily satisfied with long poems that are brilliant failures. They have not demanded structure; and since they have not demanded structure, they have not particularly looked for it.

Baudelaire said that a writer of verse did not deserve the name of poet until, growing in power and clarity, he knew exactly what he was about. The great long poems of the world, whatever the differences otherwise, have this at least in common: they have something to say, and that something is said with clarity, power, and conviction because the poet, whether Sophocles or Milton, Racine or Whitman, brought to the poem a talent for organizing ideas into well-shaped and coherent masses.

"It stands to reason," says one critic, "that Whitman gave much thought to the planning and organizing of his poems." [1] Not enough attention, however, has been paid to the architectonics of Whitman's poems. It is, of course, a commonplace of criticism that "When Lilacs Last in the Dooryard Bloom'd" is the high-water mark of American poetry; and certainly the estimate of this poem is due to more than the exquisite phrasing of powerful emotion. But people have gone to *Leaves of Grass*,

From *The English Journal*, College Edition (September, 1938), XXVII, 597–607. Reprinted with the permission of the National Council of Teachers of English and the author.

[1] Killis Campbell, "The Evolution of Whitman as Artist," *American Literature*, VI, (November, 1934), 256.

as they should, of course, for novel ideas vigorously expressed rather than for an encounter with magnificent structure. Whitman has been a seer, a prophet; he has called people to a new religion.

It was an experience to hear an elderly man—looking a venerable seer—with absolute abandonment tell how *Leaves of Grass* had meant for him spiritual enlightenment, a new power in life, new joys in a new existence on a plane higher than he had ever hoped to reach. All this with the accompanying physical exaltation expressed by dilated pupils and intensity of utterance that were embarrassing to uninitiated friends. This incident illustrates the type of influence exercised by Whitman on his disciples —a cult of a type such as no other literary man of our generation has been the object. . . .[2]

That Walt Whitman could inspire such loyalty, such faith, was well—was, in fact, marvelous.

But of three methods of approach to the poet, one, it seems to me, offers for the moment the richest returns. Many critics of varying degrees of either hostility or sympathy have dealt with the religion of Whitman. Other students, feeling that his ideas have been sufficiently reviewed, have occupied themselves with certain problems of his life. As this investigation, highly important and certainly interesting, comes to a successful end or degenerates into futile scholarship, it may be both profitable and zestful to shift our attention to the significance of Whitman as an artist—as a creator, for example, of such an admirable long poem as "Song of Myself." Out of the study of the structure of such a poem may arise a new realization of the greatness of this greatest American poet.

In submitting "Song of Myself" to analysis, I am at present not particularly interested in various readings, changes, or improvements. The study of these is valuable in estimating any poet; Tennyson, for example, shows us his growth in taste and power by his rejections and improvements, and Whitman's revisions are almost always for the better. But while I recognize the value of such a study, I do not think we need now consider any more than "Song of Myself" as it appears in any good edition of *Leaves of Grass*.[3]

Two other matters must be briefly mentioned before the analysis proceeds. First, I am not at all concerned in this scrutiny of a great philosophic poem with ideas except in their relation to form. There can, consequently, be no discussion of them. Second, and I am aware that mention of this is probably superfluous, there need be no apology to the lovers of Whitman for a piece of schoolroom pedantry. A proper analysis always enhances the richness and the appeal of a work of art.

As a matter of convenience let me immediately put down the results of analysis. There are five large divisions in the poem.

[2] Sir William Osler writing about Dr. Bucke in Harvey Cushing's *The Life of Sir William Osler* (Oxford: Clarendon Press, 1925), I, 266.

[3] Dr. Triggs has given variorum readings in *Leaves of Grass* (ed. Emory Holloway [Doubleday, Doran, 1931]). For convenience' sake all references will be made to this edition.

1. Paragraphs 1–18, the Self; mystical interpenetration of the Self with all life and experience
2. Paragraphs 19–25, definition of the Self; identification with the degraded, and transfiguration of it; final merit of Self withheld; silence; end of first half
3. Paragraphs 26–38, life flowing in upon the Self; then evolutionary interpenetration of life
4. Paragraphs 39–41, the Superman
5. Paragraphs 42–52, larger questions of life—religion, faith, God, death; immortality and happiness mystically affirmed

This synopsis will serve as a guide throughout the more elaborate analysis which now proceeds.

To begin, in the first paragraph [4] Whitman announces three important themes: the Self, the identification of Self with others, and "Nature without check with original energy." Transitions in this poem, as in others by Whitman, are clear; the last line of one paragraph frequently suggests the theme, either by way of contrast or by way of continuation, of the next paragraph. So here. In paragraph two the Self declares its independence of "civilization," which is represented by "houses and rooms." The poet then indulges in a catalogue of the scattered and diverse phenomena of nature and the ecstasies of the Self in nature.

". . . . the song of me rising from bed and meeting the sun." The paragraph concludes with an invitation to others to have this firsthand primary relationship with the universe. We are assured in paragraph three that we are being invited to something worth our attention. The world is still good and productive.

"Clean and sweet is my soul, and clean and sweet is all that is not my soul." Whitman is satisfied; he dances, laughs, and sings. This third paragraph may be characterized as the abundance of nature and the poet's satisfaction with nature. The section ends with the parable of the loving bedfellow and the "baskets cover'd with white towels."

The fourth paragraph introduces a theme of hesitation. The major theme, which has been announced, may be too startling; in its dismissal of the temporal it may be too shocking for most readers. After all, Whitman would ruthlessly tear us out of our social context, friends, dinners, clothes, authors, and the like; so that for a moment he hesitates and balances on the periphery of his ideas, stormy, husky, and brawling, certainly not polite and well mannered. For Whitman our social context is a "game."

Paragraph five shows a marked advance; now the picture of companionship in nature is more vivid than in paragraph two, and here also there is a more emphatic declaration of the basis of the universe than in three. Here Whitman says that "a Kelson of the creation is love." The music of the poem has grown into a larger and nobler mood of acceptance. The symbol of the grass, as the most universal and common and even meanest phenomenon, is employed in paragraph six and leads to the themes of pantheism and immortality. Toward the close of this paragraph Whit-

---

[4] I shall call the numbered sections of "Song of Myself" paragraphs.

man speaks of dying as "different from what any one supposed, and luckier." This theme floods over into paragraph seven, which, like four, marks an important transition. Here the poet emphasizes his universal quality by stating that he passes "death with the dying and birth with the new-wash'd babe." More emphatically than in paragraph three, the universal Self finds all things good; all are "as immortal and fathomless" as he himself. There is here a tentative beginning of the vast catalogue which gets under way in eight and storms through to eighteen, abating only in nineteen with a few iridescent drops. This catalogue is the procession of his mystical interpenetration of all life. "I am there," he says, "I saw the marriage," "I behold the picturesque giant." In paragraph eleven there is the marvelous picture of the twenty-eight young men bathing and of the young woman who "owns the fine house by the rise of the bank." This mystical interpenetration of the universe floods over into paragraph nineteen, a very important transition, in which the impetuosity of the previous paragraphs has largely abated. Whitman is a master of change of pace; here the music is slower; there are fewer instruments.

> This hour I tell things in confidence,
> I might not tell everybody, but I will tell you.[5]

So far in this poem there has been only declaration of the Self, nature, love, immortality, and closely allied themes; there has been only invitation to ecstasy; Whitman has audaciously omitted definition or analysis. Now, however, the rhythm, the movement of the music have ceased their tantivy. "Who goes there?" he asks in paragraph twenty. He describes himself. He is "hankering, gross, mystical, nude"; he is a great ego, a representative ego, an ego no prouder than Nature itself—

> I see that the elementary laws never apologize,
> (I reckon I behave no prouder than the level I plant my house by, after all.)[6]

In paragraph twenty-one there is a clear presentation of what Whitman includes under the name of Self: (a) body, (b) soul, (c) good, (d) evil, (e) man, (f) woman. The conclusion of this paragraph is among the most lyrical passages Whitman ever wrote; and the crowning touch to this ecstasy is love.

> Prodigal, you have given me love—therefore I to you give love!
> O unspeakable passionate love.

This lyrical rush surges over into the twenty-second paragraph, in which, after an apostrophe to the sea, Whitman comes to grips with the meaning of what he has been so variously trying to say. "I moisten the roots of all that has grown," says Whitman, and as the poet of balance he accepts both good and evil. It is because he moistens the roots of all that has grown that Whitman is able to call himself "a kosmos." [7] All students of Whitman know how this audacious term aroused disgust or tickled easily tickled risibilities in various quarters when *Leaves of Grass* was re-

---

[5] *Leaves of Grass*, p. 39.
[6] *Ibid.*, p. 40.
[7] *Ibid.*, p. 43.

viewed. But Whitman certainly had a right to the word. Its occurrence is well timed, for it comes immediately after the long catalogue of mystical interpenetration and constitutes another definition of the Self. The word could not have been very well understood had it occurred earlier in the poem; but there was no reason for delaying its use beyond this point or for not employing it at all; it fits admirably into the scheme of the poem in the position it occupies. So well calculated is the artistic and philosophic justness of the word that the cavil of earlier critics must be set down as stupid; today there is no reason for denying to Whitman the highest attributes of the conscious artist, all of whose effects, or certainly the most important of them, are precisely calculated. For, of course, I have no intention of claiming that Whitman is careful of all detail; he is not. But an analysis of "Song of Myself" reveals in him an artist who is conscious of the movement and direction of his ideas, an artist who goes from climax to climax like a god striding mountain peaks.

In linking the word "kosmos" with the clause "I moisten the roots of all that has grown," I have anticipated somewhat. In paragraph twenty-three Whitman accepts reality, materialism, and science. But these, the poet says, are not his dwelling; he but enters them to an area of his dwelling. Then, after opening the twenty-fourth paragraph with the word "kosmos," he gives in a third catalogue his ethical inter-penetration of life. Now we have not mere *presence* at a scene, as in the previous interpenetration of life, but a *transfiguration* of life, for Whitman is now assuming the burden of all evil:

> Through me forbidden voices,
> Voices of sexes and lusts, voices veil'd and I remove the veil,
> Voices indecent by me clarified and transfigur'd.[8]

If Walt Whitman is to "moisten the roots of all that has grown" he must accept all life; accordingly he must identify himself with the manifestations and phenomena that are somewhat less pleasant than the fire of roses or the rush of lovers' kisses. It is interesting to note, however, what some have missed, that he accepts these phenomena "only to lift them up." This interpenetration is highly ethical. It is ethical because life as Whitman conceives it is ethical. He could not accept these phenomena on their own level, because he stands always in a primary relation to the universe, which in its goodness acts as a challenge to him.

> Dazzling and tremendous how quick the sun-rise would kill me,
> If I could not now and always send sun-rise out of me.[9]

But the final merit of the Self cannot be spoken. There is always a mystery; a hush on his lips. In silence the first great half of the poem ends, all instruments mute, the mystical Being quiescent, passive, not storming out upon the world, not identify-ing itself with all the varied life-forms, but ready to receive into itself the magic flow of life.

The second half of the poem begins with twenty-six. Here instead of expression

[8] *Ibid.*, p. 44.
[9] *Ibid.*, p. 46.

we have impression—phenomena flowing in. Now that the great and expressing Self is passive, bathing in a flood of impressions, these phenomena are puzzling.

> . . . . I lose my breath,
> Steep'd amid honey'd morphine, my windpipe throttled in fakes of death,
> At length let up again to feel the puzzle of puzzles,
> And that we call Being.[10]

In twenty-seven and twenty-eight Whitman records his sensitive reaction to this puzzle, this experience of other existences; and in twenty-nine there is record of the returns, in spite of aches, of this experience—"rich showering rain, and recompense richer afterward." The conclusion at which he arrives as a result of this experience is that "all truths wait in all things." This is preparation for the fifth catalogue, which begins in thirty-one and goes through thirty-eight. This catalogue is different from the other two great and most important catalogues. In eight to eighteen we have mystical interpenetration as mere *presence* at a scene; twenty-four gives us an *ethical* interpenetration ending in transfiguration; in the present catalogue we have *evolutionary* interpenetration. For the character of this catalogue we had been prepared in thirty, in which Whitman says, "I believe the soggy clods shall become lovers and lamps." This is interpenetration under space and time, announced in thirty-three, and the range is greater and the identification closer than in eight to eighteen. He is "stucco'd with quadrupeds and birds all over"; he "could turn and live with animals"; he walked "the old hills of Judea with the beautiful gentle God"; he is "the hounded slave." Those who are interested in such a study as this article is pursuing have undoubtedly noticed the close identification of the poet with his subjects. The contrast of this catalogue to that from eight to eighteen is interesting:

8–18	31–38
I lift the gauze	I find I incorporate gneiss
I witness the corpse	I am the man, I suffer'd, I was there
I am there, I help	All these I feel or am
I hunt	I am the hounded slave
I saw the marriage	I am the mash'd fireman
I heard his motions (a runaway slave)	I am an old artillerist
I had him sit next me at table	Askers embody themselves in me
I behold the picturesque giant	

I think we have assured ourselves that there has been a profound movement from the objective to the subjective. And since the mystical experience in this last catalogue is encompassing and universal under space and time, Walt Whitman justifies the use at the beginning of thirty-nine of the term "the friendly and flowing savage." This phrase is as accurately and as consciously employed as was the word "kosmos." The phrase is pivotal; it not only refers to the immediately preceding evolutionary interpenetration but it also shoots forward into the announcement of the Superman, which is given us in forty and forty-one in the sixth catalogue, another mystical

[10] *Ibid.*, p. 48. Paragraph twenty-six is the fourth catalogue.

interpenetration of life, this time that of the man of power who can "dilate you with tremendous breath," and "buoy you up." Here is the Superman flowing through life.

> I seize the descending man and raise him with resistless will,
> O despairer, here is my neck,
> By God, you shall not go down! hang your whole weight upon me.[11]

The Superman brushes aside the old gods, for god is in all. The growth in the poem can be noted by contrasting the questions asked in paragraph twenty to those asked now in forty-two: "What is a man anyhow? what am I? what are you?" (par. 20). "And what is reason? and what is love? and what is life?" (par. 42). Between these two sets of questions is packed a tremendous experience of life. The more universal questions of forty-two indicate the character of the close of the poem, the flight upward and onward into the Unknown. In paragraph forty-three Whitman tells us his faith is all faiths; and there is a final grand utterance of optimism. From forty-four to the end the poet launches all men and women forward with him into the Unknown. There is the doctrine of progress, from "the huge first Nothing" to "my robust soul." [12] Life promulgates life, he says in forty-five, and all creation ends in God. Eternity is the theme of forty-six; each must have the experience for himself. Whitman is the teacher of athletes, those who will have the experience for themselves. In paragraph forty-seven, which is the seventh catalogue, he tells us that nature and those living naturally understand him. In forty-eight there is appropriate emphasis on the universal presence of God; in the remainder of the poem Whitman goes beyond death and announces eternal life and happiness as central. The poem concludes with the emphasis on the ego, "I stop somewhere waiting for you."

For a recapitulation, let me refer the reader to the synopsis with which I have introduced the analysis.

I do not by any means labor under the delusion that this scrutiny of "Song of Myself" establishes for the first time the fact that Whitman was a conscious artist, careful of the design and direction of his ideas. But such an analysis as has here been prosecuted helps to show how very much Whitman was in command of his materials, how orderly was his march from climax to climax, how effectually he secured the unimpeded progress forward and upward in his ideas by well-placed transitional passages and even single words which gather into themselves the whole meaning of large sections of the poem. That he was not the most meticulous and refined artist is rather obvious; and I should acquiesce in Mr. Santayana's judgment that there is an "absence of any principle of selection," [13] if that stricture were limited to the catalogues, the materials for which are gathered without the selective principle the absence of which Mr. Santayana feels. But this judgment carries with it a wholesale indictment to which in defense of Whitman one may be permitted to reply that Mr. Santayana was overwhelmed by the abundance of a poet who had taken all life

---

[11] *Ibid.*, p. 63.
[12] *Ibid.*, pp. 68–69.
[13] George Santayana, *Interpretations of Poetry and Religion* (New York: Scribner, 1900), p. 181.

for his theme and from it had made a wide but representative selection after his own manner. Overwhelmed by this abundance and perhaps fatigued and bored by the rich catalogues, Mr. Santayana entirely missed the magnificent and consciously directed structure of such a poem as "Song of Myself"; otherwise he could not have delivered himself of the opinion that there is in Whitman's poetry an abundance of detail without organization.[14] The obvious inaccuracy of such a judgment is undoubtedly the result of an impatience with a poetry that appeared chaotic, and the consequent failure to examine any one poem to discover either a presence or an absence of organization. That "Song of Myself" is an artistically organized poem, this analysis, I think, has sufficiently demonstrated.

But I have no argument with an essay that was written many years ago and which people will condemn or praise as their sympathies toward either Santayana or Whitman move them. One can only deplore the inaccuracy of one of our greatest critics; for it is obvious that in spite of occasional indifference to relatively unimportant details, Whitman is one of the great artists in poetry.

[14] *Ibid.*, p. 180.

"SONG OF MYSELF" AS POETRY

SOME LINES FROM WHITMAN

by Randall Jarrell

WHITMAN, Dickinson, and Melville seem to me the best poets of the 19th Century here in America. Melville's poetry has been grotesquely underestimated, but of course it is only in the last four or five years that it has been much read; in the long run, in spite of the awkwardness and amateurishness of so much of it, it will surely be thought well of. (In the short run it will probably be thought entirely too well of. Melville is a great poet only in the prose of *Moby Dick*.) Dickinson's poetry has been thoroughly read, and well though undifferentiatingly loved—after a few decades or centuries almost everybody will be able to see through Dickinson to her poems. But something odd has happened to the living changing part of Whitman's reputation: nowadays it is people who are not particularly interested in poetry, people who say that they read a poem for what it says, not for how it says it, who admire Whitman most. Whitman is often written about, either approvingly or disapprovingly, as if he were the Thomas Wolfe of 19th Century democracy, the hero of a de Mille movie about Walt Whitman. (People even talk about a war in which Walt Whitman and Henry James chose up sides, to begin with, and in which you and I will go on fighting till the day we die.) All this sort of thing, and all the bad poetry that there of course is in Whitman—for any poet has written enough bad poetry to scare away anybody—has helped to scare away from Whitman most "serious readers of modern poetry." They do not talk of his poems, as a rule, with any real liking or knowledge. Serious readers, people who are ashamed of not knowing all Hopkins by heart, are not at all ashamed to say, "I don't really know Whitman very well." This may harm Whitman in your eyes, they know, but that is a chance that poets have to take. Yet "their" Hopkins, that good critic and great poet, wrote about Whitman, after seeing five or six of his poems in a newspaper review: "I may as well say what I should not otherwise have said, that I always knew in my heart Walt Whitman's mind to be more like my own than any other man's living. As he is a very great scoundrel this is not a very pleasant confession." And Henry James, the leader of "their" side in that awful imaginary war of which I spoke, once read Whitman to Edith Wharton (much as Mozart used to imitate, on the piano, the organ) with such power and solemnity that both sat shaken and silent; it was after this reading

From Randall Jarrell, *Poetry and the Age* (New York: Alfred A. Knopf, 1953), pp. 112–132. Reprinted by permission of the publisher.

that James expressed his regret at Whitman's "too extensive acquaintance with the foreign languages." Almost all the most "original and advanced" poets and critics and readers of the last part of the 19th Century thought Whitman as original and advanced as themselves, in manner as well as in matter. Can Whitman really be a sort of Thomas Wolfe or Carl Sandburg or Robinson Jeffers or Henry Miller—or a sort of Balzac of poetry, whose every part is crude but whose whole is somehow great? He is not, nor could he be; a poem, like Pope's spider, "lives along the line," and all the dead lines in the world will not make one live poem. As Blake says, "all sublimity is founded on minute discrimination," and it is in these "minute particulars" of Blake's that any poem has its primary existence.

To show Whitman for what he is one does not need to praise or explain or argue, one needs simply to quote. He himself said, "I and mine do not convince by arguments, similes, rhymes,/ We convince by our presence." Even a few of his phrases are enough to show us that Whitman was no sweeping rhetorician, but a poet of the greatest and oddest delicacy and originality and sensitivity, so far as words are concerned. This is, after all, the poet who said, "Blind loving wrestling touch, sheath'd hooded sharp-tooth'd touch"; who said, "Smartly attired, countenance smiling, form upright, death under the breast-bones, hell under the skull-bones"; who said, "Agonies are one of my changes of garments"; who saw grass as the "flag of my disposition," saw "the sharp-peak'd farmhouse, with its scallop'd scum and slender shoots from the gutters," heard a plane's "wild ascending lisp," and saw and heard how at the amputation "what is removed drops horribly in a pail." This is the poet for whom the sea was "howler and scooper of storms," reaching out to us with "crooked inviting fingers"; who went "leaping chasms with a pike-pointed staff, clinging to topples of brittle and blue"; who, a runaway slave, saw how "my gore dribs, thinn'd with the ooze of my skin"; who went "lithographing Kronos . . . buying drafts of Osiris"; who stared out at the "little plentiful mannikins skipping around in collars and tail'd coat,/ I am aware who they are, (they are positively not worms or fleas)." For he is, at his best, beautifully witty: he says gravely, "I find I incorporate gneiss, coals, long-threaded moss, fruits, grain, esculent roots,/ And am stucco'd with quadrupeds and birds all over"; and of these quadrupeds and birds "not one is respectable or unhappy over the whole earth." He calls advice: "Unscrew the locks from the doors! Unscrew the doors from their jambs!" He publishes the results of research: "Having pried through the strata, analyz'd to a hair, counsel'd with doctors and calculated close,/ I find no sweeter fat than sticks to my own bones." Everybody remembers how he told the Muse to "cross out please those immensely overpaid accounts,/ That matter of Troy and Achilles' wrath, and Aeneas', Odysseus' wanderings," but his account of the arrival of the "illustrious emigré" here in the New World is even better: "Bluff'd not a bit by drainpipe, gasometer, artificial fertilizers,/ Smiling and pleas'd with palpable intent to stay,/ She's here, install'd amid the kitchenware." Or he sees, like another Breughel, "the mechanic's wife with the babe at her nipple interceding for every person born,/ Three scythes at harvest whizzing in a row from three lusty angels with shirts bagg'd out at their waists,/ The snag-toothed hostler with red hair redeeming sins past and to come"—the passage has enough wit not only (in Johnson's phrase) to keep it sweet, but enough to make it believable. He says:

> I project my hat, sit shame-faced, and beg.
>
> Enough! Enough! Enough!
> Somehow I have been stunn'd. Stand back!
> Give me a little time beyond my cuff'd head, slumbers, dreams, gaping,
> I discover myself on the verge of a usual mistake.

There is in such changes of tone as these the essence of wit. And Whitman is even more far-fetched than he is witty; he can say about Doubters, in the most improbable and explosive of juxtapositions: "I know every one of you, I know the sea of torment, doubt, despair and unbelief./ How the flukes splash! How they contort rapid as lightning, with splashes and spouts of blood!" Who else would have said about God: "As the hugging and loving bed-fellow sleeps at my side through the night, and withdraws at the break of day with stealthy tread,/ Leave me baskets cover'd with white towels, swelling the house with their plenty"?—the Psalmist himself, his cup running over, would have looked at Whitman with dazzled eyes. (Whitman was persuaded by friends to hide the fact that it was God he was talking about.) He says, "Flaunt of the sunshine I need not your bask—lie over!" This unusual employment of verbs is usual enough in participle-loving Whitman, who also asks you to "look in my face while I snuff the sidle of evening," or tells you, "I effuse my flesh in eddies, and drift it in lacy jags." Here are some typical beginnings of poems: "City of orgies, walks, and joys. . . . Not heaving from my ribb'd breast only. . . . O take my hand Walt Whitman! Such gliding wonders! Such sights and sounds! Such join'd unended links. . . ." He says to the objects of the world, "You have waited, you always wait, you dumb, beautiful ministers"; sees "the sun and stars that float in the open air,/ The apple-shaped earth"; says, "O suns— O grass of graves— O perpetual transfers and promotions,/ If you do not say anything how can I say anything?" Not many poets have written better, in queerer and more convincing and more individual language, about the world's *gliding wonders*: the phrase seems particularly right for Whitman. He speaks of those "circling rivers the breath," of the "savage old mother incessantly crying,/ To the boy's soul's questions sullenly timing, some drown'd secret hissing"—ends a poem, once, "We have voided all but freedom and our own joy." How can one quote enough? If the reader thinks that all this is like Thomas Wolfe he *is* Thomas Wolfe; nothing else could explain it. Poetry like this is as far as possible from the work of any ordinary rhetorician, whose phrases cascade over us like suds of the oldest and most-advertised detergent.

The interesting thing about Whitman's worst language (for, just as few poets have ever written better, few poets have ever written worse) is how unusually absurd, how really ingeniously bad, such language is. I will quote none of the most famous examples; but even a line like O *culpable! I acknowledge. I exposé!* is not anything that you and I could do—only a man with the most extraordinary feel for language, or none whatsoever, could have cooked up Whitman's worst messes. For instance: what other man in all the history of this planet would have said, "I am a habitan of

Vienna"? (One has an immediate vision of him as a sort of French-Canadian half-breed to whom the Viennese are offering, with trepidation, through the bars of a zoological garden, little mounds of whipped cream.) And *enclaircise*—why, it's as bad as *explicate!* We are right to resent his having made up his own horrors, instead of sticking to the ones that we ourselves employ. But when Whitman says, "I dote on myself, there is that lot of me and all so luscious," we should realize that we are not the only ones who are amused. And the queerly bad and merely queer and queerly good will often change into one another without warning: "Hefts of the moving world, at innocent gambols silently rising, freshly exuding,/ Scooting obliquely high and low"—not good, but *queer!*—suddenly becomes, "Something I cannot see puts up libidinous prongs,/ Seas of bright juice suffuse heaven," and it is sunrise.

But it is not in individual lines and phrases, but in passages of some length, that Whitman is at his best. In the following quotation Whitman has something difficult to express, something that there are many formulas, all bad, for expressing; he expresses it with complete success, in language of the most dazzling originality:

> The orchestra whirls me wider than Uranus flies,
> It wrenches such ardors from me I did not know I possess'd them,
> It sails me, I dab with bare feet, they are lick'd by the indolent waves,
> I am cut by bitter and angry hail, I lose my breath,
> Steep'd amid honey'd morphine, my windpipe throttled in fakes of death,
> At length let up again to feel the puzzle of puzzles,
> And that we call Being.

One hardly knows what to point at—everything works. But *wrenches* and *did not know I possess'd them;* the incredible *it sails me, I dab with bare feet; lick'd by the indolent; steep'd amid honey'd morphine; my windpipe throttled in fakes of death*—no wonder Crane admired Whitman! This originality, as absolute in its way as that of Berlioz' orchestration, is often at Whitman's command:

> I am a dance—play up there! the fit is whirling me fast!
> I am the ever-laughing—it is new moon and twilight,
> I see the hiding of douceurs, I see nimble ghosts whichever way I look,
> Cache and cache again deep in the ground and sea, and where it is neither
>   ground nor sea.
> Well do they do their jobs those journeymen divine,
> Only from me can they hide nothing, and would not if they could,
> I reckon I am their boss and they make me a pet besides,
> And surround me and lead me and run ahead when I walk,
> To lift their sunning covers to signify me with stretch'd arms, and resume
>   the way;
> Onward we move, a gay gang of blackguards! with mirth-shouting music
>   and wild-flapping pennants of joy!

If you did not believe Hopkins' remark about Whitman, that *gay gang of blackguards* ought to shake you. Whitman shares Hopkins' passion for "dappled" effects, but he slides in and out of them with ambiguous swiftness. And he has at his command a language of the calmest and most prosaic reality, one that seems to do no more than present:

> The little one sleeps in its cradle.
> I lift the gauze and look a long time, and silently brush away flies with my hand.
> The youngster and the red-faced girl turn aside up the bushy hill,
> I peeringly view them from the top.
>
> The suicide sprawls on the bloody floor of the bedroom.
> I witness the corpse with its dabbled hair, I note where the pistol has fallen.

It is like magic: that is, something has been done to us without our knowing how it was done; but if we look at the lines again we see the *gauze, silently, youngster, red-faced, bushy, peeringly, dabbled*—not that this is all we see. "Present! present!" said James; these are presented, put down side by side to form a little "view of life," from the cradle to the last bloody floor of the bedroom. Very often the things presented form nothing but a list:

> The pure contralto sings in the organ loft,
> The carpenter dresses his plank, the tongue of his foreplane whistles its wild
>   ascending lisp,
> The married and unmarried children ride home to their Thanksgiving dinner,
> The pilot seizes the king-pin, he heaves down with a strong arm,
> The mate stands braced in the whale-boat, lance and harpoon are ready,
> The duck-shooter walks by silent and cautious stretches,
> The deacons are ordain'd with cross'd hands at the altar,
> The spinning-girl retreats and advances to the hum of the big wheel,
> The farmer stops by the bars as he walks on a First-day loafe and looks at the
>   oats and rye,
> The lunatic is carried at last to the asylum a confirm'd case,
> (He will never sleep any more as he did in the cot in his mother's bed-room;)
> The jour printer with gray head and gaunt jaws works at his case,
> He turns his quid of tobacco while his eyes blur with the manuscript,
> The malform'd limbs are tied to the surgeon's table,
> What is removed drops horribly in a pail; . . .

It is only a list—but what a list! And how delicately, in what different ways—likeness and opposition and continuation and climax and anticlimax—the transitions are managed, whenever Whitman wants to manage them. Notice them in the next quotation, another "mere list":

> The bride unrumples her white dress, the minute-hand of the
>   clock moves slowly,
> The opium-eater reclines with rigid head and just-open'd lips,
> The prostitute draggles her shawl, her bonnet bobs on her tipsy
>   and pimpled neck. . . .

The first line is joined to the third by *unrumples* and *draggles, white dress* and *shawl*; the second to the third by *rigid head, bobs, tipsy, neck*; the first to the second by *slowly, just-open'd,* and the slowing-down of time in both states. And occasionally one of these lists is metamorphosed into something we have no name for; the man who would call the next quotation a mere list—anybody will feel this—would boil his babies up for soap:

Ever the hard unsunk ground,
Ever the eaters and drinkers, ever the upward and downward sun, ever the air and
    the ceaseless tides,
Ever myself and my neighbors, refreshing, wicked, real,
Ever the old inexplicable query, ever that thorned thumb, that breath of itches and
    thirsts.
Ever the vexer's *hoot! hoot!* till we find where the sly one hides and bring him forth,
Ever love, ever the sobbing liquid of life,
Ever the bandage under the chin, ever the trestles of death.

Sometimes Whitman will take what would generally be considered an unpromising subject (in this case, a woman peeping at men in bathing naked) and treat it with such tenderness and subtlety and understanding that we are ashamed of ourselves for having thought it unpromising, and murmur that Chekhov himself couldn't have treated it better:

Twenty-eight young men bathe by the shore,
Twenty-eight young men and all so friendly,
Twenty-eight years of womanly life and all so lonesome.

She owns the fine house by the rise of the bank,
She hides handsome and richly drest aft the blinds of the window.

Which of the young men does she like the best?
Ah the homeliest of them is beautiful to her.

Where are you off to, lady? for I see you,
You splash in the water there, yet stay stock still in your room.

Dancing and laughing along the beach came the twenty-ninth bather,
The rest did not see her, but she saw them and loved them.

The beards of the young men glisten'd with wet, it ran from their long hair,
Little streams pass'd all over their bodies.

An unseen hand also pass'd over their bodies,
It descended tremblingly from their temples and ribs.

The young men float on their backs, their white bellies bulge to the sun, they do not
    ask who seizes fast to them,
They do not know who puffs and declines with pendant and bending arch,
They do not think whom they souse with spray.

   And in the same poem (that "Song of Myself" in which one finds half his best work) the writer can say of a sea-fight:

Stretch'd and still lies the midnight,
Two great hulls motionless on the breast of the darkness,
Our vessel riddled and slowly sinking, preparations to pass to the one we have
    conquer'd,
The captain on the quarter-deck coldly giving his orders through a countenance white
    as a sheet,
Near by the corpse of the child that serv'd in the cabin,
The dead face of an old salt with long white hair and carefully curl'd whiskers,
The flames spite of all that can be done flickering aloft and below,
The husky voices of the two or three officers yet fit for duty,
Formless stacks of bodies and bodies by themselves, dabs of flesh upon the masts
    and spars,
Cut of cordage, dangle of rigging, slight shock of the soothe of waves,
Black and impassive guns, litter of powder-parcels, strong scent,
A few large stars overhead, silent and mournful shining,
Delicate sniffs of sea-breeze, smells of sedgy grass and fields by the shore, death-
    messages given in charge to survivors,
The hiss of the surgeon's knife, the gnawing teeth of his saw,
Wheeze, cluck, swash of falling blood, short wild scream, and long, dull, tapering
    groan,
These so, these irretrievable.

There are faults in this passage, and they *do not matter*: the serious truth, the complete realization of these last lines make us remember that few poets have shown
more of the tears of things, and the joy of things, and of the reality beneath either
tears or joy. Even Whitman's most general or political statements sometimes are
good: everybody knows his "When liberty goes out of a place it is not the first to
go, nor the second or third to go,/ It waits for all the rest to go, it is the last"; these
sentences about the United States just before the Civil War may be less familiar:

Are those really Congressmen? are those the great Judges? is that the President?
Then I will sleep awhile yet, for I see that these States sleep, for reasons;
(With gathering murk, with muttering thunder and lambent shoots we all
    duly awake,
South, North, East, West, inland and seaboard, we will surely awake.)

How well, with what firmness and dignity and command, Whitman does such passages! And Whitman's doubts that he has done them or anything else well—ah, there
is nothing he does better:

The best I had done seemed to me blank and suspicious,
My great thoughts as I supposed them, were they not in reality meagre?
I am he who knew what it was to be evil,
I too knitted the old knot of contrariety . . .
Saw many I loved in the street or ferry-boat or public assembly, yet never
    told them a word,
Lived the same life with the rest, the same old laughing, gnawing, sleeping,

> Played the part that still looks back on the actor and actress,
> The same old role, the role that is what we make it . . .

Whitman says once that the "look of the bay mare shames silliness out of me." This is true—sometimes it is true; but more often the silliness and affection and cant and exaggeration are there shamelessly, the Old Adam that was in Whitman from the beginning and the awful new one that he created to keep it company. But as he says, "I know perfectly well my own egotism,/ Know my omnivorous lines and must not write any less." He says over and over that there are in him good and bad, wise and foolish, anything at all and its antonym, and he is telling the truth; there is in him almost everything in the world, so that one responds to him, willingly or unwillingly, almost as one does to the world, that world which makes the hairs of one's flesh stand up, which seems both evil beyond any rejection and wonderful beyond any acceptance. We cannot help seeing that there is something absurd about any judgment we make of its whole—for there is no "point of view" at which we can stand to make the judgment, and the moral categories that mean most to us seem no more to apply to its whole than our spatial or temporal or causal categories seem to apply to its beginning or its end. (But we need no arguments to make our judgments seem absurd—we feel their absurdity without argument.) In some like sense Whitman is a world, a waste with, here and there, systems blazing at random out of the darkness. Only an innocent and rigidly methodical mind will reject it for this disorganization, particularly since there are in it, here and there, little systems as beautifully and astonishingly organized as the rings and satellites of Saturn:

> I understand the large hearts of heroes,
> The courage of present times and all times,
> How the skipper saw the crowded and rudderless wreck of the steam-ship, and Death
>   chasing it up and down the storm,
> How he knuckled tight and gave not back an inch, and was faithful of days and
>   faithful of nights,
> And chalked in large letters on a board, Be of good cheer, we will not desert you;
> How he follow'd with them and tack'd with them three days and would not give it up,
> How he saved the drifting company at last,
> How the lank loose-gown'd women looked when boated from the side of their
>   prepared graves,
> How the silent old-faced infants and the lifted sick, and the sharp-lipp'd unshaved
>   men;
> All this I swallow, it tastes good, I like it well, it becomes mine,
> I am the man, I suffered, I was there.

In the last lines of this quotation Whitman has reached—as great writers always reach—a point at which criticism seems not only unnecessary but absurd: these lines are so good that even admiration feels like insolence, and one is ashamed of anything that one can find to say about them. How anyone can dismiss or accept patronizingly the man who wrote them, I do not understand.

The enormous and apparent advantages of form, of omission and selection, of the highest degree of organization, are accompanied by important disadvantages—and there are far greater works than *Leaves of Grass* to make us realize this. But if we compare Whitman with that very beautiful poet Alfred Tennyson, the most skillful of all Whitman's contemporaries, we are at once aware of how limiting Tennyson's forms have been, of how much Tennyson has had to leave out, even in those discursive poems where he is trying to put everything in. Whitman's poems *represent* his world and himself much more satisfactorily than Tennyson's do his. In the past a few poets have both formed and represented, each in the highest degree; but in modern times what controlling, organizing, selecting poet has created a world with as much in it as Whitman's, a world that so plainly *is* the world? Of all modern poets he has, quantitatively speaking, "the most comprehensive soul"—and, qualitatively, a most comprehensive and comprehending one, with charities and concessions and qualifications that are rare in any time.

"Do I contradict myself? Very well then I contradict myself," wrote Whitman, as everybody remembers, and this is not naive, or something he got from Emerson, or a complacent pose. When you organize one of the contradictory elements out of your work of art, you are getting rid not just of it, but of the contradiction of which it was a part; and it is the contradictions in works of art which make them able to represent to us—as logical and methodical generalizations cannot—our world and our selves, which are also full of contradictions. In Whitman we do not get the controlled, compressed, seemingly concordant contradictions of the great lyric poets, of a poem like, say, Hardy's "During Wind and Rain"; Whitman's contradictions are sometimes announced openly, but are more often scattered at random throughout the poems. For instance: Whitman specializes in ways of saying that there is in some sense (a very Hegelian one, generally) no evil—he says a hundred times that evil is not Real; but he also specializes in making lists of the evil of the world, lists of an unarguable reality. After his minister has recounted "the rounded catalogue divine complete," Whitman comes home and puts down what has been left out: "the countless (nineteen-twentieths) low and evil, crude and savage . . . the barren soil, the evil men, the slag and hideous rot." He ends another such catalogue with the plain unexcusing "All these—all meanness and agony without end I sitting look out upon,/ See, hear, and am silent." Whitman offered himself to everybody, and said brilliantly and at length what a good thing he was offering:

> Sure as the most certain sure, plumb in the uprights, well entretied,
>   braced in the beams,
> Stout as a horse, affectionate, haughty, electrical,
> I and this mystery here we stand.

Just for oddness, characteristicalness, differentness, what more could you ask in a letter of recommendation? (Whitman sounds as if he were recommending a house —haunted, but what foundations!) But after a few pages he is oddly different:

> Apart from the pulling and hauling stands what I am,
> Stands amused, complacent, compassionating, idle, unitary,
> Looks down, is erect, or bends an arm on an impalpable certain rest

> Looking with side curved head curious what will come next,
> Both in and out of the game and watching and wondering at it.

Tamburlaine is already beginning to sound like Hamlet: the employer feels uneasily, "Why, I might as well hire myself. . . ." And, a few pages later, Whitman puts down in ordinary-sized type, in the middle of the page, this warning to any *new person drawn toward me*:

> Do you think I am trusty and faithful?
> Do you see no further than this façade, this smooth and tolerant manner of me?
> Do you suppose yourself advancing on real ground toward a real heroic man?
> Have you no thought O dreamer that it may be all maya, illusion?

Having wonderful dreams, telling wonderful lies, was a temptation Whitman could never resist; but telling the truth was a temptation he could never resist, either. When you buy him you know what you are buying. And only an innocent and solemn and systematic mind will condemn him for his contradictions: Whitman's catalogues of evils represent realities, and his denials of their reality represent other realities, of feeling and intuition and desire. If he is faithless to logic, to Reality As It Is—whatever that is—he is faithful to the feel of things, to reality as it seems; this is all that a poet has to be faithful to, and philosophers have been known to leave logic and Reality for it.

Whitman is more coordinate and parallel than anybody, is *the* poet of parallel present participles, of twenty verbs joined by a single subject: all this helps to give his work its feeling of raw hypnotic reality, of being that world which also streams over us joined only by *ands*, until we supply the subordinating conjunctions; and since as children we see the *ands* and not the *becauses*, this method helps to give Whitman some of the freshness of childhood. How inexhaustibly interesting the world is in Whitman! Arnold all his life kept wishing that he could see the world "with a plainness as near, as flashing" as that with which Moses and Rebekah and the Argonauts saw it. He asked with elegiac nostalgia, "Who can see the green earth any more/ As she was by the sources of Time?"—and all the time there was somebody alive who saw it so, as plain and near and flashing, and with a kind of calm, pastoral, Biblical dignity and elegance as well, sometimes. The *thereness* and *suchness* of the world are incarnate in Whitman as they are in few other writers.

They might have put on his tombstone WALT WHITMAN: HE HAD HIS NERVE. He is the rashest, the most inexplicable and unlikely—the most impossible, one wants to say—of poets. He somehow *is* in a class by himself, so that one compares him with other poets about as readily as one compares *Alice* with other books. (Even his free verse has a completely different effect from anybody else's.) Who would think of comparing him with Tennyson or Browning or Arnold or Baudelaire?—it is Homer, or the sagas, or something far away and long ago, that comes to one's mind only to be dismissed; for sometimes Whitman *is* epic, just as *Moby Dick* is, and it surprises us to be able to use truthfully this word that we have misused so many times. Whitman *is* grand, and elevated, and comprehensive, and real with an astonishing reality, and many other things—the critic points at his qualities in despair and wonder, all method failing, and simply calls them by their names. And the range of these qualities is the most extraordinary thing of all. We can surely say about him, "He was a man, take him for all in all. I shall not look upon his like again"—and wish that people had seen this and not tried to be his like: one Whitman is miracle enough, and when he comes again it will be the end of the world.

I have said so little about Whitman's faults because they are so plain: baby critics who have barely learned to complain of the lack of ambiguity in *Peter Rabbit* can tell you all that is wrong with *Leaves of Grass*. But a good many of my readers must have felt that it is ridiculous to write an essay about the obvious fact that Whitman is a great poet. It is ridiculous—just as, in 1851, it would have been ridiculous for anyone to write an essay about the obvious fact that Pope was no "classic of our prose" but a great poet. Critics have to spend half their time reiterating whatever ridiculously obvious things their age or the critics of their age have found it necessary to forget: they say despairingly, at parties, that Wordsworth is a great poet, and *won't* bore you, and tell Mr. Leavis that Milton is a great poet whose deposition *hasn't* been accomplished with astonishing ease by a few words from Eliot. . . . There is something essentially ridiculous about critics, anyway: what is good is good without our saying so, and beneath all our majesty we know this.

Let me finish by mentioning another quality of Whitman's—a quality, delightful to me, that I have said nothing of. If some day a tourist notices, among the ruins of New York City, a copy of *Leaves of Grass*, and stops and picks it up and reads some lines in it, she will be able to say to herself: "How very American! If he and his country had not existed, it would have been impossible to imagine them."

"SONG OF MYSELF" AS MYSTICISM

"SONG OF MYSELF" AS INVERTED
MYSTICAL EXPERIENCE

by James E. Miller, Jr.

WHITMAN'S "Song of Myself" has long been considered a loosely organized, perhaps even chaotic poem which is held together, if at all, by his own robust personality.
He himself may have contributed to this concept of the poem. Untitled when it
appeared in the first edition of *Leaves of Grass* in 1855, it was called "Poem of
Walt Whitman, an American" in the 1856 edition; "Walt Whitman" in the 1860
edition, and was given the present title in the 1881 edition. This frequent change
of title together with the many revisions made in the numbering of the sections and
in the text itself suggests one of two possibilities: either Whitman was uncertain,
perhaps confused as to the basic nature of what he was writing; or he was struggling
to perfect a work of art the execution of which had fallen short of the conception.
Too frequently the critics have assumed as self-evident the first of these possibilities.[1]
Inability to find a structure in "Song of Myself" has resulted, I believe, from a failure
to find a center of relevancy, an "informing idea," to which the parts of the poem
may be related. It is the purpose of this paper to propose such a center, to show how
it gives structure to the poem, and to examine the parts of the poem in detail to test
their relevancy to this central "informing idea."

"Song of Myself" is the dramatic representation of a mystical experience. The term
"dramatic representation" indicates an important distinction: it is not my contention
that the poem is a transcript of an actual mystical experience; rather it is a work of
art in which such an experience, conceived in the imagination, is represented dramatically, with the author assuming the main or title role. The mystical experience
is dramatically represented in the sense that the poet portrays his preparation for
and his entry into a state of mystical consciousness (sections 1–5), his progressively

From James E. Miller, Jr., *A Critical Guide to Leaves of Grass* (Chicago: University of
Chicago Press, 1957), pp. 6–35. Copyright © 1957 by The University of Chicago Press and
reprinted with their permission.

[1] A notable exception is Carl F. Strauch, "The Structure of Walt Whitman's 'Song of
Myself,'" *English Journal*, xxvii (Sept. 1938), 597–607. Strauch's analysis of the poem, in
which he combines sections 1–18, 19–25, 26–38, 39–41, 42–52, has been widely quoted.
Although my analysis differs considerably from his, I agree thoroughly with his basic thesis
that the poem has a structure and that "Whitman was in command of his materials." Gay
Wilson Allen's valuable *Walt Whitman Handbook* (Chicago: Packard, 1946) also contains
an illuminating discussion of "Song of Myself" (pp. 114–121).

significant and meaningful experience while in this state (sections 6–49), and, finally, his emergence from the mystical state (sections 50–52).

The central portion of the poem, sections 6–49, may be related, step by step, to the "Mystic Way," as described by Evelyn Underhill in her valuable study.[2] In what she herself labels an "arbitrary classification," she analyzes five "phases of the mystical life": 1. The Awakening of Self; 2. The Purification of Self; 3. Illumination; 4. The Dark Night of the Soul; 5. Union. These phases, she insists, answer only "loosely and generally to experiences which seldom present themselves in so rigid and unmixed a form" (p. 205). "Song of Myself" conforms, in framework, remarkably well to these five stages, but with some significant differences from the traditional mystical concepts or attitudes. These differences, central to the poet's meaning and intention, represent an inversion of some of the steps in the Mystic Way or a reversal of values held by the traditional mystic.

"Song of Myself," considered as the dramatic representation of an inverted mystical experience, may be analyzed as follows:

    I. Sections 1– 5: Entry into Mystical State.
    II. Sections 6–16: Awakening of Self.
    III. Sections 17–32: Purification of Self.
    IV. Sections 33–37: Illumination and the Dark Night of the Soul.
    V. Sections 38–43: Union (Faith and Love).
    VI. Sections 44–49: Union (Perception).
    VII. Sections 50–52: Emergence from Mystical State.

The third and fourth stages in the Mystic Way (Illumination and the Dark Night of the Soul) have been combined in sections 33–37; Miss Underhill indicates that, in reality, the fourth phase sometimes accompanies, intermittently, the third, and that her separation of the two is somewhat arbitrary (p. 206). Each of the two parts of "Song of Myself" devoted to the fifth stage of the Mystic Way is concerned with separate, distinct characteristics of Union as described by Miss Underhill.

Portrayal of the entry into and emergence from the mystical state of consciousness in sections 1–5 and 50–52 conforms to the popular concept of the behavior of the mystic, his "going into" and "coming out of" the mystic trance. This portrayal represents what William James called the "sporadic type" of mystical experience in which the individual gains sudden, fleeting insight or transcendent knowledge.[3] But between the beginning and end of this trance-like state, the poet portrays the laborious steps of the traditional mystic in his efforts to achieve Union with the Transcendent. The poet not only fuses the two kinds of mystical experience into one, but also, for poetic economy and dramatic intensity, portrays the five stages of the Mystic Way as following each other immediately in time, whereas in reality the mystic might take years to reach his goal of Union. Justification for this departure from reality may be found

[2] *Mysticism: A Study in the Nature and Development of Man's Spiritual Consciousness* (London: Methuen, 1926), 11th ed., used here. The 1st ed. appeared in 1911.

[3] *Varieties of Religious Experience* (New York, 1920), pp. 395–396. James cites section 5 of "Song of Myself" as an expression of the "sporadic type" of mystical experience.

in the requirements of a work of art: "Song of Myself" is a poem, not a historical, philosophical, or religious document.

I. Sections 1–5: Entry into the Mystical State

In the opening section of "Song of Myself," the poet, while in the passive and receptive state of "leaning" and "loafing," "observing a spear of summer grass," sends forth what is to prove a significant invitation: "I loafe and invite my soul." [4] In section 5, the soul not only accepts the invitation but also consummates a union with the poet. The intervening sections of the poem portray the poet's mental and physical preparation for this union. "Creeds and schools," second-hand knowledge, are to be held "in abeyance," and the poet will "permit to speak at every hazard, Nature without check with original energy." Surroundings congenial to the experience must be found: "I will go to the bank by the wood and become undisguised and naked." In order for nature to speak "with original energy," all man-made objects—houses, rooms, clothes—must be, at least for the moment, forsaken. The importance of the senses to the anticipated experience is suggested in the catalogue in the middle of section 2, in which the poet expresses delight in and implies unqualified acceptance of each of the senses: of taste ("the smoke of my own breath"); of sound ("echoes, ripples, buzz'd whispers"); of odor ("the sniff of green leaves and dry leaves"); of touch ("a few light kisses, a few embraces"); of sight ("the play of shine and shade on the trees").

The nature of the knowledge to be gained through the experience is indicated when the poet invites the reader to "stop this day and night" with him and discover "the origin of all poems," "the good of the earth and sun." There are further hints in sections 3 and 4 of the kind of knowledge which nature will bestow. The "talkers" of section 3 and the "trippers and askers" of section 4, with their doubt and their skepticism and debate about a "beginning" and "end," are too much involved in the minutiae of daily living and accept too readily inherited beliefs, to experience the "felt" order in the apparent chaos of existence: "Out of the dimness opposite equals advance, always substance and increase, always sex." The knowledge to be gained is to reconcile "opposite" yet "equals," the "distinction" and "breed" yet "knit of identity": "To elaborate is no avail, learn'd and unlearn'd feel that it is so." The pastime of the age, "showing the best and dividing it from the worst," is futile and misleading. The poet will not engage in the talk about the beginning and end, nor will he, with the age, make judgments about the best and the worst, nor will he surrender himself to the trippers and askers: "Apart from the pulling and hauling stands what I am." At the close of section 4, the poet, "both in and out of the game and watching and wondering at it," portrays himself as withdrawn, withholding comment and judgment —prepared for the imminent union with his soul: "I witness and wait."

In section 5, while the poet is in this state of bemused detachment, the soul ma-

---

[4] All quotations from "Song of Myself" may be easily located by my references to the sections of the poem. I have used the so-called Deathbed edition of *Leaves of Grass* as it appears in *The Complete Writings of Walt Whitman* (New York, 1902), ed. Oscar Lovell Triggs.

terializes and is invited to loaf on the grass, to loose the "stop" from his throat, to "lull" and "hum" with his "valvèd voice." The poet then portrays his entry into the mystical state of consciousness:

> I mind how once we lay such a transparent summer morning,
> How you settled your head athwart my hips and gently turn'd over upon me,
> And parted the shirt from my bosom-bone, and plunged your tongue to my bare-
>   stript heart,
> And reach'd till you felt my beard and reach'd till you held my feet.

The sexual connotations are unmistakable: implicit in the imagery is the consummated marriage of body and soul. The preceding sections of the poem have given ample preparation for such a symbolic marriage: "Clear and sweet is my soul, and clear and sweet is all that is not my soul." Throughout sections 1–5 of the poem, the senses have been defiantly accepted and even celebrated, with the suggestion that they are to have a significant part in the approaching union with the soul. This attitude toward the senses constitutes the basic paradox in the poem. Whereas normally the mystical state is achieved only through a mortification of or escape from the senses, the poet of "Song of Myself" asserts that it is through the transfigured senses that he reaches mystical consciousness.

In "Song of Myself" the self is not, as in the traditional mystical experience, submerged or annihilated, but rather celebrated, the senses are not humbled, but glorified. When the soul plunges his tongue to the "bare-stript heart" of the poet, the physical becomes transfigured into the spiritual, the body from beard to feet is held in the grip of the soul, and body and soul become one: "Lack one lacks both." The imagery of the tongue and heart is ingenious: the spiritual tongue informs; the physical heart receives. Such imagery suggests that it is only through the intimate fusion of the physical and spiritual, the ennobling of the physical through the spiritual, that one can come to know transcendent Reality. The poet's mystical state of consciousness results in immediate "knowledge":

> Swiftly arose and spread around me the peace and knowledge that pass all the argu-
>   ment of the earth,
> And I know that the hand of God is the promise of my own,
> And I know that the spirit of God is the brother of my own,
> And that all the men ever born are also my brothers, and the women my sisters and
>   lovers,
> And that a kelson of the creation is love.

This knowledge would confound the trippers, askers, and talkers: it is not rational knowledge at all, but the "peace and knowledge," or love, which the tongue of the soul imparts to the heart of the body. It is, in short, the beginning of the spiritual awakening of the physical self.

II. SECTIONS 6–16: AWAKENING OF SELF

The sudden certitude which the poet feels that the "hand of God" is the "promise" of his own and that the "spirit of God" is the "brother" of his own is the mystic's awakening to "consciousness of Divine Reality." [5] The poet's intense vision brings an intuitive awareness of the relationship of self to God, to other men and women, and to nature, and the sum of the knowledge is, "a kelson of the creation is love." The awakening of self begins, as with the mystic, in "a disturbance of the equilibrium of the self, which results in the shifting of the field of consciousness from lower to higher levels, with a consequent removal of the centre of interest from the subject to an object now brought into view." [6] The nature imagery at the end of section 5 trails off with "elder, mullein, poke-weed," which leads naturally to the question posed in section 6, "What is the grass?"

The grass becomes, in this important section, a key to the ultimate enigma of Divine Reality. The poet, now become intensely aware and perceptive, searches out the grass's significance in relation to self (the "flag of my disposition"), to God (the "handkerchief of the Lord"), to life ("a uniform hieroglyphic . . . sprouting alike in broad zones and narrow zones"), and to death ("the beautiful uncut hair of graves"). These large subjects (self, God, life, death) introduce the areas into which insight is to be sought and perhaps gained through the Mystic Way. The poet seems most fascinated by the puzzle of death, and he attempts to "translate the hints" given by the grass of the fate of the dead:

The smallest sprout shows there is really no death,
And if ever there was it led forward life, and does not wait at the end to arrest it,
And ceas'd the moment life appear'd.

All goes onward and outward, nothing collapses,
And to die is different from what any one supposed, and luckier.

The imagery is complex, suggesting a threefold view of death. The "smallest sprout" of grass offered as proof that there is no death suggests pantheism. But the lines which follow suggest that faith is placed in evolution: death is the void that existed on earth before life existed; the "moment life appear'd" death ceased and now all "goes onward and outward"—the race has eternal life though the individual dies. But implicit in, "And if there was it [death] led forward life, and does not wait at the end to arrest it," is the suggestion of the eternal life of the individual; death is the nonentity of the individual before birth rather than after death. Once the individual achieves existence, eternal life is bestowed; there is change ("onward and outward"— material and spiritual) but not disintegration ("collapse").

But all of these thoughts to which contemplation of the grass has given rise are merely hints, a groping about for insight by the newly awakened self. They indicate to the reader the nature of the journey on which the poet is embarking, the kind of knowledge after which he is striving. In section 7 there is a return to the probing of self, an attempt to express what the self really is. The poet is "not contain'd between [his] hat and boots," nor is he "an earth nor an adjunct of an earth." This indication of what the self is *not* launches the poet into an expanding vision of what the self *is*, a vision which begins in section 7 and runs through to a climax in section 16. These

[5] Underhill, p. 205.
[6] Underhill, p. 213.

sections represent a gradual intensification of the poet's awakening of self, and, as in the traditional mystical experience, the awakening tends not inward but outward: the "object now brought into [the poet's] view" is other life of all kinds, in all emotional states, in all conditions and situations.

Section 8 introduces the poet observing the cycle of life—birth ("The little one sleeps in its cradle"), love ("The youngster and the red-faced girl turn aside up the bushy hill"), and death ("The suicide sprawls on the bloody floor"). This cycle fades into the montage of city street-life, beginning with "the blab of pave" and concluding with the poet's observation, "I mind them or the show or resonance of them—I come and I depart." In section 9 the scene changes from city to country, with a full picture of a farm; the poet is there: "I help, I came stretch'd atop of the load [of the wagon]." In section 10 there is a series of pictures in which the poet sees himself or observes others in activities which isolate the individual: he hunts "alone far in the wilds" and he sails on the Yankee clipper; he observes the "marriage of the trapper in the open air in the far west," and he plays generous and tender host to the runaway slave. The observation of the lonely and isolated reaches a climax in section 11, which is devoted in its entirety to the vivid picture of the young woman, whose life has been "all so lonesome," secretly observing, longing for, and imagining herself joining, the twenty-eight young swimmers, whose "bellies bulge to the sun." In section 12 the poet shifts his observation to the lowly, as he loiters and enjoys the "repartee" of the butcherboy and follows the movements of the blacksmith. Section 13 continues with the life of the humble in the full portrait of the negro holding "firmly the reins of his four horses."

This portrait brings into focus another element of life which, after a brief reference to the role of self, causes another shift in the poet's vision:

I behold the picturesque giant and love him, and I do not stop there,
I go with the team also.

In me the caresser of life wherever moving, backward as well as forward sluing,
To niches aside and junior bending, not a person or object missing,
Absorbing all to myself and for this song.

"Caresser of life" suggests the role of the poet throughout this first phase of his mystical experience. The love which the soul has bestowed on the heart has awakened the poet to a sympathetic awareness of life outside of self—to all life, "backward" or "forward." The "niches" is an ingenious image connoting all of the lonely, the isolated, whom others—but not the poet—pass by. And the poet's love is extended to life other than human. With "I go with the team also," the poet begins a series of pictures of such life, from the oxen, wood-drake, wood-duck, tortoise, jay, and bay mare of the latter part of section 13 through the gander, moose, cat, chickadee, prairie-dog, sow, and turkey hen of the first half of section 14. All of this life, like the wild gander, finds "its purpose and place," and, like the tortoise, is not "unworthy because [it] is not something else." Through this animal life, the poet awakens further to self: "I see in them and myself the same old law." The poet is "enamour'd of growing out-doors," where such self-awareness or self-knowledge is granted so freely and easily. Section 14 closes with the first clear indication that the poet identifies himself with those whom he observes—the "commonest, cheapest, nearest, easiest." In going in for his chances, "spending for vast returns," the poet is asserting that he will have ample reward for the love and affection which he seems to be bestowing so indiscriminately—the reward of awakened self and the resulting insight into the riddle of existence.

Good will is indeed scattered freely in section 15, a long catalogue of rapid one-line pictures, ranging from contralto to lunatic, from opium-eater and prostitute to flatboatmen and coon-seekers, ending

> And these tend inward to me, and I tend outward to them,
> And such as it is to be of these more or less I am,
> And of these one and all I weave the song of myself.

The awakening of self has been an awakening to the realization of the potentiality in the self to be all of these, to have all of their varied emotions, to engage in all of their sundry activities. The awakening has caused the eyes to turn not inward but outward, and has resulted in not contraction but expansion of self, excluding none, including all.

The poet insists on even greater diversity of self in section 16: "I am of old and young, of the foolish as much as the wise." Emphasis in this section, in contrast with the preceding, is placed on the merging of sectional or geographical differences. The poet is "one of the Nation of many nations," a Southerner, a Northerner, a Yankee, a Kentuckian, a Louisianian, a Californian and many more: "Of every hue and caste am I, of every rank and religion." What had started, in section 8, as observation, coming and departing, has become by now complete identification—the poet no longer watches, or is "of" what he sees, but actually *is* all that he observes. Self has been expanded to include the whole of America, high and low, far and near, divine or degraded. And accompanying this vision of the diversity of self is the sense of the fitness of things as they are. Section 16 closes with the poet asserting

> [I] am not stuck up, and am in my place.
>
> (The moth and the fish-eggs are in their place,
> The bright suns I see and the dark suns I cannot see are in their place,
> The palpable is in its place and the impalpable is in its place.)

In the first phase of the mystical experience, the poet has achieved an acute awareness of an expanded self and a supreme confidence in the fitness of that self in its place. Implied in this sense of "place," not only for the self but for all else, is the sense of design or plan transcending the self and all things, animate and inanimate, seen and unseen. Awakening of self has bestowed an intuitive glimpse of this design—the Divine Reality.

III. SECTIONS 17–32: PURIFICATION OF SELF

In section 17 of "Song of Myself" there is a pause in the long catalogues, and the poet appears to assess the value of what he has so far learned:

These are really the thoughts of all men in all ages and lands, they are not
    original with me,
If they are not yours as much as mine they are nothing, or next to nothing.

The poet's thoughts on himself are in reality thoughts on selfhood and belong not to just one but to all. And these thoughts are the "riddle and the untying of the riddle." The awakening of self, the realization of the otherness or diversity of self, is a riddle, but in the awakening lies the clue to the solution of the riddle. As the first lines of section 17 comment on the foregoing experiences, so the last lines introduce, metaphorically, a change in the direction of the mystical journey:

This is the grass that grows wherever the land is and the water is,
This is the common air that bathes the globe.

As contemplation of the meaning of the grass launched the first phase of the mystical experience, so one particular symbolic quality of it is used to begin the second phase. The image of the grass is joined with the image of the air to suggest, particularly through the word "common," the equality of all. Although the subject matter ranges widely in sections 17–32, the theme of equality is constant. It is through this insistent theme that the poet achieves purification of self.

As it has been through acceptance of the body, not through mortification of it as something evil, that the mystical experience has been launched in "Song of Myself," it should not be surprising that in the "purification" phase the traditional values of the mystic are inverted. Purification is achieved not through "purgation," not through "discipline and mortification," [7] but by an ennobling and acceptance of what has been mistakenly reviled and degraded. Whitman's reversal of the traditional mystic values, values not necessarily peculiar to the mystic, is the heart of his meaning: man's sense of sin is his greatest sin, his greatest delusion; in order to purify himself, he must purge this false sense.

Throughout sections 18–32, the degraded and rejected are ennobled and accepted through a reconciliation of opposites usually considered irreconcilable: in section 18, the vanquished and victor; in section 19, the wicked and righteous; in section 20, the self and others; in section 21, the body and soul, and woman and man; in section 22, vice and virtue; in section 23, the present and past, and science and spirit (or reality and spirituality); in section 24, the self and others, and body and soul (or the lusts of the body and the desires of the soul); in section 25, the unseen and the seen, or the felt and the provable; in section 26, the inflow and the outflow, or the heard and the spoken; in sections 27 through 30 (the well-known sections on the poet's sensitivity to touch), the body and soul, or the physical and spiritual; in section 31, the common and the miraculous, or the known and the unknown, or the familiar and the unfamiliar; in section 32, the animal and man.

The dropping and subsequent return to a particular subject, what has frequently been called the symphonic treatment of theme, may be justified on the basis of the dramatic situation of the poet: in the emotional state imposed by the mystical ex-

[7] Underhill, p. 205.

perience, something approaching ecstatic frenzy, it is natural that the poet's thought lacks logical continuity. But the disunity is more apparent than real: when a subject is reintroduced it is treated in a new light, from a different point of view; such periodic and gradual treatment builds up to a climax. The most notable example is the celebration of the body, begun in section 21, returned to in section 24, and become an ecstatic eulogy in sections 27–30.

The act of purification begins in section 18 with "conquer'd and slain persons," as the poet imagines himself a band, with cornets and drums, beating and pounding "for the dead": "it is good to fall, battles are lost in the same spirit in which they are won." In section 19 the poet elevates the wicked alongside the righteous. His "meal [is] equally set" for the kept-woman, sponger, thief, slave, venerealee: "There shall be no difference between them and the rest." And to those who question his motive, the poet answers,

Do you guess I have some intricate purpose?
Well I have, for the Fourth-month showers have, and the mica on the side of a
  rock has.

His motive is no different from nature's; in him exist the same "elementary laws." In section 20 there is an almost arrogant egotism which has frequently been found objectionable: "I wear my hat as I please indoors or out." But, as the poet insists, this seeming arrogance is not meant to be an expression of superiority: "In all people I see myself, none more and not one a barley-corn less." The source of the poet's strong feeling of equality is his knowledge that he is "deathless," but his immortality is no more than any other man's:

My foothold is tenon'd and mortis'd in granite,
I laugh at what you call dissolution,
And I know the amplitude of time

The only superiority he has is his intuitive knowledge of immortality—he knows that man is deathless; others do not.

The first lines of section 21 announce the theme which is crucial to the purification of self:

I am the poet of the Body and I am the poet of the Soul,
The pleasures of heaven are with me and the pains of hell are with me,
The first I graft and increase upon myself, the latter I translate into a new tongue.

As the poet will, through self, "increase" the "pleasures of heaven" (the spiritual), so he will "translate into a new tongue"—transfigure, purify—the "pains of hell" (the physical). Although the poet momentarily passes on to other aspects of his central theme of equality ("I am the poet of the woman the same as the man"; "I show that size is only development"), he returns to the body-soul theme in the celebrated passage, extending into section 22, which delicately fuses imagery of night, earth, and sea with sexual imagery:

> I am he that walks with the tender and growing night,
> I call to the earth and sea half-held by the night.

The night is masculine, "bare-bosom'd night," "mad naked summer night," while the earth is feminine—"voluptuous cool-breath'd earth!" "earth of the mountains misty-topt!" Whereas the earth's lover is the descending night, the poet himself is beckoned by the "crooked inviting fingers" of the sea and hurries to it, undresses, and is dashed by "amorous wet." This delicate portrayal of sexual feeling in nature imagery is the "translation into a new tongue" promised by the poet. The gross language in which such feelings are usually embodied, with its connotations of sin and evil, is abandoned, and the sensitive, delicate imagery of nature transfigures the emotions and ennobles them. When, later in section 22, the poet exclaims, "I am not the poet of goodness only, I do not decline to be the poet of wickedness also," "wickedness" must be interpreted in the context of what has preceded: inasmuch as the word has been associated with the body, the physical, the sexual impulse and fulfillment, then the poet does not decline to be the "poet of wickedness." The physical may be reconciled with the spiritual: "I find one side a balance and the antipodal side a balance."

The theme of the equality of the present with the past is introduced in the latter part of section 22 ("This minute that comes to me over the past decillions,/ There is no better than it and now") and is carried over into the first part of section 23 ("Endless unfolding of words of ages!/ And mine a word of the modern, the word En-masse"). The poet accepts "Time absolutely" and accepts "Reality and dare[s] not question it." Reality is "materialism," symbolized by "positive science," which the poet enthusiastically accepts but by no means considers final:

> Gentlemen, to you the first honors always!
> Your facts are useful, and yet they are not my dwelling,
> I but enter by them to an area of my dwelling.

Acceptance of the body would necessarily entail the acceptance of the physical world, or materialism; but just as the body offered the way into the mystical state, so positive science offers the way to something other than itself, to "life untold."

Section 24 reintroduces the egotistic tone of section 20, but again emphasis is placed on equality, not superiority. The poet is "no stander above men and women or apart from them":

I speak the pass-word primeval, I give the sign of democracy,
By God! I will accept nothing which all cannot have their counterpart of on the same terms.

Following this passionate outburst asserting equality, championing the "rights of them the others are down upon," there is a return to the body-soul theme:

> Through me forbidden voices,
> Voices of sexes and lusts, voices veil'd and I remove the veil,
> Voices indecent by me clarified and transfigur'd.

The aim of the poet is, clearly, transfiguration, purification, spiritualization of the physical self. The senses, "seeing, hearing, feeling, are miracles" as much as are faculties of the soul. But the transfiguration is not to be accomplished through mere assertion only; it is to be accomplished poetically through association of the physical with the innocence, beauty and divine mystery of nature. The poet sees the innocence of the sensual and sexual in the primitive, natural, eternal world about him, in such symbolic products of nature as "root of wash'd sweet-flag! timorous pond-snipe! nest of guarded duplicate eggs!"

Sections 25 and 26 of "Song of Myself" complement each other; in the first the poet conceives of himself as imparting, in the latter, as receiving. When, in section 25, he says, "My voice goes after what my eyes cannot reach," he is asserting the importance of the unseen alongside the seen. But when, further on, he says, "you conceive too much of articulation," he is asserting the importance of the felt or inexpressible alongside the provable, the demonstrable. The desire to impart of section 25 becomes a desire to receive in section 26:

> Now I will do nothing but listen,
> To accrue what I hear into this song, to let sounds contribute toward it.

Underlying these two sections is the theme of the equal validity of the outflow and the inflow, the imparted and the received. The sounds accrued range from the sounds of the city to the sounds of the country, from the sounds of the day to the sounds of the night, and they conclude with an orchestra which "wrenches such ardors" from the poet that he reacts with emotional violence:

> . . . . I lose my breath,
> Steep'd amid honey'd morphine, my windpipe throttled in fakes of death,
> At length let up again to feel the puzzle of puzzles,
> And that we call Being.

Sections 27 through 30 are an exploration of this puzzle of "Being": "To be in any form, what is that?" Is "Being" the body or the soul, or the one transfigured by the other into a new self infinitely more significant than either alone? The answer lies only in the self: "I merely stir, press, feel with my fingers, and am happy." The body cannot be denied; the instinctive reaction to touch confirms it as a basic truth, not lie—good, not evil. Through touch the poet is quivered "to a new identity"— the purified self. The remarkable imagery in which the poet's other senses, bribed by touch, "go and graze at the edges" of him, suggests sexual ecstasy and fulfillment, reaching a climax as the poet cries out, "Unclench your floodgates, you are too much for me." Section 29 portrays the poet, after the departure of "blind loving wrestling . . . sheath'd hooded sharptooth'd touch," emotionally fulfilled but exhausted, and section 30 shows him reflecting on the significance of his ecstatic encounter with touch: "All truths wait in all things . . . (What is less or more than a touch?)." As touch, in spite of "logic and sermons," "proves itself" to the poet, the body is accepted. The self, through instinctive insight, has been purified by a purgation, not of the senses, but of the illusion of the senses as vile.

The grass imagery, which has appeared previously at key points in the poem, is reintroduced in section 31: "I believe a leaf of grass is no less than the journey-work of the stars." The leaf of grass here becomes a symbol of the insignificant which to the poet is "as big as any." The miraculous may be found in the smallest or the most commonplace object. In the latter part of section 31, the poet shows an awareness of self as the product of a long, evolutionary development. When he says, "[I] have distanced what is behind me for good reasons," he suggests that he too, like the leaf of grass, the pismire, the grain of sand, and the rest, is "miracle enough to stagger sextillions of infidels."

Section 32, which closes the second phase of the mystical experience, celebrates the primitive life of the animals. When the poet exclaims, "I think I could turn and live with animals," he is acknowledging that he has achieved purification of self, a purification that the animals do not need to struggle to attain inasmuch as they are born with an innate primitive purity:

They do not sweat and whine about their condition,
They do not lie awake in the dark and weep for their sins,
They do not make me sick discussing their duty to God,
Not one is dissatisfied, not one is demented with the mania of owning things,
Not one kneels to another, nor to his kind that lived thousands of years ago,
Not one is respectable or unhappy over the whole earth.

In the animals exist all of the traits which the poet has attempted, in sections 17–32, to ennoble and celebrate, traits frequently considered evil.[8] It is this sense of evil that the poet has purged in the purification of self. These traits are now so much the poet's own that he wonders where the animals got them: "Did I pass that way huge times ago and negligently drop them?" Man, in the primitive state of his evolution, had such traits, but, in the development of his civilization, lost them to the animals. The section closes with the vivid picture of the poet riding the "gigantic beauty of a stallion," whose "well-built limbs tremble with pleasure": the stallion is symbolic of all the primitive innocence which the poet admires and has achieved. But the poet says,

> I but use you a minute, then I resign you, stallion,
> Why do I need your paces when I myself out-gallop them?
> Even as I stand or sit passing faster than you.

The poet realizes that the animal, with all of his innocence and purity, cannot achieve what a man of similar nature can achieve—what the poet is to achieve in the next stage of his mystical experience.

---

[8] Among these traits, the only one which resembles the ideal of the mystic is the indifference to "owning things." In the purification of self, the traditional mystic cultivates poverty, chastity, and obedience, all of which results in the desired humility. (Underhill, pp. 247–248.)

IV. Sections 33–37: Illumination and the Dark Night of the Soul

Illumination, when it comes to the purified self, is swift; the poet at the opening of section 33 bursts forth with the "knowledge of Reality" [9] which is suddenly his:

> Space and time! now I see it is true, what I guess'd at,
> What I guess'd when I loaf'd on the grass,
> What I guess'd while I lay alone in my bed,
> And again as I walk'd the beach under the paling stars of the morning.

It is as though the poet, after the struggles of awakening and purification of the previous two phases of the experience, has finally achieved existence outside space and time and has sudden insight, like the mystic's, into the "secret of the world." [10] What had only been felt before, or "guess'd," receives confirmation through intuitive but certain knowledge. The emotional feeling accompanying the insight is evoked in the image of the balloon, its ties and ballasts cast off, ascending above the world. But this image merges immediately with that of a giant self, whose "elbows rest in sea-gaps" and whose "palms cover continents." The one image suggests upward movement or flight, while the other suggests immense power; together the images imply greater physical sight, symbolic of the greater spiritual insight which has been attained. The poet is "afoot" with his vision at last; the self, awakened and purified, apprehends directly Divine Reality.

The increase in energy of the "intuitional or transcendental self" [11] is manifested in the poet's sense of ubiquity or all-inclusiveness. The first half of section 33, the longest section in the poem, consists of the long catalogue in which the poet imagines himself "by the city's quadrangular houses," "where the panther walks," "scaling mountains," "where the human heart beats with terrible throes under its ribs," "under Niagara," and elsewhere, near and distant, placid and dangerous. This catalogue has, however, a significant difference from those found in the sections describing the poet's awakening of self (particularly in sections 8, 15, and 16). For the first time the poet imagines himself out of time, "Walking the old hills of Judaea with the beautiful gentle God by my side," and not confined to this world, hampered by space: "Speeding through space, speeding through heaven and the stars." A sense of existing outside both space and time is conveyed in

> I visit the orchard of spheres and look at the product,
> And look at quintillions ripen'd and look at quintillions green.

All of this imagery of movement up and down, over, through, in and out, flung out in an almost frenzied state though it may seem, evokes the feeling of ecstatic insight appropriate to the emotional state of the poet. He is flying the flight of a "fluid and swallowing soul," and his course runs "below the soundings of plummets."

---

[9] Underhill, p. 205.

[10] Underhill, p. 289: One of the characteristics of the stage of Illumination is that the "self perceives an added significance and reality in all natural things: is often convinced that it knows the 'secret of the world.'"

[11] Underhill, p. 289. Another characteristic of Illumination.

In the latter part of section 33 the imagery becomes increasingly morbid: the man's body, fetched up "dripping and drown'd"; the "wreck of the steamship, and Death chasing it up and down the storm"; the "old-faced infants and the lifted sick"; the "mother of old, condemn'd for a witch"; the "hounded slave." The poet not only observes but becomes what he observes: "I am the man, I suffer'd, I was there"; "Hell and despair are upon me, crack and again crack the marksmen." After reaching the emotional heights of the ecstasy of Illumination, the poet seems suddenly plunged into the depths of "hell and despair":

Agonies are one of my changes of garments,
I do not ask the wounded person how he feels, I myself become the wounded person,
My hurts turn livid upon me as I lean on a cane and observe.

In the experience of the traditional mystics the Dark Night of the Soul (also "mystic pain" and "mystic death") sometimes accompanied the preceding stage, Illumination. In this fourth phase of the experience, the "consciousness which had, in Illumination, sunned itself in the sense of the Divine Presence, now suffers under an equally intense sense of the Divine Absence." There is a feeling of "great desolation in which the soul seems abandoned by the Divine." [12]

The Dark Night into which the poet's soul is plunged brings an acute consciousness of identity with the sinful, the suffering, the down-trodden, the injured, the sick, the wounded. The poet assumes the agony and despair of the world. The imagery of war, of fighting, of battles, of violence, introduced in the latter part of section 33, continues through section 36. Section 34 is the narrative of the "murder in cold blood of four hundred and twelve young men." The most ghastly aspects of the massacre are dwelt upon, from the "maim'd and mangled" digging in the dirt to the "burning of the bodies." This narrative is a story of tragedy in defeat, as the seafight in sections 35 and 36 is a story of tragedy in victory. Again, the details emphasized point up the terrible human woe resulting from the battle. The triumphant captain's "countenance [is] white as a sheet," as near him lies the "corpse of the child that serv'd in the cabin." On deck are "formless stacks of bodies and bodies by themselves," and nearby is heard,

The hiss of the surgeon's knife, the gnawing teeth of his saw,
Wheeze, cluck, swash of falling blood, short wild scream and long, dull tapering
    groan,
These so, these irretrievable.

Although the land battle and the sea-battle exhibit man courageous in the face of defeat and victory, such courage tends to become meaningless in the face of the resulting misery and suffering and death, in the face of the "irretrievable."

In section 37 the poet reaches the climax in his Dark Night of the Soul. First he imagines himself imprisoned:

. . . . I am possess'd!
Embody all presences outlaw'd or suffering,

[12] Underhill, p. 206.

> See myself in prison shaped like another man,
> And feel the dull unintermitted pain.

In quick succession the poet becomes a convict, a mutineer, a "youngster" taken for larceny, a cholera patient. And it is not with courage and optimism that the poet assumes these roles; he feels and shows suffering and despair when he is the "hand cuff'd" mutineer or the cholera patient with "ash-color'd" face. Certain it is that he no longer feels a sense of the Divine Presence, nor does he any longer feel the exultation of sudden insight felt when he was "afoot" with his vision. At the end of this section, the poet identifies himself with the beggar:

> Askers embody themselves in me and I am embodied in them,
> I project my hat, sit shame-faced, and beg.

Here the poet reaches the nadir in degradation, particularly in the emotion of shame, an emotion foreign to his mystical experience up to this point. But it is with this emotion that his Dark Night of the Soul draws to a close.

V. SECTIONS 38–43: UNION (FAITH AND LOVE)

In sections 38 through 43 of "Song of Myself," the poet seems filled with "peaceful joy" and "intense certitude," and seems granted "enhanced powers." He is intoxicated with a "consciousness of sharing" the strength of the "Infinite," of "acting by Its authority." [13] Section 38 opens with strong repudiation of the attitudes and emotions expressed in the preceding section, the emotions of the Dark Night of the Soul:

> Enough! enough! enough!
> Somehow I have been stunn'd. Stand back!
> Give me a little time beyond my cuff'd head, slumbers, dreams, gaping,
> I discover myself on the verge of a usual mistake.

The "usual mistake" is the exclusion of the Divine, the Infinite. What seems lost is not, as the poet had thought, "irretrievable." The hell, the despair, the shame are illusion, false reality; genuine reality may be perceived by Union with the Transcendent, out of time, out of space. Such Union results not in identification with the lowly, the degraded, the sinful and suffering, an acceptance of them on their own terms, but in infinite sympathy and tenderness and granted power for them.

The poet suggests his Union with the Transcendent through imagery of the Crucifixion of Christ:

That I could forget the mockers and insults!
That I could forget the trickling tears and blows of the bludgeons and hammers!
That I could look with a separate look on my own crucifixion and bloody crowning.

I remember now,
I resume the overstaid fraction.

[13] Underhill, pp. 207, 497. These are characteristics of Union.

The insight of the Illumination ("I see it is true, what I guess'd at"), though intense, had not been complete; a "fraction" had been "overstaid," a fraction large enough to plunge the poet into the Dark Night of the Soul. Now, however, the "overstaid fraction" is "resumed"; the poet achieves the complete insight brought with Union with the Transcendent. Whereas in Illumination the poet's apprehension of Divine Reality was symbolized by his "walking the old hill of Judaea" with Christ, in Union, the poet's merge with the Transcendent is symbolized by outright identification of self with Christ. As the Crucifixion of Christ resulted not in death, meaningless suffering, or shame, but in eternal life and joy, so the poet's Dark Night results in renewed vigor and life ("corpses rise, gashes heal, fastenings roll from me") and in supreme power. Through Union, the poet is suddenly changed from the passive sufferer into the powerful healer, issuing "swift ordinances . . . over the whole earth." The "bloody crowning" is transfigured into the "blossoms we wear in our hats."

The Christ figure merges with the "friendly and flowing savage" in section 39. Like Christ, wherever the savage goes, men and women "desire he should like them, touch them, speak to them, stay with them." The savage, like Christ, is God become man: his behavior is "lawless as snow-flakes" and his words "simple as grass." He does not conform to man's law but to divine or nature's law; his teachings are simple, cast in the common language and the homely figure which all can understand. In him the "common features" and "common modes . . . descend in new forms from the tips of his fingers" and "fly out of the glance of his eyes." Through him the common is transfigured into the divine. In this description, the poet, Christ, and the savage merge into one. The savage, man in his primitive original state, becomes the symbol of the divinity which civilized man has lost. The poet has had to strip away the errors and delusions of civilization in order to achieve his Union.

Throughout the remainder of the sections (40–43) devoted to this phase of the mystical experience, the "I" is the poet as Christ-savage. The supreme power resulting from Union enables the poet, like the mystic, to become "an actual parent of spiritual vitality in other men." [14] He will not give "lectures or a little charity" when he gives, but will give himself. He has "stores plenty and to spare" and will never "deny" the lowliest "cottonfield" drudge. He takes the place of the physician and the priest at the bedside of the dying, and he calls to the "descending" man, "here is my neck . . . hang your whole weight upon me." His power is sufficient for all, as he exclaims, "I dilute you with tremendous breath, I buoy you up."

But, as the first lines in section 41 indicate, the poet in his new-found power is not concerned solely with the down-trodden and suffering: "for strong upright men I bring yet more needed help." This "help" is a supreme faith in the order and harmony of the universe. The poet has heard "what was said of the universe," but finds these theories—these religions—insufficient, incomplete. He does not reject them. He takes them all—Jehovah, Kronos, Zeus, Brahma, Buddha, and the rest—"for what they are worth," but fills out the "rough deific sketches" in himself, in the "framer

14 Underhill, pp. 497–498.

framing a house," in the "mechanic's wife with her babe," in common people and in the commonplace. The poet's divinity is derived from and freely dispensed to all.

In section 42, the poet imagines himself as orator, perhaps like Christ delivering his Sermon on the Mount, bringing his message to the multitude. A feeling of flux, of eternal change, movement, recurrence, is evoked by the seven-line stanza in which each line begins with "ever" ("ever the upward and downward sun, ever the air and the ceaseless tides"), followed by the five-line stanza, with each line ending with the gerundive form. The latter stanza is suggestive of a biblical parable:

Here and there with dimes on the eyes walking,
To feed the greed of the belly the brains liberally spooning,
Tickets buying, taking, selling, but in to the feast never once going,
Many sweating, ploughing, thrashing, and then the chaff for payment receiving,
A few idly owning, and they the wheat continually claiming.

The selfish rich are the spiritually dead ("with dimes on the eyes walking"), who devote their minds "to feed the greed of the belly," who take the wheat and leave the chaff to the laborers, but who in reality never go into the significant feast, where spiritual sustenance may be gained—perhaps the "feast" of labor itself, with its intercourse with other human beings.[15] The latter part of section 42 places, as did the previous section, the ultimate value on man as against the material or "things":

> Not words of routine this song of mine,
> But abruptly to question, to leap beyond yet nearer bring.

The intent is to "leap beyond" the object or image and bring nearer the human behind it: the printer beyond the book, the wife or friend beyond the photograph, the "captain and engineers" beyond the "black ship mail'd with iron," and, finally, the "fathomless human brain" beyond the "sermons, creeds, theology."

The poet, in section 43, envisions himself as "enclosing worship ancient and modern and all between ancient and modern." As in section 41 the poet accepted religions of all kinds and varieties, so in section 43 he accepts religions of all ages, from the earliest which made "a fetich of the first rock or stump," to the latest of the "winders of the circuit of circuits" (the itinerant evangelists). Nor are the "down-hearted doubters," lost in a "sea of torment, doubt, despair, and unbelief," to be excluded. The poet's supreme power, his "spiritual vitality," is sufficient for all:

I do not know what is untried and afterward,
But I know it will in its turn prove sufficient, and cannot fail.

Each who passes is consider'd, each who stops is consider'd, not a single one can
it fail.

15 There are echoes in this stanza of several biblical passages. The reference to the spiritually dead ("dimes on the eyes walking") is similar to Christ's in His advice to let the dead bury their own dead (Luke ix.60). The rich who are so busy buying and selling that they never once go "into the feast" are similar to those who refused the invitation in Christ's parable of the great supper (Luke xiv.16–24).

"What is untried and afterward" is the Absolute, the Divine, the Transcendent, which the poet has come to know intuitively through Union; he speaks with the supreme faith of his "intense certitude." "What is untried and afterward" will not fail those who have died, the "old man who has lived without purpose," "him in the poor house tubercled by rum," the "numberless slaughter'd and wreck'd." No longer does the poet, as in his Dark Night of the Soul, accept the suffering and despair of the outcast, injured, and dying as his own; instead, he gives hope to all from his abundant faith and love derived from his Union. It remains for him to convey to the reader what he can of his transcendent mystical knowledge.

VI. Sections 44–49: Union (Perception)

The final stage of the mystical experience is announced abruptly in the opening line of section 44: "It is time to explain myself—let us stand up." And the intent of conveying hints of the "supreme perception" [16] granted in Union is made immediately clear:

> What is known I strip away,
> I launch all men and women forward with me into the Unknown.

"What is known" is that which is usually considered reality but which, by the mystic, is designated illusion: it is the world familiar to man through his senses. The "Unknown" is that which is not perceived by the senses, known only to the mystic, and designated by him the "transcendent reality." At the beginning of the Illumination stage, the stage of intuitive insight, the poet exclaimed, "Space and Time! now I see it is true"; through the supreme perception of Union, the poet becomes intensely aware of the relation of self to Time (section 44) and to Space (section 45).

When, in section 44, the poet asks, "The clock indicates the moment—but what does eternity indicate?" he is suggesting that man's relation to the moment is trivial compared to his relation to eternity, that eternity is the transcendent reality, the moment illusion. The remainder of section 44 is filled with imagery the purpose of which is to evoke a vision of eternity and the self's relation to it:

> We have thus far exhausted trillions of winters and summers,
> There are trillions ahead, and trillions ahead of them.

It is through time, through the symbolic "trillions" suggesting infinity, that eternity is to be conceived: eternity is endless time before and after "now." The self, at a point in time, is intimately related to before and after: "I am an acme of things accomplish'd, and I an encloser of things to be." Eternity has its only existence in self, flows with self from the before to the after. There are no "before" and "after" to the self:

[16] Evelyn Underhill, p. 100: "True mystical experience is the most complete and most difficult expression of life which is as yet possible to man. It is at once an act of love, an act of union, and an act of supreme perception; a trinity of experiences which meets and satisfies the three activities of self."

> My feet strike an apex of the apices of the stairs,
> On every step bunches of ages, and larger bunches between the steps,
> All below duly travel'd, and still I mount and mount.

In this striking imagery, the self is conceived as coeval with eternity, mounting the stairway of time. There was never a period when the self did not exist: "Afar down I see the huge first Nothing, I know I was even there." Using the imagery of physics and evolution,[17] the poet says that he "slept through the lethargic mist" and took "no hurt from the fetid carbon," that for him the "stars kept aside in their own rings," that for his embryo the "nebula cohered to an orb" and that "monstrous sauroids transported it [his embryo] in their mouths and deposited it with care." The cumulative effect of this startling imagery is to convey the impression of form and plan in the flow of time, the impression of the oneness of self and eternity.

In the closing line of section 44, the poet exults, "Now on this spot I stand with my robust soul." The opening lines of section 45 express the self's ecstatic joy in the "now," from youth, through manhood, to old age, and faith in the future: "And the dark hush promulges as much as any." But after this outburst of joy in existence, the poet opens his "scuttle" and looks at the "far-sprinkled systems." Using the imagery of astronomy, he evokes the endlessness of space:

> My sun has his sun and round him obediently wheels,
> He joins with his partners a group of superior circuit,
> And greater sets follow, making specks of the greatest inside them.

Time, "a few quadrillions of eras," cannot "hazard the span," cannot affect space. "Limitless space" and "limitless time," and the form and plan implicit in their infinity, instead of shrinking the self into insignificance, give certain assurance of the "rendezvous" with the "great Camerado," assurance of the ultimate Union with the Transcendent—Union after death similar to the Union in life of the mystic. The poet's description of the "great Camerado" as "the lover true for whom I pine" is suggestive of symbolism of the "Mystical Marriage" with which, as Evelyn Underhill has noted (p. 207), many mystics describe their Union with the Absolute.

When the poet states, at the opening of section 46, "I know I have the best of time and space, and was never measured and never will be measured," he is presenting the essence of his transcendent knowledge or "supreme perception." It is not a static knowledge which can be codified for church or philosophy, expressed in a book, conveyed through logic. Rather it is dynamic, intuitive insight which each man must gain for himself. The poet can only point the way. Travel imagery dominates the section, beginning with the poet's "I tramp a perpetual journey," and extending through his direct address to the reader:

> Not I, not any one else can travel that road for you,
> You must travel it for yourself.

[17] Joseph Beaver's *Walt Whitman—Poet of Science* (New York: King's Crown Press, 1951) gives many excellent interpretations of the passages in "Song of Myself" containing scientific imagery.

The poet's exhortation to the reader to begin the journey ("Shoulder your duds dear son"), to rely on self, continues into section 47: "The boy I love, the same becomes a man not through derived power, but in his own right." As the poet achieved his "supreme perception" through the contemplation of a spear of summer grass, so others may discover his meaning in observation of the most commonplace objects: "The nearest gnat is an explanation, and a drop or motion of the waves a key." In the latter part of section 47, the poet identifies both self and meaning with a series of familiar objects with which people are intimately associated: the poet and his "meaning" exist in the axe and jug which the woodman takes to his work, in the blanket which rubs the hunter's face when he sleeps at night. For each individual there lies near at hand the poet's meaning to decipher; in each individual lies the potentiality of discovering for himself the transcendent Reality.

As the vision began in section 6 with "guesses" about the significance of the grass in relation to self, God, life, and death, so the mystical experience draws to a close in sections 48 and 49 with observations on these same subjects, but now the poet speaks with the authority given him by his Union with the Transcendent. Assured that he has "the best of time and space," he can speak with conviction on these great and eternal questions. Self is both body and soul, the one not more than the other, and "nothing, not God, is greater to one than one's self is." As the poet has discovered, it is only through the united self that God may be apprehended; self, then, cannot be abased or considered subordinate. The poet admonishes, "Let your soul stand cool and composed before a million universes . . . Be not curious about God." With the proper perspective on the relation of self to infinity, one is not curious but is "at peace about God." No one can "understand" God, but can see Him "each hour of the twenty-four," "in the faces of men and women," in "letters . . . dropt in the street." God may be apprehended, "known," anywhere, any time, for He is in "limitless space" and in "limitless time."

Death, the "bitter bug of mortality," cannot "alarm" the poet: he marks the "outlet" and marks the "relief and escape." Death is not an end of the self, but an outlet for it into the Transcendent, a relief from life, an escape into permanent Union with the Absolute. The corpse, the body deprived of the soul, becomes "good manure," and has its eternity in the life it gives to the white roses and the melons—and to succeeding generations. Thus life is the "leavings of many deaths." This pantheistic belief is not necessarily in conflict with the belief in God as the great Camerado. The eternity of the soul exists in God, in the transcendent Reality, outside time and space; the eternity of the body exists in life, in the material world, inside time and space; the latter serves as a symbol (a letter "from God") for the former. Such a reconciliation of the two points of view is suggested in the "whispering" the poet hears from the "stars of heaven" and from "the grass of graves": "O perpetual transfers and promotions." The whispering of the "grass of graves" gives insight into the "perpetual" *transfer* of life from the dead to the living; the whispering of the "stars of heaven" gives insight into the "perpetual" *promotion* of souls to the Transcendent. Eternal life is granted to both body and soul, both the material and spiritual.

The mystical experience ends in a series of vivid images connotative of death. The "turbid pool that lies in the autumn forest," reflecting the twilight moon, is surrounded by "black stems that decay in the muck," and above all is heard the "moaning gibberish of the dry limbs." But the poet perceives the illusion in this scene of desolation, decay and death:

> I ascend from the moon, I ascend from the night,
> I perceive that the ghastly glimmer is noonday sunbeams reflected,
> And debouch to the steady and central from the offspring great or small.

Paradoxical, but surely intentional, is the use of the scientific to symbolize the spiritual truth. The "ghastly glimmer" of the moon is but "sunbeams reflected." The moon and night, suggestive of death, are but the "offspring" of the "steady and central" sun. The figure is apt: death is an "offspring" of God, a birth into the "steady and central" transcendent Reality. The poet sees in death the ultimate permanent Union which he has fleetingly achieved in his mystical experience.

VII. Sections 50–52: Emergence from the Mystical State

The lucidity with which the poet spoke during his mystical experience disappears when he emerges from the mystical state in section 50:

There is that in me—I do not know what it is—but I know it is in me.

Wrench'd and sweaty—calm and cool then my body becomes,
I sleep—I sleep long.

I do not know it—it is without name—it is a word unsaid,
It is not in any dictionary, utterance, symbol.

Two aspects of the typical mystical experience are described. First, the physical condition of the poet, upon emergence from the mystical state, is one of exhaustion. There has been nervous excitement and tension which, when it releases the poet, leaves him "wrench'd and sweaty," and sleep is needed as a restorative. Second, it becomes extremely difficult for the poet, after the mystical state of consciousness has passed, to formulate its significance in words. The poet is portrayed as groping about for what is "without name," for the word that "is not in any dictionary." He can only hint at the significance of the knowledge his mystical experience has bestowed:

> Something it swings on more than the earth I swing on,
> To it the creation is the friend whose embracing awakes me.

"It" is not tied to the earth as is the poet; it is outside time and space. To it the creation of the universe is no greater miracle than the love of a friend for the poet.

But the desire to sum up the knowledge of the experience in an inadequate word is compulsive; the poet continues to grope:

Perhaps I might tell more. Outlines! I plead for my brothers and sisters.

Do you see O my brothers and sisters?
It is not chaos or death—it is form, union, plan—it is eternal life—it is Happiness.

The searching about for the precise word is almost frenzied; the motive is love, love for those "brothers and sisters" intuitively discovered after entry into the mystical state in section 5 ("And that all the men ever born are also my brothers, and the women my sisters and lovers"). Outside space, outside time, from the point of view of the Transcendent, life is not "chaos or death"; there are "form, union, plan" and there is "eternal life." And the key to human existence is not rejection, not the "beginning" and "end" of the talkers, or the division of the best from the worst, but, simply—"Happiness." As "form, union, plan" refer to the not-self, so "Happiness" points to the self and indicates the proper or ideal relationship of man to the universe.

Happiness is the ultimate state of that self assured that "Chaos and death" are illusion, that "form, union, plan" and "eternal life" are reality. Such a self, firmly rooted in supreme faith, may indeed sing. Each individual may, like the poet, go forth on his journey singing the "Song of Myself." As Whitman's dramatization of the entry into the mystical state is inverted, so also is the hint at the meaning of self and existence grasped from the quickly receding mystical consciousness. At some stage in the traditional mystical experience, "the human instinct for personal happiness must be killed." [18] Whitman has used the mystical experience as a framework within which to deny some of its basic traditions. The form of the experience is adhered to, but its substance is transfigured.

The last two sections of "Song of Myself" show the poet, the agony and the ecstasy of the mystical experience now behind him, pleading for a response from the reader. There is, as the poet holds back the evening ("snuff[s] the sidle of evening"), an acute sense of urgency in the plea: "Will you speak before I am gone? will you prove already too late?" The emotional tone suggests here and elsewhere the religious fervor of the will to convert: the poet urgently feels the need for acceptance of his startling new insight; when he exclaims

> Do I contradict myself?
> Very well then I contradict myself,
> (I am large, I contain multitudes.)

he is asserting the importance of reliance on self which is in reality obedience to the Transcendent in self. Consistency in transient ideas is irrelevant; consistency in faith to self is supreme.

The last section of the poem introduces a series of images of swift movement and departure. The poet is like the spotted hawk, swooping over the rooftops sounding his "barbaric yawp," or he is like a meteor, shaking his "white locks at the runaway sun." Each of these images has connotations which relate to the mystical experience from which the poet has just emerged: the yawp of the hawk is "barbaric," like the "nature" which has been permitted to speak "without check with original energy"; the meteor, in its shaking, effusing, drifting, suggests the intensity, in both depth and height, of the experience as well as its defiant exultation in self. Like the hawk, the poet is "untranslatable," impossible to comprehend except in his own language,

18 Underhill, p. 206.

upon his own terms. When he bequeaths himself "to the dirt to grow from the grass" he loves, and confides to the reader, "If you want me again look for me under your boot-soles," he returns to the central symbol of the poem, the grass, the contemplation of which at the opening of the poem launched him on his journey into the unknown. More important than the pantheism on the surface of the line is the suggestion that every man has easily within his grasp, his for the taking, the means for his own mystical journey. The reader is under the "boot-soles" only in the sense that the clue to what he has hinted at is there for each man to discover for himself. The poet is one with the riddle whose unravelling each man, each self, must undertake on his own.

"SONG OF MYSELF" AS COMEDY

"ONE'S SELF I SING"

by Richard Chase

THE MAIN ITEM of the 1855 edition of *Leaves of Grass* was, of course, "Song of Myself," the profound and lovely comic drama of the self which is Whitman's best poem and contains in essence nearly all, yet not quite all, there is to *Leaves of Grass*. The comic spirit of the poem is of the characteristic American sort, providing expression for a realism at once naturalistic and transcendental, for the wit, gaiety, and festive energy of all good comedy, and also for meditative soliloquy, at once intensely personal and strongly generic.

One circumstance that contributes to the general spontaneity of "Song of Myself" is, in fact, Whitman's unsuccessful attempt to be an Emersonian or Wordsworthian moralist. In his preface, he wrote that "of all mankind the poet is the equable man. Not in him but off from him things are grotesque or eccentric or fail of their sanity . . . He is the arbiter of the diverse and he is the key. He is the equalizer of his age and land." Whitman tries, indeed, to install himself in his poem on this high moral ground: he will, he says, first regenerate himself by leaving the fallacious artificialities of modern life and getting back to fundamentals; then, having perfected himself as the norm, he will summon all the world to him to be freed of its abnormalities. But although in the poem the self remains pretty much at the center of things, Whitman finds it impossible to accept the idea that it is a norm. To the sententious prophet who "promulges" the normative self, the comic poet and ironic realist keep introducing other, disconcertingly eccentric selves.

> Who goes there? hankering, gross, mystical, nude. . . .

Whoever he is, he is not in a position to utter morality. The self in this poem *is* (to use Lawrence's phrase) "tricksy-tricksy"; it does "shy all sorts of ways" and is finally, as the poet says, "not a bit tamed," for "I too am untranslatable." So that as in all true, or high, comedy, the sententious, the too overtly insisted-on morality (if any) plays a losing game with ironical realism. In the social comedy of Molière, Congreve, or Jane Austen, moral sententiousness, like other deformities of comportment or personality, is corrected by society. But this attitude is, of course, foreign to Whitman, who has already wished to invite society to correct itself by comparing itself

From Richard Chase, *Walt Whitman Reconsidered* (New York: William Sloane Associates, 1955), pp. 58–76. Copyright © 1955 by Richard Chase and reprinted by permission of the publishers.

with him and who, furthermore, cannot even sustain this democratic inversion of an aristocratic idea. Whitman's comic poetry deflates pretensions and chides moral rigidity by opposing to them a diverse, vital, indeterminate reality.

"I resist anything better than my own diversity," says Whitman, and this is the characteristic note of "Song of Myself." Not that by referring to "Song of Myself" as a "comic" poem I wish too narrowly to limit the scope of discussion—nor do I suggest in using the term a special theory of Whitman or of American literature. I simply respond to my sense that "Song of Myself" is on the whole comic in tone and that although the poem's comic effects are of universal significance, they often take the specific form of American humor. If one finds "Song of Myself" enjoyable at all, it is because one is conscious of how much of the poem, though the feeling in many of its passages need not perhaps have been comic at all, nevertheless appeals to one, first and last, in its comic aspect. The poem is full of odd gestures and whimsical acts; it is written by a neo-Ovidian poet for whom self-metamorphosis is almost as free as free association, who can write "I am an old artillerist" or "I will go to the bank by the wood, and become undisguised and naked" as easily as he can write:

> Askers embody themselves in me and I am embodied in them,
> I project my hat, sit shame-faced, and beg.

The sense of incongruous diversity is very strong in "Song of Myself," and although one does not know how the sly beggar projecting his hat or the martial patriot is transformed into the "acme of things accomplish'd," and "encloser of things to be" who suddenly says:

> I find I incorporate gneiss, coal, long-threaded moss, fruits, grains, esculent roots,
> And am stucco'd with quadrupeds and birds all over,

one is nevertheless charmed with the transformation.

Whitman conceives of the self, one might say, as James conceives of Christopher Newman in *The American*—as having the "look of being committed to nothing in particular, of standing in an attitude of general hospitality to the chances of life." In other words, the "self" who is the protagonist of Whitman's poem is a character portrayed in a recognizable American way; it illustrates the fluid, unformed personality exulting alternately in its provisional attempts to define itself and in its sense that it has no definition. The chief difference between "Song of Myself" and *The American* is, of course, the difference between the stages on which Whitman and James allow the self to act, James confining the action to his international scene and Whitman opening his stage out into an eventful universe which is a contradictory but witty collocation of the natural and the transcendent, the imperfect and the utopian, the personal and the generic—a dialectic world out of whose "dimness opposite equals advance" and in which there is "always a knot of identity" but "always distinction."

The very scope of Whitman's universe and the large freedom he assumes to move about in it allowed him to appropriate new areas of experience and thus to make of "Song of Myself" the original and influential poem it is. For one thing, this is the first American poem to invade that fruitful ground between lyric verse and prose fiction that so much of modern poetry cultivates, and one may suppose that "Song of Myself" has had at least as much effect on the novel as, let us say, *Moby Dick* or *The Golden Bowl* have had on poetry. The famous lines in Section 8 are, at any rate, both "imagistic" and novelistic:

> The little one sleeps in its cradle;
> I lift the gauze and look a long time, and silently brush away flies with my hand.

> The youngster and the red-faced girl turn aside up the bushy hill;
> I peeringly view them from the top.

> The suicide sprawls on the bloody floor of the bedroom;
> I witness the corpse with its dabbled hair, I note where the pistol has fallen.

It is probably true that more than anyone else, more than Blake or Baudelaire, Whitman made the city poetically available to literature:

> The blab of the pave, tires of carts, sluff of boot-soles, talk of the promenaders,
> The heavy omnibus, the driver with his interrogating thumb, the clank of the
>   shod horses on the granite floor . . .

Such lines as these have been multitudinously echoed in modern prose and poetry, they have been endlessly recapitulated by the journey of the realistic movie camera up the city street. One might argue that Whitman's descriptions of the city made possible T. S. Eliot's *Waste Land*. The horror of Eliot's London, as of Baudelaire's "*cité pleine de rêves*," is unknown in *Leaves of Grass*, but was not Whitman the first poet, so to speak, who put real typists and clerks in the imaginary city?

There can be no doubt that "Song of Myself" made sex a possible subject for American literature, and in this respect Whitman wrought a great revolution in, for example, his beautiful idyllic scene in which the "handsome and richly drest" woman imagines herself to join the "twenty-eight young men" who "bathe by the shore." In such a passage as this (as Henry Adams was to point out) American literature was moving toward the freedom and inclusiveness that came more naturally to Europeans —to Flaubert, or Chekhov, whose panoramic novelette *The Steppe* includes a similarly idyllic scene of bathing and sexuality. It is sex, too, although of an inverted kind, that allows Whitman to write the following unsurpassable lines in which love is at once so sublimely generalized and perfectly particularized:

And [I know] that a kelson of the creation is love,
And limitless are leaves stiff or drooping in the fields,
And brown ants in the little wells beneath them,
And mossy scabs of the worm fence, and heap'd stones, elder, mullein and poke-weed.

No summary view of "Song of Myself" would be complete without reference to the elegiac tone of the concluding lines. If, as we have been saying, Whitman's poem is remarkable for its gross inclusive scope, his elegiac verse is a great act of discrimination and nicety. Where else, in the generally grandiose nineteenth-century melodrama of love and death, shall we find anything like the delicate precision of these incomparable lines?

> The last scud of day holds back for me;
> It flings my likeness after the rest and true as any, on the shadow'd wilds,
> It coaxes me to the vapor and the dusk.
>
> I depart as air, I shake my white locks at the runaway sun,
> I effuse my flesh in eddies, and drift it in lacy jags.
>
> I bequeath myself to the dirt, to grow from the grass I love;
> If you want me again look for me under your boot-soles.
>
> You will hardly know who I am or what I mean,
> But I shall be good health to you nevertheless,
> And filter and fibre your blood.
>
> Failing to fetch me at first keep encouraged,
> Missing me one place, search another,
> I stop somewhere, waiting for you.

As every poet does, Whitman asks us provisionally to accept the imagined world of his poem. It is a fantastic world in which it is presumed that the self can become identical with all other selves in the universe, regardless of time and space. Not without precedent in Hindu poetry, this central metaphor is, as an artistic device, unique in American literature, as is the extraordinary collection of small imagist poems, versified short stories, realistic urban and rural genre paintings, inventories, homilies, philosophizings, farcical episodes, confessions, and lyric musings it encompasses in "Song of Myself." Yet as heavily taxing our powers of provisional credence, as inventing a highly idiosyncratic and illusory world, "Song of Myself" invites comparison with other curious works of the American imagination—*Moby Dick*, let us say, and *The Scarlet Letter* and *The Wings of the Dove*. It is of the first importance at any rate to see that Whitman's relation of the self to the rest of the universe is a successful aesthetic or compositional device, whatever we may think of it as a moral assertion.

If we look at Whitman's implicit metaphor more closely, we see that it consists in the paradox of "identity." The opening words of *Leaves of Grass*, placed there in 1867, state the paradox:

> One's-self I sing, a simple separate person,
> Yet utter the word Democratic, the word En-Masse.

In more general terms the opening lines of "Song of Myself" state the same paradox:

> I celebrate myself and sing myself;
> And what I assume you shall assume;
> For every atom belonging to me, as good belongs to you.

Both politically and by nature man has "identity," in two senses of the word: on the one hand, he is integral in himself, unique, and separate; on the other hand, he is equal to, or even the same as, everyone else. Like the Concord transcendentalists,

Whitman was easily led in prophetic moods to generalize the second term of the paradox of identity beyond the merely human world and with his ruthless equalitarianism to conceive the All, a vast cosmic democracy, placid, without episode, separation or conflict, though suffused, perhaps, with a bland illumination. More than anything else, it is this latter tendency which finally ruined Whitman as a poet, submerging as it did, his chief forte and glory—his entirely original, vividly realistic presentation of the comedy and pathos of "the simple separate person."

What finally happens is that Whitman loses his sense that his metaphor of self vs. en-masse is a *paradox*, that self and en-masse are in dialectic opposition. When this sense is lost the spontaneously eventful, flowing, and largely indeterminate universe of "Song of Myself" is replaced by a universe that is both mechanical and vaguely abstract. Whatever, in this universe, is in a state of becoming is moving toward the All, and the self becomes merely the vehicle by which the journey is made.

In some of his best as well as in some of his worst poems, Whitman actually conceives of the self as making a journey—for example, "Song of the Open Road," "Crossing Brooklyn Ferry," and "Passage to India." In others the self journeys, as it were, not forward and outward but backward and inward, back to the roots of its being, and discovers there a final mystery, or love, comradeship, or death—for example, the *Calamus* and *Sea Drift* poems. (Notably among the latter are "Out of the Cradle Endlessly Rocking" and "As I Ebb'd with the Ocean of Life.") In "Song of Myself," however, the self is not felt to be incomplete; it has no questing odyssey to make. It stands aggressively at the center of things, "Sure as the most certain sure, plumb in the uprights, well entretied, braced in the beams." It summons the universe, "syphons" universal experience through its dilating pores, calls "anything back again when I desire it." Or the self imagines itself to be infinitely expandable and contractible (like the web of the spider in Whitman's little poem called "A Noiseless Patient Spider"), so that there is no place where at any moment it may not be, no thing or person with whom it may not merge, no act in which it may not participate. Of great importance is the fact that most of "Song of Myself" has to do not with the self searching for a final identity but with the self escaping a series of identities which threaten to destroy its lively and various spontaneity. This combination of attitudes is what gives "Song of Myself" the alternately ecstatic and gravely musing, pastoral-godlike stability one feels at the center, around which, however, the poet is able to weave the most astonishing embellishments of wit and lyric song.

This is perhaps a valid way of feeling the shifting modes of sensibility in the poem. Yet it would be wrong to attribute any clear cut structure to "Song of Myself." "The United States themselves are essentially the greatest poem," wrote Whitman in his preface. A Jacksonian Democrat, Whitman was not an admirer of federal unity, either in a nation or a poem. He was content to make his poem a loose congeries of states and half-settled territories. He was content that his poem should mirror that "freshness and candor of . . . physiognomy," that "picturesque looseness of carriage," and that "deathless attachment to freedom" which, in his preface, he attributed to his countrymen. His style would be organic; he would "speak in literature with the perfect rectitude and insouciance" of animals and growing things. Although capable of finely pictorial images, Whitman composed more by ear than by eye, and his ear being attuned to music of the looser, more variable sort, such as the Italian operas, he strung his poems together on a free melodic line and by means of motifs, voices, recapitulations, recitatives, rests, *crescendi* and *diminuendi*.

The motif of "Song of Myself" is the self taking on a bewildering variety of identities and with a truly virtuoso agility extricating itself from each one. The poem begins with the exhortation to leave the "rooms full of perfume," the "creeds and schools." Apart from conventions,

> Apart from the pulling and hauling stands what I am,
> Stands amused, complacent, compassionating, idle, unitary.

Having put society and convention behind, "What I am" finds itself in an Edenlike, early-morning world, wherein one easily observes the portentous dialectics of the universe:

> Urge and urge and urge,
> Always the procreant urge of the world.
> Out of the dimness opposite equals advance, always substance and
>   increase, always sex,
> Always a knit of identity, always distinction, always a breed of life.

But of more importance is the fact that in this idyllic world the veil is lifted from the jaundiced eye, the cramped sensibility is set free, the senses and pores of the body receive the joyful intelligences dispatched to them by a friendly and providential nature. The self appears to be the offspring of a happy union of body and soul; sublime and delightful thoughts issue from the mind in the same miraculous way as the grass from the ground. Death itself is seen to be "lucky." And, in short, "what I am" can well afford to be complacent, to be certain that it is "unitary." Nor is the feeling of power denied to the self. It derives power from nature, as does the horse—"affectionate, haughty, electrical"—with which the poet compares himself. It derives power, too, from identification with others—the "runaway slave," "the butcher-boy," the "blacksmiths," "the boatmen and clam-diggers," the "trapper," the "red girl"—and finally with America itself.

> In me the caresser of life wherever moving, backward as well as forward sluing,
> To niches aside and junior bending, not a person or object missing,
> Absorbing all to myself and for this song.

Sections 24–28, though in places rather obscure, contain the essence of Whitman's drama of identity. The poet begins by proclaiming himself a Kosmos, and commanding us to "unscrew the locks from the doors!/ Unscrew the doors themselves from their jambs!" so that the universe may flow through him—"through me the current and index" (that is, the undifferentiated flux and the "identities" that emerge therefrom). This proclamation announces not only the unshakable status and palpable reality but also the redemptive powers of the self. In a world which has been created by banishing social sanctions and social intelligence, what will keep man from being lost in idiocy, crime, squalor? What of that underground realm inhabited by

> . . . the deform'd, trivial, flat, foolish, despised,
> Fog in the air, beetles rolling balls of dung?

The threat of madness, crime, and obscenity is to be allayed by the curative powers of that Adamic world where wisdom consists in uttering "the pass-word primeval," "the sign of democracy." Siphoned through the haughty, electrical self or discussed frankly by persons not inhibited by prudery (the discourses seem perilously interchangeable), the crimes and obscenities will be redeemed:

> Voices indecent by me clarified and transfigur'd.

The poet then records a dreamlike idyl of auto-erotic experience, in which the parts of the body merge mysteriously with natural objects, and a great deal of diffuse and wistful love is generated. And, when dawn comes, the redemption is symbolized in these astonishing metaphors:

> Hefts of the moving world at innocent gambols silently rising, freshly exuding,
> Scooting obliquely high and low.

> Something I cannot see puts upward libidinous prongs,
> Seas of bright juice suffuse heaven.

The poem then speaks anew of how the self may be distorted or destroyed. The poet's "identity" is said to be assailed and warped into other "identities" by agents referred to as "traitors," "wasters," and "marauders." Somewhat elusive in particular, these appear to have in common a quality of aggressiveness and imperiousness. They act as a radical individualist conceives society to act. They break down the self, they swagger, they assert convention, responsibility and reason, they dominate and impose passivity and furtiveness on the individual.

The beautiful, diffuse, kindly dawn is succeeded by a more formidable, a more imperious, apparition. The "dazzling and tremendous" sun leaps over the horizon and cries, "See then whether you shall be master!" The poet replies to this challenge by saying that the sunrise would indeed "kill me/ If I could not now and always send sunrise out of me." The power with which the poet defeats what seeks to destroy him is asserted to be "my vision" and "my voice."

> My voice goes after what my eyes cannot reach,
> With the twirl of my tongue I encompass worlds.

In Section 26 both the metaphorical effects and the subject matter shift from the visual to the auditory. The "bravuras of birds, bustle of growing wheat, gossip of flames, clack of sticks cooking my meals"—these and myriad other sounds amplify into a symphonic orchestration. The crescendo and dying fall of the conclusion are rendered with full tone and exquisite wit.

> I hear the train'd soprano (what work, with hers, is this?)
> The orchestra whirls me wider than Uranus flies,

It wrenches such ardors from me I did not know I possess'd them,
It sails me, I dab with bare feet, they are lick'd by the indolent waves,
I am cut by bitter and angry hail, I lose my breath,
Steep'd amid honey'd morphine, my windpipe throttled in fakes of death,
At length let up again to feel the puzzle of puzzles,
And that we call Being.

But again the poet is confronted with "Being"—that is, form or identity—and is not certain that this is the Being he wants to be. It is therefore dissipated and generalized, in Section 27, into a universal process of reincarnation.

In Section 28 there occurs the famous auto-erotic pastoral dream in which "prurient provokers," like nibbling cows, "graze at the edges of me." The "provokers," conceived as symbolic of the sense of touch, arouse and madden the dreaming poet and then they all unite "to stand on a headland and worry me." After touch has "quivered" him "to a new identity"—has left him confused, vexed, self-reproachful, and isolated—he proceeds in the following sections to resume a "true," "real," or "divine" identity. This act of restoration is accomplished through love, natural piety, pastoral and cosmic meditations, symbolic fusions of self with America, allegations of the "deific" nature of democratic man, ritual celebrations, and fatherly preachments, and finally, in the last Section, by the assertion that death is also merely an extrication of the self from an identity.

Everyone has noticed that the large, bland exterior of Walt Whitman concealed a Dionysus or Pan—one of the first was Moncure Conway, who visited Walt in Brooklyn in the summer of 1857, found him basking in the sun on a hill near the Whitman house, and later noticed that the only decorations in the poet's room were two engravings, "one of Silenus and the other of Bacchus." And surely no one can read "Song of Myself" without seeing that Whitman recreates there something of the spirit of the Greek cults out of which comedy evolved. Does he not summon us, his boon companions, to the outdoor revel, to "dance, laugh, and sing," to celebrate the phallic god? Are not masks donned and removed, "identities" concealed and exchanged? Do we not have a ritual celebration of "Nature without check with original energy," of the cycle of death and rebirth, the *agon*, sacrifice, and *gamos* of the protagonist, i.e. the self? Do we not have in Whitman's image of the diffusion of the self in nature a religious feeling akin to that engendered in the Dionysian mysteries by the dismemberment and assimilation of the sacrificial victim?

To be sure, the "mysticism" we ordinarily associate with Whitman is less akin to Dionysian than to Oriental and Quaker religion. His mode of religious contemplation, taking it by and large, ends toward passivity and quietism. There is much of this quietism even in "Song of Myself." But the poem as a whole takes its tone from something more vital, indeterminate, violent, and primitive. And it is only to find the most appropriate name for this that one hits on the word "Dionysian." The ritual submovement of comedy asserts itself with a brilliant if spasmodic energy in "Song of Myself." It provides a metaphorical foundation for even the most elaborately artificial of verbal fancies such as "I recline by the sills of the exquisite flexible doors" or "I depart as air. I shake my white locks at the runaway sun"—lines which in point of rococo refinement rival anything that Congreve's Millamant might say to Mirabell.

Historically, Whitman's "American humor" is indeed related, however remotely, to the Restoration comedy. Broadly speaking, there have been in English since 1660 three manifestations of the comic spirit: the aristocratic high comedy of Congreve, the bourgeois sentimental or genteel comedy (by far the most pervasive and influential sort ever since the Restoration), and that American humor which has been practiced in one way or another and at one time or another by nearly all of our best writers. This is not the place to attempt a history of comedy or an analysis of American humor—the latter has been done exquisitely, if a little impressionistically, by Constance Rourke. One may merely venture the idea that, historically, American humor is a radical modification of sentimental comedy. At its best—in Mark Twain, Melville, Thoreau, or Whitman—it retains the capacity of sentimental comedy for pathos but escapes its sentimentality and its hypocrisy. It achieved this by rejecting the cardinal ethical values of bourgeois comedy—money and domestic fidelity. American humor is contemptuous of, or at least feels remote from, the family and money as ethical norms. In this respect and in its tendency toward cruelty and sheer verbal brilliance it is akin to high comedy.

Considered as a comic poem, "Song of Myself" combines Dionysian gaiety and an impulse toward verbal artificiality with the tone and cultural presuppositions of American humor—a striking feat of hybridization certainly, yet no more so than that which produced Moby Dick. The intention here is not to deny the justice of Emerson's remark that Whitman's poem was "a remarkable mixture of the Bhagvadgita and the New York Herald" or of the voluminous but one-sided academic scholarship which, following Emerson's remark, has regarded "Song of Myself" as an amalgam of Oriental philosophy and American realism. The intention is rather to shift the ground of discourse toward a more strictly literary view—the view which Emerson also adumbrated in his remark that the first edition of Leaves of Grass was an "extraordinary piece of wit and wisdom."

In 1889 Whitman said to his Camden friends, "I pride myself on being a real humorist underneath everything else" and when it was suggested that he might after all go down in history as a "comedian" he replied that one "might easily end up worse." He will certainly not go down in history as, purely and simply, a comedian. But humor was always a strong part of his sensibility, and it is difficult to see how it ever came to be a cliché about Whitman that "he had no sense of humor." There is substantial evidence that in his early life his mind turned naturally toward comic writing. Much of his newspaper work, particularly the "Sun-Down Papers From the Desk of a Schoolmaster," which he wrote for the Long Island Democrat and the sketches he did for the New Orleans Crescent (1848) show that he had mastered at least the easier tricks of the native folk humor. At various times during the 1840's Whitman expressed in newspaper articles his partiality to Dickens and Carlyle— Dickens whom "I love and esteem . . . for what he has taught me through his writings"; Carlyle, whose Sartor Resartus exhibits in abundance the author's "strange wild way." From these two writers Whitman seems to have learned that a great book might be eloquent, crotchety, full of curious events and observations, or a humorous compound of realism, philosophy, and sentiment. He surely learned this even more directly from Emerson's essays. If indeed there are so many parallels between "Song of Myself" and "Self-Reliance" that we almost think the poem a versification of the essay, it is nevertheless true that the parallels are not confined to the philosophic or moral message. There is a good deal of humor in Emerson's essay of the spontaneous, odd, yeasty sort noticed by Santayana, who said that Emerson "was like a young god making experiments in creation: he botched the work and always began on a new and better plan. Every day he said, 'Let there be light,' and every day the light was new." More specifically, what Whitman may have sensed in "Self-Reliance" is the humorous touch-and-go between the self and the author, which underlies the elaborate web of portentous epigram. Surely, one of the Emersonian passages that brought the simmering Whitman to a boil (as the poet himself phrased it) was the one near the end of "Self-Reliance" where Emerson is speaking of the fatuity of foreign travel and says that although he should wake up in Naples, "there beside me is the stern fact, the sad self, unrelenting, identical, that I fled from."

But aside from the question of literary influences there is the more fundamental question of cultural influence. Whitman emulated our democratic American ideals to an extent unexampled among our great writers, and there can be no doubt that many of his moral utterances and even his poetic effects are produced by the sublime literalness of the democratic assumptions which were so faithfully registered on his plastic mind and temperament. Tocqueville (whom we shall have occasion to cite more fully in a later passage) based a part of his discussion of language and literature in the United States upon his observation that

In democratic communities each citizen is habitually engaged in the contemplation of a very puny object, namely, himself. If he ever raises his looks higher, he then perceives nothing but the immense form of society at large, or the still more imposing aspect of mankind. His ideas are all either extremely minute and clear, or extremely general and vague; what lies between is an open void.

This habit of mind has induced in American writing a style capable of very great and sudden extremes and has drawn from such writers as Melville, Emerson, Thoreau, and Emily Dickinson their idiosyncratic styles—the common denominator among them being a tendency of the language to shift rapidly from the homely and the colloquial to a rhetoric at once highly self-conscious, highly abstract, and highly elaborate. Since such shifts of ground between incongruous extremes are of the essence of wit, it is proper to speak of wit, or as we say, of "American humor," as a central problem in any exact investigation of the language of American literature—so long as we keep in mind how very pervasive an attitude is American humor. For indeed this form of wit is not confined to rural hoe-downs, minstrel shows, or tall tales about Paul Bunyan. It is a style, a habit of thought which allows for the different combinations of the native vernacular and traditional English created by the American authors, as well as their common habit of shifting with such brilliant effect from the particular to the general, from the small to the great, from the concrete to the transcendent. To encompass such effects a language must be highly flexible, capable not of subtle and sustained modulations, as is the prose of Edmund Burke or the poetry of Shakespeare,* but—as Selincourt observed in writing about Whitman's language—of rapid transpositions, rapid shifts of language and of levels of discourse. And if these remarks are generally true of all American authors, they seem more literally true of Whitman than of anyone else.

Thus Whitman's struggle for a language in the years before 1855 was not essentially different from that of his peers among American writers. It was easy to combine the literary with the vernacular as a joke, and Whitman often did this in his newspaper writing, as in (a sentence from one of his New Orleans sketches) "a beautiful, enameled, filigree, inlaid morceau of *bijouterie*, whose value intrinsically, *per se*, was perhaps about six bits," or "we will e'en just have to give the go-by." It was more difficult to learn the trick of producing similar transpositions without being silly or bathetic—such a trick as is turned toward the end of "Song of Myself" where the last line of Section 43 and the first of 44 are:

> Nor the present, nor the least wisp that is known.
> It is time to explain myself—let us stand up.

And most difficult of all was to achieve the standard accomplishment of the poetry at its best—a style, that is, which is "literary" and conversational at the same time, a style which has one eye on the individual and the concrete and one eye on the general and the transcendent.

One had better hasten to admit that a good deal of caution is called for in arguments which adduce the culture a poet lives in to explain his aesthetics. For one thing, it is of course impossible to say just what American culture is or to be sure that one traces aright its manifold influences on poetry. Then, again, no culture is perfectly unique. France has had democratic poets, there are moments in Rabelais and Kafka which seem indistinguishable from "American humor," Heine and Arnold wrote relatively "free verse," Whitman's own ideals were not only national but international. Yet the fact remains that we do have an observable national culture as well as an inherited European one, and that a truly historical critique of Whitman's poetry must begin with a view of the spoken and unspoken assumptions, the myths and habits of mind, the manners and "sentiments," of the culture the poet lived in.

---

* Shakespeare's style, wrote Whitman (sounding for the moment like Burke), is determined by "the exquisite and seductive transfiguration of caste."

"SONG OF MYSELF" AS EPIC

"SONG OF MYSELF"

by Roy Harvey Pearce

THAT there could be no American epic in the traditional sense of the word was quite clear to a group of young Harvard juniors and seniors who in 1836 submitted essays for the Bowdoin Prize on a topic set for them: "What reasons are there for not expecting another great epic poem?" Their meditations are interesting because in effect they agree with Barlow's conclusions: Perhaps there will not be another American *epic*; but there will surely be something greater. In effect, they accepted the eighteenth-century dictum that the epic was a poem of a non-civilized society; that appropriately it had focused on the *actions* of a primitive hero; that progress had brought civilization, Christianity, and a hero whose high *thoughts* distinguished him from other men. The most adventurous of the students, Jones Very (who won the senior prize) concluded grandly:

"To complain of this [progressive] tendancy [sic] of the human mind and its influence on literature, to sigh that we cannot have another Homeric poem is like weeping for the feeble days of childhood; and shows an insensibility to the ever-increasing beauty and grandeur developed by the Spirit in its endless progress; a forgetfulness of those powers of soul, which result from this very progress; which enable it, while enjoying the present, to add to that joy by the remembrance of the past, and to grasp at a higher form the anticipations of the future. By the progress of the arts power is manifested by an agency almost as invisible as itself—it almost speaks, and it is done; it almost commands, and it stands fast. Man needs no longer a vast array of physical means to effect his loftiest purpose—he seizes the quill, the mere toy of a child, and stamps on the glowing page the copy of his own mind, his thoughts pregnant with celestial fire; and sends them forth, wherever the winds of heaven blow or its light penetrates, the winged messengers of his pleasure. He is learning to reverse the order, in which the ancients looked at the outward creation; he looks at the world with reference to himself, and not at himself with reference to the world." [1]

This evinces a progressivism somewhat more sophisticated than Barlow's; evinces, moreover, an attempt to counter the prevailing sentiment as to the impossibility of

From Roy Harvey Pearce, *The Continuity of American Poetry* (Princeton, N.J.: Princeton University Press, 1961), pp. 69–83. Reprinted by permission of the publisher.

[1] I quote from K. W. Cameron's transcription of the manuscript version of the essay, *Emerson Society Quarterly*, No. 12 (1958), pp. 25–32. The essay was first published in a form revised from the ms. in *Christian Examiner* xxiv (1838), pp. 201–202.

an epic *per se* with the possibility of something grander than the epic. Also, it evinces a step toward the Walt Whitman of *Song of Myself*.

As everyone knows, Whitman sat and looked out, travelled, read, wrote, talked, planned, dreamed, aspired. He admitted that he was often puzzled, even confused. But one thing he was always sure he wanted: freedom for self-realization for himself and all the myriad persons who populated the world he contemplated with such hypnagogic diligence. Quite early in his career he came to understand the way that such self-realization could be achieved—in poetry, in a new, autochthonous American poem which would celebrate its culture so as to make the power for self-realization for the first time spontaneously available to all comers. His readers would thus become celebrants; with him they would celebrate themselves in their world, hence really come to know themselves. In the familiar words of the 1855 Preface:

"The Americans of all nations at any time upon the earth have probably the fullest poetical nature. The United States themselves are essentially the greatest poem. In the history of the earth hitherto the largest and most stirring appear tame and orderly to their ampler largeness and stir. . . . [*these* points indicate my elision, not, like the rest, Whitman's pauses] Here is the hospitality which forever indicates heroes. . . ."

And later:

"The greatest poet hardly knows pettiness or triviality. If he breathes into anything that was before thought small it dilates with the grandeur and life of the universe. He is a seer . . . he is individual . . . he is complete in himself . . . the others are as good as he, only he sees it and they do not."

And still later:

". . . but folks expect of the poet to indicate more than the beauty and dignity which always attach to dumb real objects . . . they expect him to indicate the path between reality and their souls."

Such words—and their substance is repeated too often and too feverishly by Whitman to make any multiplication of them necessary here—take on a special import when read in the light of Barlow's performance in *The Columbiad*. They exhibit a Whitman who feels that he has finally discovered the way to the poem made out of that "living language" which will "warm the world with one great moral soul." Such a poem can only be epic in scope. In the Preface Whitman says further of it that it must be "creative" and have "vista" and that "*it is to be indirect and not direct or descriptive or epic*" (the italics are his). Thus it is to do for modern man what the epic did for men of the outworn past. Yet it cannot be in form like the traditional epic; its form must be self-transcending, as must its heroes. Whitman's world is overflowing with that "hospitality" which, as he says, forever "indicates heroes." If all men are heroes, then the heroism of modern society has infinitely more aspects and qualities than can be fused in the single hero of the traditional epic. Moreover, if this modern equivalent of the epic is to join the reality (that is, the *realia*) of the world to the souls which inhabit it, it cannot teach by example, as did the traditional epic, which had set up super-human models whose mythified presence would reinforce and refine its readers' (and auditors') sense of themselves living fully and freely in their world. Rather, this new poem must teach by action, by calling forth and giving form to the possibility for the heroic in its readers. The method of indirection is a means to transforming the objective world into the subjective. Otherwise, it would have to be directly described and would thereby hold sway over the souls of its readers—a state of affairs manifestly outmoded in a society of genuinely free men.

Thus Whitman, feeling no such bothersome ties to the traditional past as had Barlow, conceived of an American equivalent of the epic and strove throughout his life to create one. Writing in 1867 and 1868 the two essays which he finally put together as *Democratic Vistas*, he admitted: ". . . we have to say there can be no complete or epical presentation of democracy in the aggregate, or anything like it, at this day, because its doctrines will only be effectually incarnated in one branch, when, in all, their spirit is at the root and centre." An American epic, then, would be one whose spirit would totally satisfy the needs of democracy in the aggregate. It would be propaedeutic—the working of its form and its language so managed as immediately to relate the reader to the milieu and the ambiance, the culture, which the form and the language project. Making it new, in the later Poundian phrase, the new epic would make the reader new. As the traditional epic had achieved its authenticity through confirmation, so the new epic would achieve its authenticity through creation and re-creation. The modern poet could confirm only his readers' sense of themselves as being "effectually incarnated."

Acting out of his exquisite feeling for the deep and terrible need of his culture to find an adequate poetic image of its very being, Whitman wrote *Song of Myself*. Indeed, he repeatedly revised and rearranged the whole of *Leaves of Grass*, and *Song of Myself* with it, perhaps in order to make it into a total image—the full and complete surrogate for the traditional epic.[2] But, so it seems to me, *Song of Myself* is the clearest, surest, most self-contained and complete, and most widely gauged product of Whitman's desire to create an American epic and of the metamorphosis of genre which that desire necessarily brought about.

Most students of *Song of Myself* have wished to find in it some firm structural principle.[3] It is as though they would measure it by such dialectically unifying stand-

---

[2] See particularly James E. Miller, "America's Epic," *A Critical Guide to Leaves of Grass* (Chicago, 1957), pp. 256–261. Mr. Miller urges that we read *Leaves of Grass in toto* as an "epic." But the evidence from Whitman's later prefaces would urge us to read it as a set of holy scriptures. Moreover, Whitman wrote (in the 1872 Preface to *As a Strong Bird on Pinions Free*) that *Leaves of Grass* consisted "of New World songs, and an epic of Democracy." The "epic" could only have been *Song of Myself*.

[3] For example: Carl Strauch, "The Structure of Walt Whitman's 'Song of Myself,' " *English Journal*, xxvii (1938), pp. 597–607; Gay Wilson Allen, *Walt Whitman Handbook* (Chicago, 1946), pp. 115–121; Gay Wilson Allen and Charles T. Davis, *Walt Whitman's Poems* (New York, 1955), pp. 127–131; and James E. Miller, "Song of Myself as Inverted Mystical Experience," *A Critical Guide to Leaves of Grass*, pp. 6–35. Thomas J. Rountree's "Whitman's Indirect Expression and Its Application to 'Song of Myself,' " (PMLA LXXIII [1958], pp. 549–555) which I read after writing this, is closer to my own view. Another characteristic view of the poem is Charles Feidelson's (*Symbolism and American Literature* [Chicago, 1953]), p. 25: ". . . [Compared to 'When Lilacs Last in the Dooryard Bloom'd,' Whitman's] other long poems generally lack . . . [a] stabilizing factor. Whatever the nominal subject, it is soon lost in sheer 'process'; all roads lead into 'Song of Myself,' in which the bare

ards and forms as those which Whitman strove to transcend. If only we look at *Song of Myself* as an exemplar of a further stage in the development of an American epic, we may see how it was necessary for the success of the poem that it be in no way externally or generically structured. In Whitman's conception, this new kind of poem was more a process than a form. True enough, he revised it considerably before he decided upon its final version in 1881; and he moved it around in successive editions of *Leaves of Grass*. But these facts argue, not that he was trying to tailor it to a form and give it a proper place, but rather that he wanted it to grow and move, as he and his world had grown and moved. It is as if Barlow's Columbus were allowed to have a vision which would be demonstrably his and his alone, not one which had been given to him; as though the structure of that vision were demonstrably the structure of his own native perceptions and his resolution of them into significance. The Whitman of *Song of Myself* surveys his whole world, his milieu and ambiance —but not according to any necessary order or chronology. He looks when he wills and interprets as he wills. There is a movement here, but not a form. It is essential to the meaning of the poem that the movement be unique; for the movement derives from the motion of the protagonist's sensibility. What is relatively stable and fixed, because it has no end and no beginning, is the world of which that sensibility becomes conscious, the world in and through which that sensibility discovers itself. The world is too large, too much, to have an imitable order or pattern. It is just there. The hero's hope in *Song of Myself*, his "altogether . . . moral and political" object, is to know that the world is there, and in the knowing, to know that *he* is there. In effect, through such a transaction he would create himself, only then to "find" himself: to discover, as though for the first time, that he exists and is free—at once, in the words of the opening inscriptive poem of *Leaves of Grass*, "a simple separate person" and "En-Masse." *Song of Myself* is a poem in which the protagonist wills himself to be at the mercy of his world; for he knows that in his world lies his only source of the creative forms, the range of experiences, which will let him complete the cycle of the self-recognition, identification with others, and self-definition which has been initiated by his original insight into his destiny. The poem recounts a struggle in which insight is wrought into destiny. What the poet might be, he wills himself to become, and so he is able to claim that this is what from the beginning he had to be. So it must be with his readers.

The "argument" of *Song of Myself* moves in gross outline something like this:

Phase I. 1–5: The initial insight into the creative nature ("the procreant urge") of the self and the initiating of creative power which follows spontaneously upon that insight.

Ego interacts with a miscellaneous world. The result is Whitman's characteristic disorder and turgidity. When the subject is endless, any form becomes arbitrary." Richard Chase (*Walt Whitman Reconsidered* [New York, 1955], pp. 58–59) in effect grants the disorder but finds that it makes for Whitman's marvelous plenitude. The difficulty arises, I think, out of such either/or decisions which such a concept as "form" has traditionally demanded of the critic.

II. 6–16: Recognition of the relation of the self to its world and a seeking after the metamorphoses which follow spontaneously upon that recognition.

III. 17–25: The roles of the self in and through its world; a return to the matter of 1–5, but with this difference—that self-knowledge now exists objectively, a product not of sheer inwardness as in 1–5 but of a spontaneously formalized relation between the self and its world. Now the poet is not simply a force, but a force defined in terms of its world; now he is fully a person and can name himself: "Walt Whitman, a kosmos, of Manhattan the son."

IV. 26–52: The poet (as person) fully at home in his newly defined world, fully sure of himself and his "procreant urge." He no longer needs to seek his world (as in 6–16); he can openly and lovingly address it, as he at once creates and controls it and as he is created and controlled by it. He is thus a religion, God-like in himself: "I am an acme of things accomplish'd, and I am encloser of things to be."

The structure of *Song of Myself*, then, evinces little of that internal-external sense of necessity (in its most extreme forms, an Aristotelian beginning, middle and end; or a New Critical paradox, tension, ambiguity, or irony) which we tend to demand of an achieved literary work. True enough, the argument of the poem centers on points of psychic intensity; nonetheless, there is no fixed rational or affective scheme whereby we may decide that a given section should or should not have begun where it begins and ended where it ends, or contain what it contains. It is this "formal" difficulty which has most often disturbed readers of Whitman and sent them to a poem like "Out of the Cradle . . . ," with its tight, firm internal design. But this is a specious difficulty; and the argument of the poem is, in its own way, entirely mean-ingful and quite of a piece with its epic (or must one now say, proto-epic?) intention. There is, in fact, a specific form and content for such insight as the poem makes pos-sible, even though the specificity is entirely a matter of a private transaction between the poet and his world. For since that world contains the poet's readers as well as the poet, his is an insight which, if his readers are bold enough, will move them to trans-form themselves as he has transformed himself. All that he demands of them is that they yield to his poem, as has the world. This done, the "procreant urge" will be spontaneously released and the readers will be on their way to their own private trans-formations. Yielding to the poem, in short, they will release in themselves the creative energies which will make them nothing less than heroic. (Barlow, we should recall, had hypothesized about a kind of poetry which would "win a pure passage to the heart of youth." Whitman strives for a kind of poetry which, in winning its passage, would make for a rebirth into youth.) Like Pound after him, Whitman worked toward a new Paideuma: one entirely of process, of guiding, strengthening, energiz-ing, and redefining the sensible self by putting it into direct contact with the world wherein it could be free, creative, and whole—a self proper to the American demo-crat. Such a poetry aimed at release and reintegration. Totally process, it could, as Whitman himself said, have no proper beginning or ending. It could have no form bound by necessities of any sort. Its greatness would lie in its resistance to that formalization which, as it was fatal to man, would also be fatal to poetry.

Whether or not such a poetry is possible is a nice but insoluble problem. Barlow *might* have thought it was. Whitman *did* think it was (as did Crane, as do Williams and Pound) and strove to realize the possibility. The language, the syntax, the articulation of *Song of Myself*—these are the terms of his realization and its unique form. They give it its style; and it well may be in the long run that the American epic is essentially no more than a style, what I have called a basic style.

Song of Myself begins epically, but immediately (unlike the traditional epic) turns inward, demanding that its reader do likewise:

> I celebrate myself, and sing myself,
> And what I assume you shall assume,
> For every atom belonging to me as good belongs to you. (1)

The whole first section establishes the dominance of the self when for the first time it is overpoweringly discovered; the language of the section is composed in such a way as to register the overpower. For example, all the verbs in the section apply only to the self and its attributes. At the end of this section Whitman writes:

> Creeds and schools in abeyance,
> Retiring back a while sufficed at what they are, but never forgotten,
> I harbor for good or bad, I permit to speak at every hazard,
> Nature without check with original energy.

In this stanza the absence of verbs for the items named in the first and last lines absolutely subordinates them to the newly (or re-) discovered self. What follows in the next sections is a retailing of a complete absorption into the self ("I am mad for it to be in contact with me") and a sense that the self possesses "the origin of all poems," (2) an elucidation of the timeless "Urge and urge and urge,/ Always the procreant urge of the world," (3) a recognition of its difference from other souls ("But they are not the Me myself" [4]), and the final account of how the soul, turning inward upon itself, discovers its true nature:

> I mind how once we lay such a transparent summer morning,
> How you settled your head athwart my hips and gently turn'd over upon me,
> And parted the shirt from my bosom-bone, and plunged your tongue to my
>   bare-stript heart,
> And reach'd till you felt my beard, and reach'd till you held my feet. (5)

At this point, consciousness of self becomes self-consciousness *in extremis*; the "I" becomes "you," yet—through the power of the poet's art—somehow remains "I"; he is witness to the marriage of his own two minds. The passage of parallelisms which follows takes its energy from this moment of self-generated apotheosis. The items that are named are chaotically scattered in their natural habitat; but the force of the parallelisms is to unify and relate them by means of the newly initiated, because integrated, powers of the creative self:

Swiftly arose and spread around me the peace and knowledge that pass all the
    argument of the earth,
And I know that the hand of God is the promise of my own,
And I know that the spirit of God is the brother of my own,
And that all the men ever born are also my brothers, and the women my sisters
    and lovers,
And that a kelson of the creation is love,
And limitless are leaves stiff or drooping in the fields,
And brown ants in the little wells beneath them,
And mossy scabs of the worm fence, heap'd stones, elder, mullein and poke-weed.

Only now—because it is wholly in control of its inner world, can the self begin to
turn toward its outer world, then surrender and undergo its outward metamorphoses.
With its inner stability assured, it now has the strength to do so. (5)

The movement of sensibility which gives Song of Myself its quality of process, not
form, is not that of the stream-of-consciousness or of associationism.[4] Rather it is
that of the hypnagogic meditation, controlled not by rules or method but by the
intensely personal pulsations and periodicities of the meditative act. Such pulsations
and periodicities are expressions of the energy of the creative self; and they cannot
be plotted in advance: they can only be released and followed out to their transforma-
tive end. Accordingly, the studious reader of Song of Myself must be somewhat dif-
fident about the detailed precision of any outline of the phasal structure of the poem.
Yet he must insist on the validity of the theory of phasal structure itself and of the
way in which it is meant to do its job. For herein lies the essence of the American
poet's attempt to create a poem and a poetry of epic proportions and significance.
There follows a phase-by-phase analysis of the rest of Song of Myself.

Phase II. Section 6: A meditation on the meaning of the "real" world, taken at
its simplest as a blade of grass; here the self ventures to interpret, but is not quite
sure ("I guess," it says, and "It may be . . ."); but grass leads to grave, and grave leads
to death, and death leads to continuity and identity:

> All goes onward and outward, nothing collapses,
> And to die is different from what any one supposed, and luckier.

7: The subject is death, newly understood; and through his understanding the poet,
as self, sees that in the very continuity of life and death lies what unites him with all
who are born to die, makes them (in a construction repeated so often that it unifies
the diverse), "For me. . . ." 8: The poet-as-self begins to explore a world compounded
of life and death, peace and violence; as yet, he is to a degree an outsider—looking,
peering, viewing, witnessing, and finally coming and departing. 9–11: He is here,
there, everywhere—on a farm, in the mountains, at sea—participating, helping, joining. In the notorious eleventh section, he is viewing twenty-eight handsome, friendly
young men bathing; here he is even more of an outsider, for whereas he had spoken
in the first person in the previous sections, here he speaks in the third—or rather,

---

[4] For an exposition of the view that stream-of-consciousness is involved here, see Frederik
Schyberg, Walt Whitman, trans. E. A. Allen (New York, 1951), p. 99.

has a woman look for him and observes that her "unseen hand also pass'd over their bodies"; it is as though the procreant urge of the self to create and transform itself is not yet quite powerful enough. 12–15: Further exploits as voyeur, but now one who can call himself (in 13) "the caresser of life." There are occasional interpretive interjections which make the self mindful of its object—e.g., of flying ducks, "I believe in those wing'd purposes" (13); the poet has discovered that "What is commonest, cheapest, nearest, easiest, is Me" (14); and at the end of the great catalogue in 15, he can declare, "And of these one and all I weave the song of myself." 16: A brave attempt to comprehend objectively the relation between self and world, in which the poet moves from the relational to the identical—at first he says, "I am of," then declares that he is "stuffed" as others are stuffed, and then he establishes identity by sheer naming; the process is beyond the logical necessity of a verb, being an "I am" beyond "I am." And finally, in the stanza beginning "I resist any thing better than my own diversity," there is a full recognition, achieved through the creative metamorphoses called forth in this phase of the poem, of the role and meaning of the self.

Phase III. The implications of that role are developed in a series of spasmodic break-throughs to heroic insight; here, above all, the unity of the poem derives, not from a necessary relation among its parts, but from the single creative power which is forcing that relation. 17–18: A meditation upon the self, the community, and the community of selves; what is at stake is establishing the total inclusiveness of the relationship and of the identity so discovered. 19–22: The subject is love of self and world and what that love entails—the recognition (in 20) that "I exist as I am, that is enough. . . ." There follows, in 23, a moment of victorious acceptance of the creative role of the self and of its difficult but joyous relation to its world: "I accept Reality and dare not question it. . . ." This in turn leads, in 24 and 25, to the poet's daring to name himself—as though the self had now earned, through its loving transaction with its world, a right to take on such substantial being as it could create in that transaction. The poet is now "Walt Whitman, a kosmos, of Manhattan the son." He can now say, "I dote on myself, there is that lot of me and all so luscious"; he is now "Divine . . . inside and out"; his world has filtered "through" him; hence the great, joyous, comic pronouncement—one of the great moments in the history of the American spirit:

> Unscrew the locks from the doors!
> Unscrew the doors themselves from their jambs!
>
> Whoever degrades another degrades me,
> And whatever is done or said returns at last to me.

25: This movement is carried to completion: "*Walt you contain enough, why don't you let it out then?*" Italicized by Whitman, the words announce the completion of the creative transaction between the self and its world; what has emerged is a man, a poet—no longer just a force, but now a substantial being, a means and an end.

Phase IV treats of the poet, full of the sense of what he has accomplished and how he has accomplished it, in his new relation to his world and his readers. 25–29: The poet listens to, touches, is touched by, the items which make up his world, and is thereby able to solve the mystery of being itself. 30–31: The mystery of being is the mystery of creativity, hence is no longer a mystery. Now the poet can both believe in and be everything in his world, for its being is grounded in his relation to it. As he has come to know it, he has made it an aspect of himself and himself an aspect of it. Thus the "I believe" and the "I incorporate" series of 31 is followed by an "In vain" series—for since the poet believes and so incorporates, in vain would anything in the world try to escape him. 32: Animals—"Why do I need your [the stallion's] paces when I myself out-gallop them?/ Even as I stand or sit passing faster than you." 33: The poet's life in time and space—again a movement from the relational to the identical (I am by, where, over, at, etc.—I visit, I fly, etc.—I understand, etc.—I am the man, I suffer'd, I was there). The poet is now a Tiresias who acts. 34–36: History, in the Alamo and a naval battle—I was there. 37: A prison—I was there. 38: The poet has also had his Gethsemane and his Crucifixion. 39: The poet as noble savage, a beloved primal being. 40: The poet meditates the creative self as it has worked in 26–39:

> I have embraced you, and henceforth possess you to myself,
> And when you rise in the morning you will find what I tell you is so.

41. The poet as Godlike—

> . . . becoming already a creator,
> Putting myself here and now to the ambush'd womb of the shadows.

42: The poet as God—

> I know perfectly well my own egotism,
> Know my omnivorous lines and must not write any less,
> And would fetch you whoever you are flush with myself.

43: The poet and the priests of the world—he takes on their role, his religion is all theirs put together and more. "It cannot fail . . ."—another affirmatory catalogue of the ineluctable destiny of a seemingly chaotic world. 44: An almost formal definition of the man who, made by his vision, now recreates it for others and makes it work on them—"I am an acme of things accomplish'd, and I am encloser of things to be." 45: The joy of that procreant urge discovered before in 2, but now known to be Godlike, forever youthful and reassertive. Now the poet knows that self-absorption is an inexhaustible source of that assertion and expression of self which is love and identity. As he makes himself Godlike, he is of God's Elect. 46: Again the milieu and ambiance are explored, and are known to be as measureless and inexhaustible as the poet's Godlike, God-given creative powers. 47: Having learned that the power of the poet-person is that of the teacher, the poet has earned the right to call himself thus for the first time:

> I teach straying from me, yet who can stray from me?

> I follow you whoever you are from the present hour,
> My words itch at your ears till you understand them.

48: The poet and God—it is enough to see God in his world and in himself. 49: The poet and death—he is not frightened; he knows that always he will "ascend." 50: The poet's triumphant state, unnamable—"It is not chaos or death—it is form, union, plan—it is eternal life—it is Happiness." 51: The time is forever now for a man, a poet, in this state. 52: The poet, having created himself in and through his world, is inevitably forever here—in the processes of life itself:

> I bequeath myself to the dirt to grow from the grass I love,
> If you want me again look for me under your boot-soles.
>
> . . . .
>
> Failing to fetch me at first keep encouraged,
> Missing me one place search another,
> I stop somewhere waiting for you.

Whitman's way of "winning a pure passage to the heart" consisted in meditating on his impressions of himself in his world and putting them into an order which would initiate in a reader an analogous process. In the end, the substance of the impressions was of worth only as it might be available to meditation. The quality of the meditation was so intense as to make process the equivalent of form, and all the items in a man's world of no account except as they might be made to minister to his growing sense of himself. A man could love them only after he had studied and mastered them. Before he could let them discipline him, he had perforce to discipline them. All would be well, however, and there would be no danger of tyranny or solipsism; for such discipline was no less than an act of love. Whitman's hero was under the constant injunction, self-imposed, to prove the world upon himself. Ideas could be put into action (to look forward to Pound's phrase for the process) not as their power for action—deriving from their role in history, tradition, and the like—might be realized, but as that power might be given them by a poet, or a reader. Thus Whitman instructed his readers in the 1855 Preface that if they read his poem aright and acted accordingly, their "flesh" would be "a great poem." Only a poet could instruct them so; for, as he concluded, "the known universe has but one complete lover and that is the greatest poet."

Another passage in the Preface calls to mind Barlow's vision of a utopian world language and what it might do for men and their poets. Whitman, however, is characteristically more energetic, and will savor the quality of the language itself: "The English language befriends the grand American expression . . . it is brawny enough and limber and full enough. On the tough stock of a race who through all change of circumstances was never without the idea of political liberty, which is the animus of all liberty, it has attracted the terms of daintier and gayer and subtler and more elegant tongues. It is the powerful language of resistance . . . it is the dialect of common sense. It is the speech of the proud and melancholy races and of all who aspire. It is the chosen tongue to express growth faith self-esteem freedom justice equality friendliness amplitude prudence decision and courage. It is the medium that shall well nigh express the inexpressible." [5]

Whitman needed such a medium; and needing it, he created it.[6] Since, as he proclaimed, it was a language of resistance, he could use it as a language of creation and love, simply by tapping the resources of the self and turning its forces outward. The theory implied is almost psychoanalytic: When the stream of libido is turned from resistance to creativity, the ego no longer has to defend itself, but is able, by virtue of the act of the poem, to love and be loved and so to achieve positive identity. In the light of his performance in Song of Myself, Whitman's views on the poet and his language do make for a kind of unity. It is the unity of psychic exhaustion, of an act of self-discovery, self-involvement, and self-creation carried through to completion. Perhaps that is why, yielding to his (mistaken) need to give "finish" to the poem, he finally settled upon fifty-two sections for Song of Myself. Its unity is that of a year, which, once having completed its seasons of birth, growth, and death, will inevitably come again. Such an eternal cycle can be known only in terms which, in its inclusiveness, it generates. So it will be with the poem and the poet, "untranslatable," sounding a "barbaric yawp over the roofs of the world."

This is a new heroic poetry—not an epic, but an American equivalent of an epic. In this proto-epic, the hero releases the full creative force of the self, defines the *realia* of his world and takes from them his name, his office, and his phenomenal, existential qualities. He fathers, delivers, and baptizes himself. To carry the act through, he must free himself from what he has learned is the false, hierarchical heroism of traditional societies. The structure (the word is too strong) of Song of Myself articulates (again, the word is too strong) this act. As the act is dynamic yet fluid, so is the structure (which, if thus qualified, is not too strong a word). The new heroic poem, the specifically American epic, is one of ordering, not of order; of creation, not confirmation; of revealing, not memorializing. When in Democratic Vistas Whitman let the trajectory of Song of Myself and what followed it carry him forward toward his utopia, he concluded: "It must still be reiterated . . . [here again the points are mine, not Whitman's] that all else in the contributions of a nation or age, through its politics, materials, heroic personalities, military eclat, &c., remains crude, and defers, in any close and thoroughgoing estimate, until vitalized by national, original archetypes in literature. They only put the nation in form, finally tell anything— prove, complete anything—perpetuate anything." Song of Myself is such a national, original archetype. As Whitman said generally of his poetry in A Backward Glance O'er Travell'd Roads, it is "to give ultimate vivification to facts, to science, and to common lives, endowing them with the glows and glories and final illustriousness which belong to every real thing, and to real things only."

---

[5] Whitman thought enough of the lines to convert them into the poem beginning "Wonderful is language!" See Schyberg, Walt Whitman, p. 83. His words, of course, recall those of his American Primer, as I have cited them above, p. 5.

[6] Feidelson (Symbolism and American Literature, p. 18) describes the theory of Whitman's poetic medium thus: "A poem, therefore, instead of referring to a completed act of perception, constitutes the act itself, both in the author and in the reader.

"SONG OF MYSELF"
AS INSPIRED PROPHECY

INTRODUCTION TO THE

FIRST (1855) EDITION

by Malcolm Cowley

ONE REASON among others why "Song of Myself" has been widely misprized and misinterpreted, especially by scholars, is that they have paid a disproportionate share of attention to its sources in contemporary culture. Besides noting many parallels with Emerson, they have found that it reflected a number of popular works and spectacles. Among these are Italian opera (notably as sung at the Astor Place Theatre in the great season of 1852–1853, when "Alboni's great self" paid her long and only visit to New York); George Sand's novel, *The Countess of Rudolstadt*, which pre-sented the figure of a wandering bard and prophet (as well as another of her novels, *The Journeyman Joiner*, in which the hero was a carpenter and a proletarian saint); Frances Wright's then famous defense of Epicurean philosophy, *A Few Days in Athens*; the Count de Volney's *Ruins*, predicting the final union of all religions; Dr. Abbott's Egyptian Museum, on Broadway; O. M. Mitchel's book, *A Course of Six Lectures on Astronomy*, as well as other writings on the subject; and a number of essays clipped from the English quarterly reviews, of which the poet seems to have been a faithful reader. All these works and shows had a discernible influence on Whit-man, but when they are listed with others and discussed at length they lead to one of the misconceptions that are the professional weakness of scholars. They tempt us to conclude that "Song of Myself" was merely a journalist's report, inspired but uneven, of popular culture in the 1850s. It was something more than that, and some-thing vastly different from any of its literary sources.

I might suggest that the real nature of the poem becomes clearer when it is con-sidered in relation to quite another list of works, even though Whitman had prob-ably read none of them in 1855. Most of them he could not have read, because they were not yet written, or not published, or not translated into English. That other list might include the *Bhagavad-Gita*, the *Upanishads*, Christopher Smart's long crazy inspired poem *Jubilate Agno*, Blake's prophetic books (not forgetting *The Marriage of Heaven and Hell*), Rimbaud's *Illuminations*, *The Chants of Maldoror*, and

Nietzsche's *Thus Spake Zarathustra*, as well as *The Gospel of Sri Ramakrishna* and a compendious handbook, *The Philosophies of India*, by Heinrich Zimmer (New York, 1951). I am offering what might seem to be a curious list of titles, but its double purpose is easy to explain. "Song of Myself" should be judged, I think, as one of the great inspired (and sometimes insane) prophetic works that have appeared at intervals in the Western world, like *Jubilate Agno* (which is written in a biblical style sometimes suggesting Whitman's), like the *Illuminations*, like *Thus Spake Zarathustra*. But the system of doctrine suggested by the poem is more Eastern than Western, it includes notions like metempsychosis and karma, and it might almost be one of those *Philosophies of India* that Zimmer expounds at length.

What is extraordinary about this Eastern element is that Whitman, when he was writing the poems of the first edition, seems to have known little or nothing about Indian philosophy. It is more than doubtful that he had even read the *Bhagavad-Gita*, one of the few Indian works then available in translation. He does not refer to it in his notebooks of the early 1850s, where he mentions most of the books he was poring over. A year after the first edition was published, Thoreau went to see him in Brooklyn and told him that *Leaves of Grass* was "Wonderfully like the Orientals." Had Whitman read them? he asked. The poet answered, "No: tell me about them." He seems to have taken advantage of Thoreau's reading list, since words from the Sanskrit (notably "Maya" and "sudra") are used correctly in some of the poems written after 1858. They do not appear in "Song of Myself," in spite of the recognizably Indian ideas expressed in the poem, and I would hazard the guess that the ideas are not of literary derivation. It is true that they were vaguely in the air of the time and that Whitman may have breathed them in from the Transcendentalists or even from some of the English quarterly reviewers. It also seems possible, however, that he reinvented them for himself, after an experience similar to the one for which the Sanskrit word is samadhi, or absorption.

What it must have been was a mystical experience in the proper sense of the term. Dr. Richard Maurice Bucke, the most acute of Whitman's immediate disciples, believed that it took place on a June morning in 1853 or 1854. He also believed that it was repeated on other occasions, but neither these nor the original experience can be dated from Whitman's papers. On the other hand, his notebooks and manuscripts of the early 1850s are full of sidelong references to such an experience, and they suggest that it was essentially the same as the illuminations or ecstasies of earlier bards and prophets. Such ecstasies consist in a rapt feeling of union or identity with God (or the Soul, or Mankind, or the Comos), a sense of ineffable joy leading to the conviction that the seer has been released from the limitations of space and time and has been granted a direct vision of truths impossible to express. As Whitman says in the famous fifth chant of "Song of Myself":

> Swiftly arose and spread around me the peace and joy and knowledge
>   that pass all the art and argument of the earth;
> And I know that the hand of God is the elderhand of my own,
> And I know that the spirit of God is the eldest brother of my own,

And that all the men ever born are also my brothers . . . and the
women my sisters and lovers.

It is to be noted that there is no argument about the real occurrence of such
ecstasies. They have been reported, sometimes in sharp detail, by men and women
of many different nations, at many historical periods, and each report seems to bear
a family resemblance to the others. Part of the resemblance is a feeling universally
expressed by mystics that they have acquired a special sort of knowledge not learned
from others, but directly revealed to the inner eye. This supposed knowledge has
given independent rise to many systems of philosophy or cosmology, once again in
many different cultures, and once again there is or should be no argument about one
feature of almost all the systems or bodies of teaching: that they too have a family
resemblance, like the experiences on which they are based. Indeed, they hold so many
principles in common that it is possible for Aldous Huxley and others to group them
all together as "the perennial philosophy."

The arguments, which will never end, are first about the nature of the mystical
state—is it a form of self-hypnosis, is it a pathological condition to be induced by
fasting, vigils, drugs, and other means of abusing the physical organism, or is it, as
Whitman believed, the result of superabundant health and energy?—and then about
the source and value of the philosophical notions to which it gives rise. Do these
merely express the unconscious desires of the individual, and chiefly his sexual desires? Or, as Jungian psychologists like to suggest, are they derived from a racial or
universally human unconscious? Are they revelations or hallucinations? Are they supreme doctrines, or are they heretical, false, and even satanic? They belong in the
orthodox tradition of Indian philosophy. In Western Christianity, as also in Moham-
medanism, the pure and self-consistent forms of mysticism are usually regarded as
heresies, with the result that several of the medieval mystics were burned at the stake
(though Theresa of Avila and John of the Cross found an orthodox interpretation for
their visions and became saints).

Whitman cannot be called a Christian heretic, for the simple reason that he was
not a Christian at any stage of his career, early or late. In some of the poems written
after the Civil War, and in revisions of older poems made at the same time, he ap-
proached the Christian notion of a personal God, whom he invoked as the Elder
Brother or the great Camerado. But then he insisted—in another poem of the same
period, "Chanting the Square Deific"—that God was not a trinity but a quaternity,
and that one of his faces was the "sudra face" of Satan. In "Song of Myself" as
originally written, God is neither a person nor, in the strict sense, even a being; God
is an abstract principle of energy that is manifested in every living creature, as well
as in "the grass that grows wherever the land is and the water is." In some ways this
God of the first edition resembles Emerson's Oversoul, but he seems much closer to
the Brahman of the *Upanishads,* the absolute, unchanging, all-enfolding Consciousness, the Divine Ground from which all things emanate and to which all living things
may hope to return. And this Divine Ground is by no means the only conception

that Whitman shared with Indian philosophers, in the days when he was writing "Song of Myself."

The poem is hardly at all concerned with American nationalism, political democracy, contemporary progress, or other social themes that are commonly associated with Whitman's work. The "incomparable things" that Emerson found in it are philosophical and religious principles. Its subject is a state of illumination induced by two (or three) separate moments of ecstasy. In more or less narrative sequence it describes those moments, their sequels in life, and the doctrines to which they give rise. The doctrines are not expounded by logical steps or supported by arguments; instead they are presented dramatically, that is, as the new convictions of a hero, and they are revealed by successive unfoldings of his states of mind.

The hero as pictured in the frontispiece—this hero named "I" or "Walt Whitman" in the text—should not be confused with the Whitman of daily life. He is, as I said, a dramatized or idealized figure, and he is put forward as a representative American workingman, but one who prefers to loaf and invite his soul. Thus, he is rough, sunburned, bearded; he cocks his hat as he pleases, indoors or out; but in the text of the first edition he has no local or family background, and he is deprived of strictly individual characteristics, with the exception of curiosity, boastfulness, and an abnormally developed sense of touch. His really distinguishing feature is that he has been granted a vision, as a result of which he has realized the potentialities latent in every American and indeed, he says, in every living person, even "the brutish koboo, called the ordure of humanity." This dramatization of the hero makes it possible for the living Whitman to exalt him—as he would not have ventured, at the time, to exalt himself—but also to poke mild fun at the hero for his gab and loitering, for his tall talk or "omnivorous words," and for sounding his barbaric yawp over the roofs of the world. The religious feeling in "Song of Myself" is counterpoised by a humor that takes the form of slangy and mischievous impudence or drawling Yankee self-ridicule.

There has been a good deal of discussion about the structure of the poem. In spite of revealing analyses made by a few Whitman scholars, notably Carl F. Strauch and James E. Miller, Jr., a feeling still seems to prevail that it has no structure properly speaking; that it is inspired but uneven, repetitive, and especially weak in its transitions from one theme to another. I suspect that much of this feeling may be due to Whitman's later changes in the text, including his arbitrary scheme, first introduced in the 1867 edition, of dividing the poem into fifty-two numbered paragraphs or chants. One is tempted to read the chants as if they were separate poems, thus overlooking the unity and flow of the work as a whole. It may also be, however, that most of the scholars have been looking for a geometrical pattern, such as can be found and diagramed in some of the later poems. If there is no such pattern in "Song of Myself," that is because the poem was written on a different principle, one much closer to the spirit of the Symbolists or even the Surrealists.

The true structure of the poem is not primarily logical but psychological, and is not a geometrical figure but a musical progression. As music "Song of Myself" is not a symphony with contrasting movements, nor is it an operatic work like "Out of the Cradle Endlessly Rocking," with an overture, arias, recitatives, and a finale. It comes closer to being a rhapsody or tone poem, one that modulates from theme to theme, often changing in key and tempo, falling into reveries and rising toward moments of climax, but always preserving its unity of feeling as it moves onward in a wavelike flow. It is a poem that bears the marks of having been conceived as a whole and written in one prolonged burst of inspiration, but its unity is also the result of conscious art, as can be seen from Whitman's corrections in the early manuscripts. He did not recognize all the bad lines, some of which survive in the printed text, but there is no line in the first edition that seems false to a single prevailing tone. There are passages weaker than others, but none without a place in the general scheme. The repetitions are always musical variations and amplifications. Some of the transitions seem abrupt when the poem is read as if it were an essay, but Whitman was not working in terms of "therefore" and "however." He preferred to let one image suggest another image, which in turn suggests a new statement of mood or doctrine. His themes modulate into one another by pure association, as in a waking dream, with the result that all his transitions seem instinctively right.

In spite of these oneiric elements, the form of the poem is something more than a forward movement in rising and subsiding waves of emotion. There is also a firm narrative structure, one that becomes easier to grasp when we start by dividing the poem into a number of parts or sequences. I think there are nine of these, but the exact number is not important; another critic might say there were seven (as Professor Miller does), or eight or ten. Some of the transitions are gradual, and in such cases it is hard to determine the exact line that ends one sequence and starts another. The essential point is that the parts, however defined, follow one another in irreversible order, like the beginning, middle, and end of any good narrative. My own outline, not necessarily final, would run as follows:

First sequence (chants 1–4): the poet or hero introduced to his audience. Leaning and loafing at his ease, "observing a spear of summer grass," he presents himself as a man who lives outdoors and worships his own naked body, not the least part of which is vile. He is also in love with his deeper self or soul, but explains that it is not to be confused with his mere personality. His joyful contentment can be shared by you, the listener, "For every atom belonging to me as good belongs to you."

Second sequence (chant 5): the ecstasy. This consists in the rapt union of the poet and his soul, and it is described—figuratively, on the present occasion—in terms of sexual union. The poet now has a sense of loving brotherhood with God and with all mankind. His eyes being truly open for the first time, he sees that even the humblest objects contain the infinite universe—

> And limitless are leaves stiff or drooping in the fields,
> And brown ants in little wells beneath them,
> And mossy scabs of the wormfence, and heaped stones, and elder and
> mullen and pokeweed.

Third sequence (chants 6–19): the grass. Chant 6 starts with one of Whitman's brilliant transitions. A child comes with both hands full of those same leaves from the fields. "What is the grass?" the child asks—and suddenly we are presented with the central image of the poem, that is, the grass as symbolizing the miracle of common things and the divinity (which implies both the equality and the immortality) of ordinary persons. During the remainder of the sequence, the poet observes men and women—and animals too—at their daily occupations. He is part of this life, he says, and even his thoughts are those of all men in all ages and lands. There are two things to be noted about the sequence, which contains some of Whitman's freshest lyrics. First, the people with a few exceptions (such as the trapper and his bride) are those whom Whitman has known all his life, while the scenes described at length are Manhattan streets and Long Island beaches or countryside. Second, the poet merely roams, watches, and listens, like a sort of Tiresias. The keynote of the sequence—as Professor Strauch was the first to explain—is the two words "I observe."

Fourth sequence (chants 20–25): the poet in person. "Hankering, gross, mystical, nude," he venerates himself as august and immortal, but so, he says, is everyone else. He is the poet of the body and of the soul, of night, earth, and sea, and of vice and feebleness as well as virtue, so that "many long dumb voices" speak through his lips, including those of slaves, prostitutes, even beetles rolling balls of dung. All life to him is such a miracle of beauty that the sunrise would kill him if he could not find expression for it—"If I could not now and always send sunrise out of me." The sequence ends with a dialogue between the poet and his power of speech, during which the poet insists that his deeper self—"the best I am"—is beyond expression.

Fifth sequence (chants 26–29): ecstasy through the senses. Beginning with chant 26, the poem sets out in a new direction. The poet decides to be completely passive: "I think I will do nothing for a long time but listen." What he hears at first are quiet familiar sounds like the gossip of flames on the hearth and the bustle of growing wheat; but the sounds rise quickly to a higher pitch, becoming the matchless voice of a trained soprano, and he is plunged into an ecstasy of hearing, or rather of Being. Then he starts over again, still passively, with the sense of touch, and finds himself rising to the ecstasy of sexual union. This time the union is actual, not figurative, as can be seen from the much longer version of chant 29 preserved in an early notebook.

Sixth sequence (chants 30–38): the power of identification. After his first ecstasy, as presented in chant 5, the poet had acquired a sort of microscopic vision that enabled him to find infinite wonders in the smallest and most familiar things. The second ecstasy (or pair of ecstasies) has an entirely different effect, conferring as it does a sort of vision that is both telescopic and spiritual. The poet sees far into space and time; "afoot with my vision" he ranges over the continent and goes speeding through the heavens among tailed meteors. His secret is the power of identification. Since everything emanates from the universal soul, and since his own soul is of the same essence, he can identify himself with every object and with every person living or dead, heroic or criminal. Thus, he is massacred with the Texans at Goliad, he fights on the *Bonhomme Richard*, he dies on the cross, and he rises again as "one of an average unending procession." Whereas the keynote of the third sequence was "I observe," here it becomes "I am"—"I am a free companion"—"My voice is the wife's voice, the screech by the rail of the stairs"—"I am the man. . . . I suffered. . . . I was there."

Seventh sequence (chants 39–41): the superman. When Indian sages emerge from the state of samadhi or absorption, they often have the feeling of being omnipotent. It is so with the poet, who now feels gifted with superhuman powers. He is the universally beloved Answerer (chant 39), then the Healer, raising men from their deathbeds (40), and then the Prophet (41) of a new religion that outbids "the old cautious hucksters" by announcing that men are divine and will eventually be gods.

Eighth sequence (chants 42–50): the sermon. "A call in the midst of the crowd" is the poet's voice, "orotund sweeping and final." He is about to offer a statement of the doctrines implied by the narrative (but note that his statement comes at the right point psychologically and plays its part in the narrative sequence). As strangers listen, he proclaims that society is full of injustice, but that the reality beneath it is deathless persons (chant 42); that he accepts and practices all religions, but looks beyond them to "what is untried and afterward" (43); that he and his listeners are the fruit of ages, and the seed of untold ages to be (44); that our final goal is appointed: "God will be there and wait till we come" (45); that he tramps a perpetual journey and longs for companions, to whom he will reveal a new world by washing the gum from their eyes—but each must then continue the journey alone (46); that he is the teacher of men who work in the open air (47); that he is not curious about God, but sees God everywhere, at every moment (48); that we shall all be reborn in different forms ("No doubt I have died myself ten thousand times before"); and that the evil in the world is like moonlight, a mere reflection of the sun (49). The end of the sermon (chant 50) is the hardest passage to interpret in the whole poem. I think, though I cannot be certain, that the poet is harking back to the period after one of his ten thousand deaths, when he slept and slept long before his next awakening. He seems to remember vague shapes, and he beseeches these Outlines, as he calls them, to let him reveal the "word unsaid." Then turning back to his audience, "It is not chaos or death," he says. "It is form and union and plan. . . . it is eternal life. . . . it is happiness."

Ninth sequence (chants 51–52): the poet's farewell. Having finished his sermon, the poet gets ready to depart, that is, to die and wait for another incarnation or "fold of the future," while still inviting others to follow. At the beginning of the poem he had been leaning and loafing at ease in the summer grass. Now, having rounded the circle, he bequeaths himself to the dirt "to grow from the grass I love." I do not see how any careful reader, unless blinded with preconceptions, could overlook the unity of the poem in tone and image and direction.

It is in the eighth sequence, which is a sermon, that Whitman gives us most of the doctrines suggested by his mystical experience, but they are also implied in the rest of the poem and indeed in the whole text of the first edition. Almost always he expresses them in the figurative and paradoxical language that prophets have used from the beginning. Now I should like to state them explicitly, even at the cost of some repetition.

Whitman believed when he was writing "Song of Myself"—and at later periods too, but with many changes in emphasis—that there is a distinction between one's mere personality and the deeper Self (or between ego and soul). He believed that the Self (or atman, to use a Sanskrit word) is of the same essence as the universal spirit (though he did not quite say it *is* the universal spirit, as Indian philosophers do in the phrase "Atman is Brahman"). He believed that true knowledge is to be acquired not through the senses or the intellect, but through union with the Self. At such moments of union (or "merge," as Whitman called it) the gum is washed from one's eyes (that is his own phrase), and one can read an infinite lesson in common things, discovering that a mouse, for example, "is miracle enough to stagger sextillions of infidels." This true knowledge is available to every man and woman, since each conceals a divine Self. Moreover, the divinity of all implies the perfect equality of all, the immortality of all, and the universal duty of loving one another.

Immortality for Whitman took the form of metempsychosis, and he believed that every individual will be reborn, usually but not always in a higher form. He had also worked out for himself something approaching the Indian notion of karma, which is the doctrine that actions performed during one incarnation determine the nature and fate of the individual during his next incarnation; the doctrine is emphatically if somewhat unclearly stated in a passage of his prose introduction that was later re-written as a poem, "Song of Prudence." By means of metempsychosis and karma, we are all involved in a process of spiritual evolution that might be compared to natural evolution. Even the latter process, however, was not regarded by Whitman as strictly natural or material. He believed that animals have a rudimentary sort of soul ("They bring me tokens of myself"), and he hinted or surmised, without directly saying, that rocks, trees, and planets possess an identity, or "eidólon," that persists as they rise to higher states of being. The double process of evolution, natural and spiritual, can be traced for ages into the past, and he believed that it will continue for ages beyond ages. Still, it is not an eternal process, since it has an ultimate goal, which appears to be the reabsorption of all things into the Divine Ground.

Most of Whitman's doctrines, though by no means all of them, belong to the mainstream of Indian philosophy. In some respects he went against the stream. Unlike most of the Indian sages, for example, he was not a thoroughgoing idealist. He did not believe that the whole world of the senses, of desires, of birth and death, was only maya, illusion, nor did he hold that it was a sort of purgatory; instead he praised the world as real and joyful. He did not despise the body, but proclaimed that it was as miraculous as the soul. He was too good a citizen of the nineteenth century to surrender his faith in material progress as the necessary counterpart of spiritual progress. Although he yearned for ecstatic union with the soul or Oversoul, he did not try to achieve it by subjugating the senses, as advised by yogis and Buddhists alike; on the contrary, he thought the "merge" could also be achieved (as in chants 26–29) by a total surrender to the senses. These are important differences, but it must be remembered that Indian philosophy or theology is not such a unified structure as it appears to us from a distance. Whitman might have found Indian sages or gurus and even whole sects that agreed with one or another of his heterodoxies (perhaps excepting his belief in material progress). One is tempted to say that instead of being a Christian heretic, he was an Indian rebel and sectarian.

Sometimes he seems to be a Mahayana Buddhist, promising nirvana for all after countless reincarnations, and also sharing the belief of some Mahayana sects that the sexual act can serve as one of the sacraments. At other times he might be an older brother of Sri Ramakrishna (1836–1886), the nineteenth-century apostle of Tantric Brahmanism and of joyous affirmation. Although this priest of Kali, the Mother Goddess, refused to learn English, one finds him delivering some of Whitman's messages in—what is more surprising—the same tone of voice. Read, for example, this fairly typical passage from *The Gospel of Sri Ramakrishna*, while remembering that "Consciousness" is to be taken here as a synonym for Divinity:

The Divine Mother revealed to me in the Kali temple that it was She who had become everything. She showed me that everything was full of Consciousness. The Image was Consciousness, the altar was Consciousness, the water-vessels were Consciousness, the door-sill was Consciousness, the marble floor was Consciousness—all was Consciousness. . . . I saw a wicked man in front of the Kali temple; but in him I saw the Power of the Divine Mother vibrating. That was why I fed a cat with the food that was to be offered to the Divine Mother.

Whitman expresses the same idea at the end of chant 48, and in the same half-playful fashion:

Why should I wish to see God better than this day?
I see something of God each hour of the twenty-four, and each moment then,
In the faces of men and women I see God, and in my own face in the glass;
I find letters from God dropped in the street, and every one is signed by God's name,
And I leave them where they are, for I know that others will punctually come
    forever and ever.

Such parallels—and there are dozens that might be quoted—are more than accidental. They reveal a kinship in thinking and experience that can be of practical value to students of Whitman. Since the Indian mystical philosophies are elaborate structures, based on conceptions that have been shaped and defined by centuries of discussion, they help to explain Whitman's ideas at points in the first edition where he seems at first glance to be vague or self-contradictory. There is, for example, his unusual combination of realism—sometimes brutal realism—and serene optimism. Today he is usually praised for the first, blamed for the second (optimism being out of fashion), and blamed still more for the inconsistency he showed in denying the existence of evil. The usual jibe is that Whitman thought the universe was perfect and was getting better every day.

It is obvious, however, that he never meant to deny the existence of evil in himself or his era or his nation. He knew that it existed in his own family, where one of his brothers was a congenital idiot, another was a drunkard married to a streetwalker, and still another, who had caught "the bad disorder," later died of general paresis in an insane asylum. Whitman's doctrine implied that each of them would have an opportunity to avoid those misfortunes or punishments in another incarnation, where each would be rewarded for his good actions. The universe was an eternal becoming for Whitman, a process not a structure, and it had to be judged from the standpoint of eternity. After his mystical experience, which seemed to offer a vision of eternity, he had become convinced that evil existed only as part of a universally perfect design. That explains his combination of realism and optimism, which seems unusual only in our Western world. In India, Heinrich Zimmer says, "Philosophic theory, religious belief, and intuitive experience support each other . . . in the basic insight that, fundamentally, all is well. A supreme optimism prevails everywhere, in spite of the unromantic recognition that the universe of man's affairs is in the most imperfect state imaginable, one amounting practically to chaos."

Another point explained by Indian conceptions is the sort of democracy Whitman was preaching in "Song of Myself." There is no doubt that he was always a democrat politically—which is to say a Jacksonian Democrat, a Barnburner writing editorials against the Hunkers, a Free Soiler in sympathy, and then a liberal but not a radical Republican. He remained faithful to what he called "the good old cause" of liberty, equality, and fraternity, and he wrote two moving elegies for the European rebels of 1848. In "Song of Myself," however, he is not advocating rebellion or even reform. "To a drudge of the cottonfields," he says, "or emptier of privies I lean. . . . on his right cheek I put the family kiss"; but he offers nothing more than a kiss and an implied promise. What he preaches throughout the poem is not political but religious democracy, such as was practiced by the early Christians. Today it is practiced, at least in theory, by the Tantric sect, and we read in *Philosophies of India:*

All beings and things are members of a single mystic family (*kula*). There is therefore no thought of caste within the Tantric holy "circles" (*cakra*). . . . Women as well as men are eligible not only to receive the highest initiation but also to confer it in the role of guru. . . . However, it must not be supposed that this indifference to the rules of caste implies any idea of revolution within the social sphere, as distinguished from the sphere of spiritual progress. The initiate returns to his post in society; for there too is the manifestation of Sakti. The world is affirmed, just as it is —neither renounced, as by an ascetic, nor corrected, as by a social reformer.

The promise that Whitman offers to the drudge of the cottonfields, the emptier of privies, and the prostitute draggling her shawl is that they too can set out with him on his perpetual journey—perhaps not in their present incarnations, but at least in some future life. And that leads to another footnote offered by the Indian philosophies: they explain what the poet meant by the Open Road. It starts as an actual road that winds through fields and cities, but Whitman is doing more than inviting us to shoulder our duds and go hiking along it. The real journey is toward spiritual vision, toward reunion with the Divine Ground; and thus the Open Road becomes Whitman's equivalent for all the other roads and paths and ways that appear in mystical teachings. It reminds us of the Noble Eightfold Path of the Buddhists, and the

Taoist Way; it suggests both the *bhakti-marga* or "path of devotion" and the *karma-marga* or "path of sacrifice"; while it comes closer to being the "big ferry" of the Mahayana sect, in which there is room for every soul to cross to the farther shore. Whitman's conception, however, was even broader. He said one should know "the universe itself as a road, as many roads, as roads for traveling souls."

I am not pleading for the acceptance of Whiman's ideas or for any other form of mysticism, Eastern or Western. I am only suggesting that his ideas as expressed in "Song of Myself" were bolder and more coherent than is generally supposed, and philosophically a great deal more respectable.

But there is more to be said in judgment of Whitman and his work. It was a truly extraordinary achievement for him to rediscover the outlines of a whole philosophical system chiefly on the basis of his own mystical experience and with little help from his reading. Frances Wright's *A Few Days in Athens*? Volney's *Ruins*? *De Rerum Natura*? The novels of George Sand? There is hardly a hint of them in Whitman's fundamental thinking, although there is more than a hint of Emerson's Neoplatonism. But Emerson, who regarded himself as a teacher not a prophet, had nothing to do with notions like metempsychosis or karma or the universe pictured as a road for traveling souls. His temporary disciple felt that he had gone far beyond the teacher and was venturing into an unexplored continent of the Self. What does it matter that his sense of discovery was largely based on ignorance of the mystical tradition! It could still encourage him to make real discoveries in style and symbol, and it could arouse a feeling of release and exhilaration in his readers.

This aspect of "Song of Myself" becomes clearer when the poem is compared with another long work about the mystical experience, T. S. Eliot's *Four Quartets*. The works have more in common than Eliot has realized, but there is a fundamental difference that leads to many others. Eliot could never have made the mistake of thinking that his experience was the first of its kind. He knows the tradition thoroughly and can always dignify his personal memories with quotations or half-quotations from the *Bhagavad-Gita* (which he read long ago in Sanskrit), from John of the Cross, *The Cloud of Unknowing*, and the anchoret Juliana of Norwich. Using craftsmanship as well as learning, he has invented a rich structure for *Four Quartets*, so that it becomes a magnificent exercise in architectonics. What we miss in the poem may be simply the exhilaration that comes from a sense of discovery. Even in his mystical experience, Eliot cannot forget the lesson of caution he has learned from his studies. He knows that his eternal moment in the rose garden will last for a moment only. He knows that he must go back to his usual state of being, and then—

> Ridiculous the waste sad time
> Stretching before and after.

Disciplined as he is by tradition, Eliot makes few mistakes of any sort; nor does he encourage his disciples to make them (except sometimes the great mistake of shrinking into dryness and pedantry). Whitman, on the other hand, misleads as much as he inspires, and there is no doubt that he has had a fatal influence on some of his disciples. There is also no doubt that he was the first to be misled, and very soon after writing "Song of Myself." At that point his exhilarating pride of discovery began to change into humorless arrogance. If he had been as familiar with the mystical tradition as Eliot shows himself to be, Whitman would have been warned against the feeling of omnipotence that, as we have seen, often follows a mystical experience. We read in *Philosophies of India* that the adept reaches a point in his spiritual progress at which he becomes identified with the personal creator of the world illusion. "He feels," Dr. Zimmer continues, "that he is at one with the Supreme Lord, partaking of His virtues of omniscience and omnipotence. This, however, is a dangerous phase; for if he is to go to Brahman, the goal, he must realize that this inflation is only a subtle form of self-delusion. The candidate must conquer it, press beyond it, so that the anonymity of sheer being (*sat*), consciousness (*cit*), and bliss (*ananda*) may break upon him as the transpersonal essence of his actual Self."

Whitman, of course, had never heard of this purely anonymous or transpersonal state. Remaining for a long time in the dangerous phase of self-inflation (or "dilation," as he called it) and regarding himself as a God-inspired prophet, he kept looking about for other new doctrines to prophesy. The first of these he found was a rather bumptious American nationalism, which is already suggested in his prose introduction to the first edition of *Leaves of Grass* (written after the poems), but which becomes more explicit in the new poems of the second or 1856 edition. Also in the second edition, he announced himself in an open letter to Emerson ("Dear Master") as the prophet of unashamed sex. In 1857 he determined to become what he called a "wander speaker"—"perhaps launching at the President, leading persons, Congressmen or Judges of the Supreme Court . . . the greatest champion America ever could know, yet holding no office or emolument whatever—but first in the esteem of men and women." Soon afterward he dreamed of founding a new religion, for which *Leaves of Grass*—expanded into 365 chapters or psalms, one to be read on each day of the year—would serve as a holy testament. Preserved among his papers is a note to himself that reads: "The Great Construction of the New Bible. Not to be diverted from the principal object—the main life work—the three hundred and sixty-five. It ought to be ready in 1859." During those years before the Civil War, Whitman was afflicted with megalomania to such an extent that he was losing touch with the realities, or at least the human possibilities, of American life.

At the same time he was making—if judged by the mystical tradition—another blunder against which the Indians might have warned him. He had once been careful to distinguish the external self or personality from the deeper Self that he was celebrating in his greatest poem. Now he forgot the distinction and began to celebrate "myself" in the guise of a simple separate person—greater than other persons, no longer standing aloof and unperturbed, but greedy for praise and tortured with desires. This person, however, laid claim to all the liberties and powers that Whitman had once ascribed to the transpersonal Self. Anything that the person felt like saying was also the right and inspired thing to say. Composing great poems was a simple matter. All the person had to do was permit Nature—*his* nature—to speak "without check with original energy."

While dreaming his crazy dreams, Whitman continued to live with his family in a little frame workingman's house in Brooklyn, where he shared a bed with his idiot brother. Thoreau on his first visit noted that the bed was unmade and that an unemptied chamber-pot stood beneath it. Other literary men described their meetings with Whitman in a tone of fascinated horror that suggests the accounts of present-day visitors to North Beach or Big Sur or Venice West. Indeed, one cannot help feeling that the Whitman of those days was a predecessor of the beatniks: he had the beard, the untrimmed hair, and although his costume was different, it might be regarded as the 1860 equivalent of sweatshirt and sandals. Some of his conduct also resembled that of the Beat Generation. He stayed out of the rat race, he avoided the squares (preferring the company of omnibus drivers and deck hands on the ferries); he was "real gone," he was "far out"; and he was writing poems in what Lawrence Lipton calls "the 'open,' free-swinging style that is prized in Beat Generation literature." Some of them should be read to loud music as a means of glossing over their faults and holding the listener's attention—not to the music of a jazz combo, like beatnik poetry, but perhaps to that of a regimental brass band.

A poet's conduct and his work are two ways of expressing the same habits of thinking. It was during those years just before the Civil War that Whitman first indulged himself in a whole collection of stylistic mannerisms. He had once planned to write in what he called "A perfectly transparent, plate-glassy style, artless, with no ornaments, or attempts at ornaments, for their own sake." He had planned to use "Common idioms and phrases—Yankeeisms and vulgarisms—cant expressions when very pat only." The effect he wanted to achieve was one of "Clearness, simplicity, no twistified or foggy sentences, at all—the most translucid clearness without variations"; and that was one of the effects he did achieve in the first edition, except in a few gangling passages and a few others where he was being deliberately hermetic. It was after 1855 that he began to cultivate his bad habits of speech—such, for example, as unnecessary or "poetic" inversions; as foreign words, often used incorrectly and without good reason (there had been only a few of them in "Song of Myself"); as ugly new words of his own coinage; as the "I" placed obtrusively at the end of a phrase ("No dainty dolce affettuoso I"); as the Quaker names for months and days, such as "Fourth-month" for April and "First-day" for Sunday (which might have been excusable if Whitman had been a Quaker); and as, worst of all, the interminable bald inventories that read like the names of parts and organs in an anatomical chart or like the index to a school geography. In the first edition he had broken most of the nineteenth-century rules for elegant writing, but now he was violating an older literary convention, that of simply being considerate of one's readers.

Whitman's beatnik period, however, proved to be only a transitory phase of a life that had several other phases. The best record of his attitude during the period is the greatly expanded text of the third or 1860 edition, which is an engaging and impressive book for all its extravagant gestures, and which, after the first, is the other vintage edition of his poems. Soon after it was published, the Civil War gave a new direction to Whitman's career. His war poems are disappointing, with two or three exceptions, but his unselfish service in army hospitals helped to establish him in still another personality, one he kept to the end: that of the good gray poet, and it was during the postwar years that he produced some of his most important work. Much of it shows that he was turning back toward the Eastern beliefs expressed in "Song of Myself." Perhaps the return was caused by another mystical experience, but although the supposition seems a likely one, the only evidence to support it consists of scattered passages in his two prose works of the time, *Democratic Vistas* and *Specimen Days*. We know, however, that he planned at the time to make "Passage to India" the title not merely of a long poem about the journey of the soul toward God, but of a whole volume "bridging the way," as he said, "from life to death."

The volume would be designed to stand beside *Leaves of Grass*, which he had come to regard as a finished work. Some of the poems he planned to put into the new book—"Proud Music of the Storm," "Prayer of Columbus," and most of all "Passage to India" itself—are truly admirable in conception and in their rich symphonic structure. The language, however, is more abstract and a great deal less vivid or Yankee than that of the first edition (besides retaining most of the mannerisms developed in his period of self-inflation). If he did have another mystical experience before writing the poems, it failed to give him the miraculously fresh vision of familiar people and objects that had followed his earlier illumination. As for the creed put forward in "Passage to India" and other poems of the same period, it is no longer purely mystical, being mixed with the ambiguous doctrine of male comradeship or "adhesiveness" that Whitman had first expressed in the "Calamus" poems of the 1860 edition, and mixed again with his still more recent doctrine of Personalism. The deeper Self is now identified with the personality (or eidólon, as he was beginning to call it). God Himself becomes personal (or four-personal, in "Chanting the Square Deific") and is addressed as the Older Brother of the soul.

Soon the notion of publishing a grand new book had to be put aside, as a result of the apoplectic stroke that Whitman suffered in January 1873. He lived nineteen years longer and wrote scores of poems, but most of them were occasional verses bearing a curious resemblance to his newspaper editorials of the 1840s. The only ambitious work he finished was "Dream of Columbus" (1874), which served as a dignified and moving peroration to his career. He retired to Camden, New Jersey, where he lived serenely and received a good many visitors, most of them his devoted followers, so that he presented the picture of an Indian guru surrounded by his *adhikarin* or disciples.

During the first years in Camden Whitman spent a good deal of time revising his early poems, in the hope of reshaping his extremely diversified work into an organic whole. Most of the revisions were designed to make his style more uniform, to bring his teaching up to date, or to gloss over the differences between what he had once said and what he now believed. "Do I contradict myself?" Once Whitman had asked the question defiantly, but now it worried him. He still regarded himself as a prophet, and a prophet's duty is to have been always right. It would have been better for his strictly poetic reputation if he had allowed the early illuminated Whitman to speak for himself, the bohemian or inflated Whitman to speak for himself, and the good gray poet to speak for himself, each in his separate fashion.

In the collection of variorum readings compiled long ago by Oscar Lovell Triggs, the revisions in "Song of Myself" occupy thirty pages. Triggs found that Whitman had changed the wording of all but five of the fifty-two chants into which he had finally divided the poem. In those five—chants 9, 27, 28, 29, and 52—the only changes are in punctuation and spelling. Of course the division into numbered chants is an important change in itself and one that has proved to be convenient for students, though it has also proved misleading.

A still more important change is in the title. By virtue of the image that holds the poem together, its title should be "Leaves of Grass," but Whitman had transferred this phrase to the book as a whole. In the first edition, the frontispiece partly takes the place of a title, since readers are being asked to interpret the poem as the testament of the idealized American workingman whom it portrays. In the second or 1856 edition, there is a title in words: "A Poem of Walt Whitman, an American." That is an awkward but accurate phrase, if we regard Walt (not Walter) Whitman as the name of the idealized figure. Beginning with the third or 1860 edition, the poem was called simply "Walt Whitman"—not so accurate a title any longer, if we remember that the name was by now completely identified with the living poet. It was not until 1881 that the poem became "Song of Myself," a phrase that I think is completely false to its original intention. "Myself" is "my personality," and Whitman had originally been writing about a not-myself, a representative figure who, by achieving union with his transpersonal soul, had realized the possibilities latent in every man and woman.

In the first edition the poet-hero presents himself, as I said, without a hint of his local or family background; he is simply "Walt Whitman, an American, one of the roughs, a kosmos." That is exactly how he should be presented, since he is speaking for all Americans and indeed for all humanity. In later editions he acquires a personal background by virtue of his complete identification with the author. As "Walt Whitman, a kosmos, of Manhattan the son," he becomes a strictly localized divinity (while ceasing to imply that each of the roughs contains in himself the entire universe). There are other changes in the same direction. In 1881 Whitman took eight lines from "Starting from Paumanok," which was written in his beatnik days, and inserted them at the end of the first chant. Four of the new lines are:

My tongue, every atom of my blood, form'd from this soil, this air,
Born here of parents born here from parents the same, and their parents the same,
I, now thirty-seven years old in perfect health begin,
Hoping to cease not till death.

He was actually thirty-four or -five when he started to write the poem, and thirty-six when it was published—but what does it matter about his age or health or his determination to cease not till death? The real point is that if he insists on presenting himself as a proud descendant of the early settlers, he can no longer presume to speak for first-generation Americans; nor can he claim to be "Not merely of the New World but of Africa, Europe or Asia. . . . a wandering savage," as he had done in the original text. He has gained an identity at the cost of ceasing to be universally representative.

There is a significant change in the first line of the poem, the addition (in 1881) of three words I have put in italics: "I celebrate myself, *and sing myself*." At first one feels that "celebrate" and "sing" are synonyms, and that the new phrase has been added partly to balance the line and partly in obedience to Whitman's old-age habit of never saying in three words what might be said in six. But the truth is that "sing" introduces a new theme into the text. In the first edition the poet-hero had "celebrated" himself by telling what he saw and did and believed. He had spoken compulsively and without self-consciousness. In the late editions, however, he also "sings" —which in Whitman's jargon means "writes a song about"—himself. When he observes the miraculous world about him, it is no longer for the pure joy of seeing, as in the first edition, but also with the intention of collecting material; he is "Absorbing all to myself and for this song." This new habit of his becomes particularly obtrusive at the beginning of chant 26. Here, in the original version, the poet-hero had been preparing to demonstrate that by merely listening, in a state of complete passivity, he could be swept forward into an ecstasy of hearing. He had said in the first two lines:

I think I will do nothing for a long time but listen,
And accrue what I hear into myself. . . . and let sounds contribute toward me.

Only four words of the second line were changed in 1881, but they were important for the meaning. The new line reads (with my italics):

To accrue what I hear into *this song, to* let sounds contribute toward *it*.

"To" implies purpose here: "in order to." If the poet is consciously trying to hear sounds that will enrich the texture of his song, he is no longer being passive, and the effect on the reader of the passage that follows is seriously weakened.

The good gray poet must have been abashed by many gestures of his earlier myself. "Washes and razors for foofoos. . . . for me freckles and a bristling beard." One can be certain that such a line would go; the wonder is that it survived until 1881. "Where the laughing gull scoots by the slappy shore and laughs her near-human laugh." The word "slappy" gives color to the line, and it was the one word to be omitted, in this case as early as 1856. There is no space to offer more than this bare suggestion of all the gay impudence and vivid Yankeeisms that were excised from later editions. I am more interested at present in apparently minor revisions that change the meaning of the poem. Among them are the phrases that introduce his accounts of the Goliad massacre in Texas (chant 34) and of the sea fight between the *Serapis* and the *Bonhomme Richard* (chants 35 and 36). In the first edition these two accounts are offered as further examples of the power of identification. The poet-hero *is* one of the murdered Texans—perhaps the "youth not seventeen years old"—and he *is* one of the sailors on the *Bonhomme Richard*, just as he had already been the mother condemned for a witch and the hounded slave that flagged in the race. By 1867, however, Whitman felt he should offer explanations. He inserted a line at the beginning of chant 34, "Now I tell what I knew in Texas in my early youth," thus falsifying his own biography, and he inserted another line at the end of the first stanza of chant 35, besides two words, which I have italicized, in the first line of the following stanza:

> List to the yarn, as my grandmother's father the sailor told it to me.

> Our foe was no skulk in his ship I tell you (*said he,*)

The result is that these great examples of the poet-hero's ability to identify himself with all creatures, living or dead, are reduced in one case to a story told long ago in Texas, in the other to an old sailor's yarn—"said he"—and thereby lose their reason for being part of the poem. Whitman can no longer say about them, "I am the man. . . . I suffered. . . . I was there." In both cases it would seem, however, that he was not so much concealing what he once meant to say as, on this occasion, honestly forgetting it.

SUGGESTED APPROACHES

THIS BOOK has been designed to give the reader glimpses into the creative process. Included are not only the initial and final versions of "Song of Myself," but also some of the early versions of the poem selected from Whitman's notebooks. Only rarely does a poem of such magnitude and importance reveal so much of its origins and history. It is perhaps best that the reader go first through the final or 1891–92 version of the poem—the version, after all, that Whitman wanted preserved—in order to understand and experience it simply as one of the great poems of our literature. Curiosity should next lead the reader to the poem's first appearance, the 1855 version. Since these texts are on facing pages in this book, a detailed comparison of passages is made relatively simple. Finally, the reader will find some still earlier versions of parts of the poem—versions that Whitman put down on paper but did not publish. Many of the lines of the published poem, however, have been shaped out of these fragmentary jottings.

The history of an individual poem can never be known in its entirety. The poet never reveals to us the versions of the poem that formed and reformed in his mind before any single line found its way to paper. Indeed, it is even doubtful that he himself knows the deepest origins of his poem in the depths of the unconscious. There are mysteries about the creative process that seem destined to remain hidden from the public gaze, mysteries that we signify when we refer to the *genius* of a poet. But although we can never penetrate to the origin of a poem and fully know its every movement toward life, we can catch glimpses of its growth if the poet saves for us his earliest trials on paper. Rarely have we had so many glimpses for so great a poem as we have in the case of "Song of Myself." These glimpses are all the more valuable because of the nature of "Song of Myself" as a kind of prophetic, inspired, or apocalyptic poem that lustily declares its own independence of the poet. Few readers have read "Song of Myself" without feeling that the poem forced itself on the poet, that he had, finally, no choice but to capitulate and commit the poem to paper. Part of this feeling stems from the deliberate dramatic pose struck by the poet in the poem. But the early fragmentary versions suggest that in part the poem did, indeed, well up from the psychic depths of the startled poet, that many of the lines shaped themselves compulsively out of the accumulated materials in the poet's unconscious.

SUGGESTED TOPICS FOR
COMPARATIVE STUDIES

1. Select one of the early fragments and trace the changes Whitman made in the published versions. Do the changes affect basic meaning? Were they made primarily for metrical or technical reasons? Is there pattern or design in the change of individual words?

2. Sometimes great compression takes place as Whitman moves toward the final version of his poem. Study Whitman's omissions and speculate as to the reason why he left out individual passages, lines, or words. Do some of the earlier versions seem to be more lucid than the later? Can the earlier versions be used on occasion as a gloss for the later? Does Whitman sometimes seem deliberately to obscure his meaning? Does he seem to be striving for particular effects or does he seem to be changing the drift of earlier meaning?

3. In moving from the 1855 to the 1891–92 version of "Song of Myself," Whitman omitted many of the lines and included new lines. Make a special study of these omissions and additions and speculate as to Whitman's motives. Does any pattern appear in this kind of revision? Are some of the omitted passages filled with excellent lines that you feel should be preserved? Discuss their merits and discuss Whitman's probable reasons for passing over them. Do the new lines added by Whitman change or shift, contract or expand meaning? Do they seem harmonious with the rest of the poem? Do the omissions and additions suggest clues to the structure of the poem?

4. Make a study of the individual words Whitman changed. How do these changes affect the tone of the poem—or do they? Is there a pattern in the changes, from informal to formal, or formal to informal, for example? Discuss the merit of these changes. Did Whitman always improve his diction, or did he sometimes blunder?

5. Were some changes made for metrical reasons? Did Whitman improve the rhythm of his lines by changing or shifting words? Are there other technical reasons that appear to lie behind some of the revisions? Did Whitman seem to have in mind the sound patterns of the line—alliteration, assonance—when he revised? Discuss some examples in detail.

6. Some critics have said that Whitman was more chauvinistic—or belligerently American—in his early editions while other critics say he became more nationalistic in the later versions of his poetry. Compare the versions of "Song of Myself" closely for evidence for one side or the other of this controversy. What are the lines that might be cited for either argument? Are these passages open to other ways of interpretation?

7. Some critics believe that as Whitman grew older, he became less physical and more spiritual in his poetry. Using the first and last versions of "Song of Myself" as

primary evidence, discuss this question. Do the revisions tend to suppress the physical or to point up the spiritual elements in the poem?

8. Perhaps the main critical controversy about "Song of Myself" is whether the first or the last version is better. After making a close examination of both versions of the poem, give your own critical judgment supported by carefully worked out reasons and examples. Consider, but do not be unduly influenced by, the problem of reversing the poet's own judgment of his work. Whitman did assert that he wanted his poems read as he last revised them. But he was then an old man. And many critics have observed that poets are not always the best judges of their own work.

CRITICAL QUESTIONS

1. When "Song of Myself" first appeared, it was untitled. Whitman called it "Poem of Walt Whitman, an American," in the 1856 edition of *Leaves of Grass* and simply "Walt Whitman" in the 1860 edition. The title "Song of Myself" appeared in the 1881 edition. What are the assets and liabilities of each of these titles? Which, finally, appears to be the best?

2. Of all the poems in *Leaves of Grass*, "Song of Myself" makes more extensive use of the title image—the leaf of grass—than any other poem. Trace the image through "Song of Myself" and investigate its relation to the poem's primary meanings and its intricate structure.

3. One of the notable techniques Whitman uses in his poetry, and especially in "Song of Myself," is the catalogue—an outpouring of images that piles detail on detail in a seemingly haphazard fashion. Particularly long catalogues appear in sections 15 and 33. Compare these catalogues for differences and likenesses. Did Whitman put down images at random, or is there a structure to the catalogues in these and other sections? Make a detailed analysis of one of the catalogues, discovering any principle of structure that appears to govern the ordering of images.

4. Whitman once said to Horace Traubel, his Boswellian biographer, "I sometimes think the *Leaves* is only a language experiment" (Horace Traubel, "Foreword," *An American Primer*). Make an intensive study of the language of "Song of Myself" as it might reveal Whitman's meaning in the statement. Note especially his use of a "nonliterary" vocabulary and his foreign borrowings. Can you find examples of both success and failure in the "experiment"?

5. Whitman wrote, in his essay "Slang in America": "Considering Language then as some mighty potentate, into the majestic audience-hall of the monarch ever enters a personage like one of Shakspere's clowns, and takes position there, and plays a part even in the stateliest ceremonies. Such is Slang, or indirection, an attempt of common humanity to escape from bald literalism, and express itself illimitably, which in highest walks produces poets and poems, and doubtless in pre-historic times gave the

start to, and perfected, the whole immense tangle of the old mythologies." Examine "Song of Myself" in the light of this statement. Does Whitman deliberately admit the clowns into the "majestic audience-hall" of his poetry? His view of slang here might be related to his statement, cited above, that "the *Leaves* is only a language experiment."

6. "Song of Myself" seems to be a serious poem, but at the same time it seems filled with humor—of one kind or another. Emerson, in his famous letter to Whitman written after reading the 1855 edition of *Leaves of Grass*, said: "I find it the most extraordinary piece of wit and wisdom that America has yet contributed." In this comment, Emerson seems to be touching on that unique combination of the serious and the humorous that makes "Song of Myself" such a remarkable poem. Analyze the wit or the humor of the poem and relate it to the poem's serious themes.

7. Whitman was the first poet to exploit fully the possibilities of free verse as a form. But although Whitman abandoned rhyme and the measured line, he used many traditional poetic techniques to give music to his verse. Many readers, in fact, feel a rhythm in his poetry even when they cannot point to it. Analyze a section of "Song of Myself," showing the various devices and techniques that Whitman used to achieve his unique effect. In what way does it seem valid to talk about Whitman's rhythms? Is it possible to discover larger patterns of rhythm in "Song of Myself" than the conventional syllabic patterns?

8. Although there are a number of personal references in "Song of Myself," readers have long understood that the speaker, or narrator, or "I" of the poem is something more than the historical Walter Whitman. Write a description of the poem's protagonist, without reference to Whitman or his biographies. Is the speaker a single, one-dimensional personality? Or are there varied, complex facets to his identity? Does he seem to fill several roles, on several levels?

9. Whitman was in advance of his time in the use of sexual imagery. Although he gathered his sex poems into the cluster of *Leaves of Grass* which he called "Children of Adam," he used sexual imagery throughout the *Leaves*, and particularly in "Song of Myself." Analyze the sexual imagery in the poem, with special attention to the sections on "touch" which reach some kind of climax in section 28. Compare Whitman's attitudes toward sex with modern psychological views.

10. Whitman has been called both a poet of life and a poet of death. If any of his poems harmonizes and balances his views, it is "Song of Myself." The poem represents a celebration of life and an acceptance of death. Analyze in detail Whitman's attitude toward death throughout "Song of Myself." Examine particularly the imagery he uses to present the drama of death. How does he reconcile his intense love of life with his welcome acceptance of death? (Compare his attitude toward death in "Song of Myself" with his attitude in "Out of the Cradle Endlessly Rocking" and "When Lilacs Last in the Dooryard Bloom'd.")

11. Whitman has been called "poet of science." What evidence is there for such a title in "Song of Myself"? Analyze the scientific imagery of the poem, with special attention to the astronomical, biological, and evolutionary. Compare Whitman's attitude toward science with other romantic attitudes—for example, Poe's in his sonnet, "To Science."

12. Another title frequently applied to Whitman is "poet of democracy." Is the title applicable in a poem like "Song of Myself"? Define the elements of Whitman's democratic belief as they are asserted or implied in the poem. (Compare the attitudes in the poem with those in Whitman's great prose work, *Democratic Vistas*.)

QUESTIONS ON ESSAYS

The six essays included here with "Song of Myself" offer rich opportunities to explore various critical methods. Though these methods are different from each other, they are not necessarily opposed or mutually exclusive. They may complement each other, or they may represent different avenues, levels, or kinds of understanding.

1. Compare and contrast the six essays by listing points of agreement and points of disagreement among them. Analyze as closely as you can what seem to be the disagreements. Select one point of disagreement and follow carefully the reasoning that led to the different conclusions. Take the role of arbiter and show how one or the other—or neither—side is right.

2. In his essay, Randall Jarrell is a poet responding to another poet's poetry. Analyze Jarrell's techniques of persuading the reader to believe his assertions about Whitman's lines. What are the virtues and limitations of Jarrell's approach? Are there brilliant lines in "Song of Myself" that he has missed? Or lines that he has praised undeservedly? Defend your statements with as much lucidity and logic as you can muster.

3. A key term in Richard Chase's essay is "comic." How does Chase's essay give definition to the term? How does this definition compare with other definitions of the comic? Does Chase cite elements in "Song of Myself" as comic which do not seem comic to you? Does he pass over some genuinely comic elements? Evaluate Chase's approach as it results in interpretation of a specific passage of "Song of Myself."

4. The key term in Roy Harvey Pearce's essay is "epic." How does Pearce seem to define the term? How does his definition compare with common notions about the epic? Evaluate Pearce's approach as it contributes to understanding the poem or its tradition.

5. Two essays (by James E. Miller, Jr. and Malcolm Cowley) make a good deal of the "mysticism" of "Song of Myself," though they differ as to the nature of the mysticism involved. How, precisely, do the Miller and Cowley essays differ in their approach or analysis? Are there ways of reconciling these approaches?

6. Four of the essays (by Carl F. Strauch, James E. Miller, Jr., Roy Harvey Pearce, and Malcolm Cowley) offer structural analyses of "Song of Myself" by dividing the poem into a number of major parts. Compare and contrast these analyses by showing how they agree and how they differ. Work out your own structure of "Song of Myself."

BIBLIOGRAPHICAL SUGGESTIONS

The student who wishes to trace "Song of Myself" with exactness and precision through all of the lifetime editions of *Leaves of Grass* must find a library which contains the nine editions, issued in 1855, 1856, 1860, 1867, 1871, 1876, 1881, 1889, and 1891–92. But he might be willing to rely on the variorum edition of the *Leaves* prepared by Oscar Lovell Triggs and published in *The Complete Writings of Walt Whitman*, edited by Richard M. Bucke, Thomas B. Harned, and Horace L. Traubel (New York: G. P. Putnam's Sons, 1902), 10 volumes. This variorum is reprinted in Emory Holloway's *Inclusive Edition: Leaves of Grass* (New York: Doubleday, Page & Co., 1926).

Three of the lifetime editions of the *Leaves* are readily available in paperback: Malcolm Cowley, ed., *Walt Whitman's Leaves of Grass: The First (1855) Edition* (New York: The Viking Press, 1959); Roy Harvey Pearce, ed., *Leaves of Grass by Walt Whitman: Facsimile Edition of the 1860 Text* (Ithaca, N. Y.: Cornell University Press, 1961); and James E. Miller, Jr., ed., *Walt Whitman: Complete Poetry and Selected Prose* (Boston: Houghton Mifflin Co., 1959)—the 1891–92 or deathbed edition.

A new edition of Whitman is in process of publication, and, when it is published in its entirety, will be the definitive edition of the poet: *The Collected Writings of Walt Whitman*, edited by Gay Wilson Allen and Sculley Bradley (New York: New York University Press, 1961–   ).

A useful and recent general introduction to the poet is: James E. Miller, Jr., *Walt Whitman* (New York: Twayne Publishers, Inc., 1962). The most comprehensive biography is: Gay Wilson Allen, *The Solitary Singer* (New York: The Macmillan Company, 1955).

For the student who wishes to explore material by or about Whitman more deeply, two books are indispensable, both containing valuable bibliographies: Gay Wilson Allen, *Walt Whitman Handbook* (Chicago: Packard and Company, 1946); and Gay Wilson Allen, *Walt Whitman as Man, Poet, and Legend; With a Check List of Whitman Publications 1945–1960* (Carbondale, Ill.: Southern Illinois University Press, 1961).